A

Al

First 24 Hours of War in the Pacific

By

Donald J. Young

 Burd Street Press

This Burd Street Press publication
was printed by
Beidel Printing House, Inc.
63 West Burd Street
Shippensburg, PA 17257-0152 USA

In respect for the scholarship contained herein, the acid-free paper used in this book meets the guidelines for permanence and durability of the Committee on Production Guidelines for Book Longevity of the Council on Library Resources.

For a complete list of available publications
please write
Burd Street Press
Division of White Mane Publishing Company, Inc.
P.O. Box 152
Shippensburg, PA 17257-0152 USA

Library of Congress Cataloging-in-Publication Data

Dedicated to the men of Wake, Guam, Hong Kong, the Philippines, Malaya, North China, and Shanghai, whose fate was sealed within the first 24 hours of war in the Pacific.

CONTENTS

ILLUSTRATIONS

MAPS

INTRODUCTION

The first the world knew of the Japanese attack on Pearl Harbor on December 7, 1941, was at 8:00 a.m., Hawaiian time, when the stunning message "AIR RAID ON PEARL HARBOR X THIS IS NO DRILL" was hurriedly flashed from Admiral Kimmel's headquarters at Pearl Harbor. Twenty-four hours and two minutes later, at 1:32 p.m., Washington time, the Congress of the United States officially declared war on the Empire of Japan.

During those first twenty-four hours of war in the Pacific, the Japanese took advantage of the element of surprise, and launched attacks against every major military installation and base that stood in the way of their primary wartime objective, the capture of Malaya and the Dutch East Indies, what they would later call the Southern Resources Area. First and foremost, the U.S. Pacific Fleet, the only real naval threat to the Japanese in the Pacific, would have to be crippled, thus the attack on Pearl Harbor. Next in line were pre-invasion attacks on Malaya, Hong Kong, the Philippines, Wake Island, and Guam, followed by land invasions of both Hong Kong and Malaya that same morning.

Just how significant to the outcome the first twenty-four hours of war in the Pacific were, can be seen by what happened in Malaya and the Philippines. Throughout the part of the Far East that had been targeted by the Japanese, the only two places where the British and American armies stood a real chance of holding back their new enemy was in Malaya and the Philippines. Although it took seventy days for the Japanese to capture Malaya and Singapore, and six months to take the Philippines, the results of their successes on that first day, without question, doomed both armies.

In Malaya, the successful Japanese invasion and capture of three crucial coastal towns, directly linking them by road to the heart of Malaya and Singapore, and the simultaneous destruction of half of the British Air Force on the first day, took away the only real chance they had of successfully holding off their invader. In the Philippines, like in Malaya, the stunning loss of half of the American Air Force took away the only hope the Americans and Filipinos had of holding back the Japanese. It was a disaster of more immediate consequences than Pearl Harbor.

Using the attack on Pearl Harbor only as the initiating event, this book focuses on what happened everywhere else throughout the Pacific in the war's first twenty-four hours.

Although the initial Japanese attack on Hawaii occurred at 7:50 a.m., Hawaii time, the first of several "AIR RAID ON PEARL HARBOR X THIS IS NO DRILL" messages, that were flashed to Washington, D.C., the Philippines, Wake, and all U.S. Navy ships present in the Hawaiian area, didn't go out until 8:00 a.m.

Since the Hawaiian Islands are located midway between Time Zone longitudes 150 and 165 degrees, at that time they were recognized as a half hour ahead of what would be their Standard Time Zone. 8:00 a.m. in Hawaii was 1:30 p.m. in Washington, 2:30 a.m. in the Philippines, and 5:30 in the morning at Wake Island.

Using the 8:00 a.m. "AIR RAID ON PEARL HARBOR..." message as the initial announcement that war had broken out, everything that happened in the Pacific from that point on within the next twenty-four hours, will be designated in this book as "PH (Pearl Harbor) plus." For example, Wake Island was attacked at 11:58 a.m., Wake Island time, exactly 6 hours and 28 minutes after the "AIR RAID ON PEARL HARBOR..." message. This will be labeled "PH plus 6 hours 28 minutes." President Roosevelt's speech to Congress on December 8, was delivered at 12:30 p.m., Washington time, or "PH plus 23 hours."

In the president's memorable "Yesterday, December 7, 1941..." speech on December 8, asking for a declaration of war on Japan, outside of Hawaii, he said the following about other targets attacked that day:

Yesterday, the Japanese government...launched an attack against Malaya.

Last night, Japanese forces attacked Hong Kong.

Last night, Japanese forces attacked Guam.

Last night, Japanese forces attacked the Philippine Islands

Last night, Japanese forces attacked Wake Island.

This morning, the Japanese attacked Midway Island.

He also said that "American ships have been reported torpedoed on the high seas between San Francisco and Hawaii."

The titles of the first seven chapters of this book have been taken from the above parts of the president's speech.

BA 12 TR 14 V AC   COMMANDER AIRCRAFT, SCOUTING FORCE   INCOMING

Heading: L Z F5L Ø71830 C8Q TART O BT

AIRRAID ON PEARL HARBOR X THIS IS NO DRILL

			ACTION	TT/1911/7 DEC/WU-PF	
Originator	Date-Time Gr. Ø71830	Date 7 DEC 41	System TT	Super WU-PF	C.W.O.	Number 338

Info.

CINCPAC

ALL U S NAVY SHIPS
PRESENT HAWAIIAN AREA

Classification Precedence

URGENT

AD	CS	OP	FS	FLT	GUN	MAT	ENG	SUP	SDO			COM	ACO

Copy of first "AIR RAID ON PEARL HARBOR..." message sent from CINCPAC (Commander in Chief Pacific). Time shown "1830" (6:30 p.m.) is Greenwich time, which was exactly 8:00 a.m. in Hawaii.

US Navy

CHAPTER I

"YESTERDAY, THE JAPANESE GOVERNMENT... LAUNCHED AN ATTACK AGAINST MALAYA..."

TIME DIFFERENCE: 8 HOURS 40 MINUTES.

12:12 p.m., December 6 (PH minus 35 hrs. 22 min.): Monsoon rains had pounded the northeast coast of Malaya for most of the first week of December. Until the morning of December 6, the weather was not good enough to allow the RAAF (Royal Australian Air Force) at Kota Bharu Air Base to launch its regular air patrol of the South China Sea.

Kota Bharu itself, the northernmost town in Malaya, was 400 air miles from Singapore, and was the most important British military outpost on the peninsula.

Sitting on the east coast of Malaya, ten miles from the border of Thailand, there was little doubt that if war came, its thirty miles of ideal landing beaches and access to the only road to the south, would make it a major focal point of any Japanese invasion attempt.

At 10:30 that morning, three Lockheed Hudson patrol planes lifted off from the monsoon-soaked Kota Bharu runway on their first reconnaissance mission in three days. At twelve minutes past noon, the crew of the plane, piloted by Lieutenant J.C. Ramshaw, who had flown northeast across the mouth of the Gulf of Siam toward Cape Cambodia, spotted what they identified as three Japanese transports and a destroyer escort heading up the gulf in a northeasterly direction.

Thirty minutes later, Lieutenant J.G. Elbertson, from a position south of Ramshaw's, reported the same convoy heading in the same direction.

British intelligence in Singapore had already been made aware that two Japanese convoys had left Camranh Bay and Saigon on December 4 and 5, respectively. With these sightings on the sixth verifying their presence in the Gulf of Siam, there seems little doubt that their objective would be to invade Kota Bharu, and Singora and Patani on the northeast coast of neighboring Thailand.

Months before, the British had put together a detailed plan for movement into Thailand if the Japanese invaded that country. Its main objective was to prevent the capture of Singora and Patani, two towns on the northeast

1

coast of Thailand with the only roads leading to the west coast of Malaya. Japanese control of these towns would post a major threat to the security of all of Malaya.

Called "Operation Matador," the success or failure of the plan hinged entirely on the British need to launch the operation from their bases in Malaya, thirty-six hours before the anticipated Japanese landings.

It would seem that the discovery of the convoy of Japanese ships entering the Gulf would be evidence enough to launch Matador, but circumstances beyond the army's control would not allow it.

It was 2:00 p.m. when British Far East commander, Sir Robert Brooke-Popham received the news that a task force of over thirty Japanese transports and war ships had been sighted entering the Gulf. Ironically, until the Japanese actually came ashore, he was hamstrung in how he could react.

The political ramifications of an invasion of Thailand by either the Japanese or the British created the main obstacle to the British plan. The Siamese government had warned that if the British crossed into Thailand before the Japanese invaded, then the Thai Army would side with the Japanese. If, on the other hand, Japan entered Thailand as part of their invasion of Malaya, the Thais would side with the British. Relative to that, British intelligence had received information on December 4, that Thai frontier guards had already set up road blocks on the roads leading to Singora and Patani.

Although not acting would mean the loss of the two towns, and give the Japanese immediate access to the vital roads to the west coast, there was a chance that they had sent their ships in hopes of provoking the British into crossing the border. This would give them an excuse to declare war on Great Britain on behalf of the Thais. The strategy of provocation was not new to the Japanese; it was the same one they had used in Manchuria in 1934 and Peking in 1937.

In anticipation of this dilemma, on December 4, Brooke-Popham sent a telegram to the War Office in London, asking for permission to initiate Matador if a situation similar to the one they were now facing was to occur. Unfortunately, London had yet to respond; a delay that would contribute greatly to the fall of Malaya and Singapore.

Air Chief Marshal Sir Robert Brooke-Popham. His unavoidable delay launching Operation Matador before December 8 led directly to the loss of Malaya and Singapore.
RAF

Unsure of Japan's intent, and handcuffed by the Thai warning and the recently reaffirmed British policy of avoiding war with Japan if at all possible, the Far Eastern commander did the only thing he could. He placed all military forces in Malaya on full alert. At the same time, he ordered the air force to continue its search and monitoring of the Japanese convoys. Despite their extra efforts to locate the enemy ships, however, bad weather over the Gulf prevented Royal Australian Air Force planes from making any further contact that day.

British Malayan Army commander, General A.E. Percival, was at III Corps Headquarters at Kuala Lampur when Brooke-Popham filled him in with information of the Japanese convoys at 3:15. Percival immediately instructed General Lewis Heath to order his 11th Indian Corps to stand by for the anticipated launch of Matador, then left for Singapore.

Eighty percent of the country was covered by dense tropical jungle growing over a rugged, mountainous interior. The key to defending the narrow, 400-mile-long Malay peninsula was the British Army's ability to hold three key roads.

Key to holding two of those roads and to the success of Matador was Major General D.M. Murray-Lyon's 11th Indian Division. Its primary job was to hold the roads from Singora to Jitra and from Patani to Kroh, the only roads with access to the west coast of Malaya.

The defense of Kota Bharu was equally important. It was ten miles below the Thailand border, in the extreme northeast corner of Malaya. Successful defense of this town would deny the Japanese access to the road running down the peninsula's east coast.

As the British anticipated, the Japanese planned to invade at all three places, Kota Bharu, Patani, and Singora. The launch and execution of Operation Matador and the defense of Kota Bharu would give the British a chance to successfully frustrate the Japanese objectives. However, the Japanese success or failure did not rely on the British Army.

7:00 p.m. (PH minus 27 hrs. 20 min.): Upon his return to Singapore at seven o'clock that night, General Percival was surprised to learn that Matador had not yet been ordered. While en route, Brooke-Popham had held a meeting with the navy to get their input on whether to launch Matador or not.

At the conference, another possible Japanese target was added to those already mentioned—the invasion of Bangkok. This possibility, along with London's silence on the issue of crossing the Thailand border first, persuaded the Far East commander to hold up Matador. He decided that if the results of aerial reconnaissance the next morning indicted Japanese intentions were to invade, there was a chance the operation could still be launched in time to be effective.

Lieutenant Sabao Takai, a squadron leader with the Imperial Japanese Air Force, recalled that their "worst fears were realized" when their troop ships were discovered by "British flying-boat patrol planes" that morning.

"Our entire invasion plan was completely exposed long before we were able to launch the invasion. It was perfectly clear to the British what a fleet composed of 30 vessels in formation represented. The possibility of an enemy aerial attack on our bases in Indochina was cause for grave concern," Takai said, "[forcing us] to disperse our bombing squadrons to bases [over] a wider area."

9:00 a.m., December 7 (PH minus 13 hrs. 10 min.): At two o'clock in the morning of December 7, two PBY patrol planes took off from the Seletar airfield in Singapore for the Gulf of Siam. Arriving over their assigned patrol areas just as dawn was breaking, the two planes separated. Before long, the Catalina piloted by Flight Sergeant James Webb discovered an unknown number of Japanese ships, prompting him to notify Seletar of what he had seen.

Unfortunately, Webb would not return from the patrol, and was apparently shot down. Outside of identifying the ships as "Japanese," nothing else was heard from the young pilot's plane. No information was given on the fleet's location, the number of ships or the direction in which they were heading. The pilot of the second Catalina reported that he had not seen a single ship, Japanese or otherwise.

Unknown to the British, Webb had probably run into one of the two enemy convoys that was heading toward its rendezvous point in the middle of the Gulf.

At 9:00 a.m., twenty-eight transports escorted by four cruisers and a division of destroyers rendezvoused at a point 100 miles off the west coast of Indochina. From there, they split into five separate invasion groups, with the bulk, twenty-one transports carrying 15,000 troops, heading for Kota Bharu, Singora, and Patani.

Along with the two PBYs from Seletar, RAAF Hudson patrol planes from Kota Bharu had been scouring the Gulf for signs of Japanese ships since first light. Fortunately for the Japanese, the weather turned in their favor about the same time the planes would have reached their area.

"What good fortune," said Colonel Masanobu Tsugi, chief of operations for the Japanese 25th Army, from his transport heading for Singora. "At about noon, the weather suddenly worsened. Fog and dense clouds hung low over Thailand Bay and it seemed as if the plan directed against Singora might be an airtight one."

It was indeed good fortune for the Japanese, as only two lone transports were spotted between dawn and 6:00 p.m.; one at 1:45 sailing west, and another, with its deck crammed with soldiers, at 3:45 heading in a southwesterly direction.

At 6:00 p.m., the communications center at Kota Bharu airfield got a message from one of its Hudsons, that it had been fired on by a cruiser that was escorting a transport heading toward Kota Bharu. Forty-five minutes later, four more ships were discovered 100 miles northeast of Singora, moving in a southwesterly direction toward that port.

For some unknown reason, between Sergeant Webb's sighting and the other four that were reported, Brooke-Popham received information on only one. It was the 6:45 sighting, and it wasn't received until close to 9:00 p.m. that night.

Although it was the most positive sighting of the four, it wasn't enough. Had he received all the reports, he probably would not have changed his mind anyhow. That afternoon, he had received a telegram from Sir Josiah Crosby, the British minister in Bangkok, who had just concluded a meeting with the Siamese foreign minister. Crosby's message included a stern reinforcement of the Thai government's earlier ultimatum on who it would side with if its soil were invaded.

Colonel Masanobu Tsugi, chief operations officer of the Japanese 25th Army that landed successfully on three west coast beaches on December 8.

Japanese Army

"For God's sake," it read, in part, "do not allow British forces to occupy one inch of Thai territory unless Japan has struck the first blow at Thailand."

Heeding Sir Josiah's warning, and advice from General Percival and Admiral Thomas Phillips, British Far East naval commander who had just arrived from Manila, Brooke-Popham knew that Britain's hands were tied until the Japanese actually attacked, and decided to wait. It was already too late for Matador to be effective, even if the Japanese did land at Singora and Patani.

As far as Kota Bharu was concerned, its defense didn't have to rely on Matador. If one of the Japanese objectives was a quick capture of Kota Bharu Air Base, just two miles inland from the beach, they would find themselves up against the best defenses the British could put up. It included eleven concrete machine gun emplacements, surrounded by mines and double-apron barbed wire strung along the entire length of landing beach. With additional support from the air force, it was hoped Kota Bharu's defenses were adequate enough to beat off an invasion.

Unknown to the British commander, at the same time the meeting broke up at 11:45, three Japanese troop transports were dropping their anchors two miles off the beach at Kota Bharu.

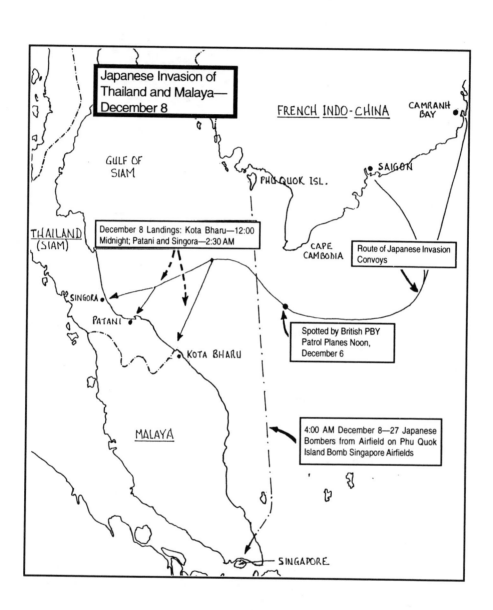

Japanese Invasion of Thailand and Malaya—December 8

FRENCH INDO-CHINA

CAMRANH BAY

GULF OF SIAM

SAIGON

PHU QUOK ISL.

THAILAND (SIAM)

December 8 Landings: Kota Bharu—12:00 Midnight; Patani and Singora—2:30 AM

CAPE CAMBODIA

Route of Japanese Invasion Convoys

SINGORA

PATANI

Spotted by British PBY Patrol Planes Noon, December 6

KOTA BHARU

MALAYA

4:00 AM December 8—27 Japanese Bombers from Airfield on Phu Quok Island Bomb Singapore Airfields

SINGAPORE

12:15 a.m., December 8 (PH minus 1 hr. 25 min.): With information on the presence of the Japanese ships, Brigadier General Berthold Key, commander of the 8th Indian Brigade, who had moved into positions along the beach at Kota Bharu, ordered one of his field guns to open fire. It was 12:15 a.m., December 8, 1941, exactly one hour and 25 minutes before the attack on Pearl Harbor.

In response, the guns from a cruiser and four Japanese destroyers answered, and the first battle of the war in the Pacific had begun.

As soon as the Japanese warships responded, General Key notified Wing Commander C.H. Noble, commanding officer at Kota Bharu air field, who quickly relayed the information to Air Headquarters in Singapore.

Ironically, before RAF commander C.W.H. Pulford would allow his planes to attack, he would wait until he got definite word from General Key that the Japanese had landed. It would take 40 minutes.

Meanwhile, on board the three Japanese transports, there had been some questions about when and if the invasion could take place. The bad weather that had helped conceal the enemy convoys from detection throughout the day, had now turned on them. Heavy wind and a ground swell producing waves over six feet had the ships rolling like a cork in a bathtub. As landing craft were being lowered into the water, they were bounced several times off the sides of the ships.

It was the same for the soldiers, who, according to Major General Hiroshi Takumi, commander of the Kota Bharu operation, "were not only encumbered with life jackets, but with rifles, light machine guns, ammunition and equipment...[making it] very hard to jump into landing craft. [Occasionally] a soldier would fall screaming into the sea, and sappers would [have to] fish him out."

Some of the boats capsized when they pulled away from the sides of the ships, drowning many of their heavily loaded occupants. It took an hour just to launch the first wave.

After several unsuccessful attempts to form into an assault formation, Takumi signaled for the boats to head for shore.

"The landing craft pushed toward the coast in four ragged lines," said their frustrated commander. "I could hear the sounds of the engines above the waves. Then a red light signal flashed twice from among the palm trees on the coast...followed by rifle fire [from] seven or more places, then artillery and machine gun fire. The enemy seemed to be in strength."

12:45 a.m. (PH minus 55 min.): About fifteen minutes later, the first Japanese soldier to land on Allied soil in World War II hit the beach at Kota Bharu. Seconds later, he was followed by the rest of the 200-man force. Darkness, rough seas, and an unyielding current had placed them directly in front of two British pill boxes, protected by a seemingly endless screen of double-apron barbed wire. When word reached General Key of where the enemy force had come ashore, he was confident his Indian troops would repel the invaders.

The way things were going, it's possible that the Japanese were also skeptical about their chances. Immediately upon disembarking, they found that to do anything but lie flat on the sand invited sure death. Fire from the two pill boxes just a few yards from where they had come ashore, was intense and deadly. It forced them to burrow down into the sand.

Colonel Masanobu Tsugi, after interviewing several survivors, wrote that the men "using their steel helmets to dig their way forward...eventually reached the wire entanglements. Those with wire-cutters kept at their work, but [suddenly] there was a thunderous [roar] and clouds of dust flew up, completely obscuring the view. [They] had reached the British mine field."

Those close enough began throwing grenades at the fire ports in the pill boxes.

"Moving over corpses," continued Tsugi, "the wire cutters continued to work, [while] behind them followed a few men, piling up sand ahead of them with their helmets and creeping forward like moles."

Meanwhile, as the first wave of Japanese troops struggled to hang on to the few yards of Malayan beach, an order came down to call off the entire operation.

At 2:00 a.m., General Takumi was preparing to launch the second wave, when the transports were attacked by RAAF Hudsons from the nearby Kota Bharu air field. The commander of the naval escort became so fearful at the sight of the British planes, that he demanded Takumi abandon the operation.

The army commander refused, pointing out that it was impossible to rescue those troops already on shore. Reluctantly, the escort commander conceded.

Moments later, however, the transport carrying Takumi, the *Awajisan Maru*, was hit by several 250-pound bombs and immediately began to burn. The other two transports, the *Ayatosen Maru* and the *Sakura Maru*, were also hit.

"Our transports," recorded Colonel Tsugi later in his 25th Army report, "soon became enveloped in flame and smoke from the bursting bombs and from shells fired from shore batteries. The *Awajisan Maru*, after ten hits, caught fire and sunk. The *Ayatosan Maru* was also sunk.."

The third transport, the *Sakura Maru*, although not sunk, was badly damaged by the valiant efforts of the five Hudsons, who, three times, landed, re-armed and returned to attack the Japanese ships.

Although two of the Hudsons were shot down, their tenacity forced the escort commander to temporarily suspend landing operations, and move his ships back out of range of British shore batteries.

Back on the *Awajisan Maru*, after it became obvious that the ship was going down, General Takumi boarded one of the landing craft and had started for the *Ayatosan Maru*, when he abruptly changed his mind and turned toward shore. As the boat neared the beach, he got a first-hand look at what was going on.

"There was the utmost confusion all along the beach," said Takumi. "Many officers and men were killed or wounded, many jumped into the water before their crafts had beached and swam ashore. The enemy positions were about 100 yards from the water, and we could see that their posts were wired in; their guns...pointing directly at us."

11:15 a.m. (PH minus 25 min.): At 1:15 a.m. the telephone rang at the Singapore home of the governor, Sir Shenton Thomas. It was a call from General Percival, informing him of the Japanese landing at Kota Bharu.

"Well," he replied, hesitating for a moment, "I suppose you'll shove the little men off?"

A minute later he was on the phone to police headquarters, ordering the roundup of the approximately 1,200 Japanese males living in Singapore—a move that had been anticipated for several weeks. All suspicious looking Japanese vessels in the harbor were also ordered seized.

After a cup of coffee with his wife on the first floor balcony of Government House, overlooking the city and the distant harbor, he told her to go back to bed. He assured her that there was no need to panic. After all, Kota Bharu was 400 miles away, and he thought there was a good chance Percival would have "shoved the little men off" by dawn anyway.

Understanding the value of radar since their success against the Luftwaffe in the Battle of Britain fifteen months earlier, the British command in Malaya had received thirteen units to detect the approach of hostile aircraft. Unfortunately, only seven of the thirteen were operational by December 8, and three of those were on Singapore Island.

A little after 3:00 a.m., one of the four radar stations operating that morning, detected a flight of planes approaching the Malayan coast from Indochina. As other stations picked up the planes, it was soon determined that they were heading for Singapore. The information was relayed to the Filter Room at Kallang Air Base, where its progress was plotted on the huge plotting table map of the area. It was estimated that there were at least 20 aircraft.

If things had gone the way the Japanese had planned, the estimate probably would have been closer to 50. Fortunately for the British, half of the original flight of 54 Japanese twin-engined "Nell" bombers, who were scheduled for the raid, were forced to turn back over the gulf because of stormy weather and poor visibility.

Lieutenant Takai, a squadron leader with that group, recalled what happened. "My fears of very bad weather," he said, "were realized when we were suddenly enveloped in thick clouds as we were climbing.

"Visibility was so poor, that it was almost impossible to recognize the formation lights of the two aircraft immediately behind me....Without changing course, I began a descent to a lower altitude. I was still losing altitude when directly below [me] there appeared the...white crests of waves streaking the black ocean surface. I pulled up and searched for the other bombers, only two of the original nine were in sight. I was still looking vainly for the other bombers...when a 'Return to base' order was received from our wing commander. All [27] bombers returned to their takeoff points."

By 3:30, with the remaining 27 planes 135 miles out and still holding on line to Singapore, the island went on full air raid alert. In other words, the military went on full alert. As for the city itself, when Governor Shenton Thomas got a call from Air Commander Pulford at 4:00 a.m., telling him hostile aircraft were within 25 miles of the city, he had quickly telephoned the Air Raid Precautions office. The ARP, as it was known, was responsible for sounding the air raid alarms and turning the lights off around the city. Unfortunately, it was Sunday night, and no one was on duty at ARP headquarters. In fact, it had been debated whether it was necessary to man the ARP stations at all at night, following a lecture given two days earlier by an RAF officer, who insisted the Japanese pilots could not see well enough to fly at night.

When the Japanese got their first glimpse of the city, they were undoubtedly surprised at what they saw. All the street lights were on, the harbor was lit up, the lights of the buildings in downtown Singapore that traditionally stayed on were burning brightly, including those illuminating the clock tower of Victoria Memorial Hall. Even more surprising was the military headquarters at Fort Canning, whose lights were still on when the first bombs were dropped.

As shocked as the Japanese were at finding a well-lit city, the civilian population and a few of the military were equally as shocked at the raid.

Cecil Brown, an American correspondent for CBS, had received a 4:00 a.m. call from Major Charles Fisher, assistant director of public relations for the military in Singapore.

"Will you come to press headquarters right away?" he said. "We have an announcement to make."

Thinking the announcement could only mean one thing—war with Japan—Brown said he'd be right there, then hung up the phone.

"I [just] put the phone down on its cradle [when] there was a heavy boom, then three more in quick succession. I know a bomb when I hear one," said Brown, "and those were bombs."

Dressing quickly, he hailed a rickshaw in front of his hotel a few minutes later.

"What is matter? What is?" asked the wide-eyed coolie, gesturing toward where the bombs had fallen.

"Bombs!" yelled Brown. "To hell with them. Take me to the Union Building."

"I no go there—not go."

"Like hell you're not," shouted the anxious correspondent. "I'll give you two dollars." Much more than the usual thirty cents.

"All right, I go."

"Hurry, hurry! Fast!" yelled Brown as they started down the street.

"There were practically no other vehicles on Beach Road," remembered Brown, "and every light in Singapore was still on. The lights in the harbor were ablaze. As I went by the Fullerton Building, I saw...where...bombs had hit in Raffles Square."

A few minutes after he arrived at press headquarters in the Union Building, Major Fisher handed him a press release.

"My story went off at 4:45 a.m.," said Brown, "which was 4:15 p.m. Sunday, New York time."

CBS correspondent Cecil Brown volunteered to sail with *Prince of Wales* and *Repulse* on night of December 8. He was one of only a handful of survivors from the *Repulse*.

AP

Along with mention of the 1:00 a.m. Japanese invasion of Kota Bharu, he cabled that the "Bombing of Singapore was totally unexpected by civilians. At this moment, numerous aircraft are roaring overhead, but I cannot tell whether they are Japanese or British."

Three hours later he phoned his friend, Captain Eugene Getchell, of the U.S. Maritime Commission, in his room at Raffles Hotel. "[I] asked him what the latest news was over the radio," said Brown. "He said he didn't know, that he had just awakened."

"For Christ's sake! The war is on."

"You're kidding," replied the startled Getchell.

"No. Singapore was bombed three hours ago. Could I come over and listen to your radio?"

Although it's doubtful many slept through the raid, some were convinced it was only practice.

An Englishwoman who had been bounced out of her bed by the concussion from a Japanese bomb, telephoned the police. "There's a raid on!" she said.

"It's only practice," replied the desk sergeant, trying to calm her.

"If it is, they're overdoing it," she yelled back. "Robinson's Department Store has just been hit."

A group of air raid wardens who had rushed to their command post when the searchlights came on and the shooting started, had also decided it wasn't the real thing. As quoted from the diary of one of the men, Reverend Jack Bennitt, "[We thought] it was a good idea to give us an unrehearsed practice as realistic as possible. The only thing that spoiled the realism was the lack of a blackout."

As far as the blackout was concerned, the lights finally did go off at 5:00 a.m., 20 minutes after the last bomb had fallen. The air raid sirens should also have sounded. They did, finally, but not until after the bombs were dropped and the anti-aircraft guns had opened up.

Charles McCormac, an officer with the RAF, and his wife, Pat, lived on the base at Seletar air field, ten miles north of the city on the northern edge of the island.

Moments after the first bomb fell, said McCormac, "Pat...tossed aside the mosquito net and was tugging frantically at my shoulder. 'Darling, wake up! We're being bombed.' "

"'Don't be silly,' replied McCormac. 'It's only thunder.'

"Then came a thin, high-pitched whine, developing into a crescendo shriek, like a train screaming its way out of a tunnel," said the now wide awake young officer. "An explosive blast echoed around the house. We picked ourselves up and rushed to the windows."

"'There!' said Pat, pointing, 'three of them there in the searchlights.'"

"We watched the tracers from the Bofors spiralling toward the spot-lit planes. I looked at my watch. It was 4:15."

After the raid, McCormac told his wife to take shelter if the planes returned, then left for the field.

Seletar had been one of the four airfields targeted by the raiders.

"A bomb had flattened part of the RAF hospital, and airmen were already working in the debris, but there were no casualties," sais McCormac.

Ironically, most of the pilots at the airfield were already up when the raid came at 4:15. A squadron of Dutch Air Force planes from Java were due in sometime after 4:30, and the pilots had just been called out to place landing flares along the edge of the runway to guide them in.

Two other airfields targeted by the Japanese, Tengah in the western part of the island, and Kallang, about a mile north of the city, were barely touched. It was thought that most of the bombs that landed in the city had been targeted for Kallang. The raid left 61 killed and 133 injured. Most of them were Chinese, since many of the bombs intended for Kallang had fallen on Chinatown.

At Sembawang Aerodrome, the northernmost of the four fields on the island, the alarm sounded a few minutes before 4:00 a.m., rousting the Australian pilots of Number 453 Squadron out of their beds and onto their bicycles, on which they grudgingly headed for their planes. Thinking it was just another of the many "bloody practice alerts" they had been put through in the past three weeks, no one was in a hurry. In fact, one of the Aussie pilots, Greg Board, cussed the man who woke him up, rolled over, and went back to sleep, until he heard "a distant crump! crump! crump!"

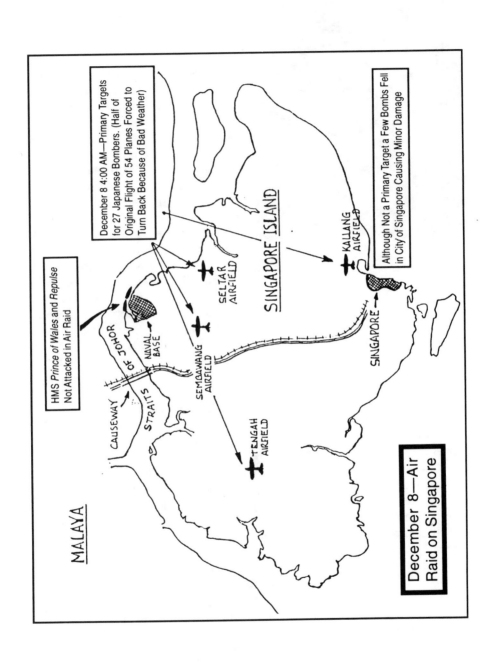

MALAYA

HMS *Prince of Wales* and *Repulse* Not Attacked in Air Raid

December 8 4:00 AM—Primary Targets for 27 Japanese Bombers. (Half of Original Flight of 54 Planes Forced to Turn Back Because of Bad Weather)

Although Not a Primary Target a Few Bombs Fell in City of Singapore Causing Minor Damage

SINGAPORE ISLAND

CAUSEWAY

STRAITS OF JOHOR

NAVAL BASE

SEMBAWANG AIRFIELD

TENGAH AIRFIELD

SELTAR AIRFIELD

KALLANG AIRFIELD

SINGAPORE

December 8—Air Raid on Singapore

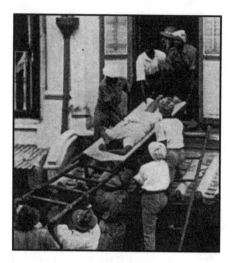

Wounded man from Singapore's Chinese quarter being lowered on a makeshift stretcher to the street below. Most of the damage from the December 8 bombing of Singapore was to the Chinese quarter.
Reuters News Service

Realizing, as he slipped into his clothes, that it was not a practice drill, Board quickly ran outside, grabbed his bicycle, and took off pedaling toward his plane.

Intelligence had said the Japanese planes they would be facing were "all fabric-covered biplanes which wouldn't stand a chance against the Buffalos," Board remembered as he headed for the airstrip, realizing this might be his chance to find out.

He did find out, but not that night. By the time the pilots had reached their planes, searchlights had come on, and, as Board remembered, "every goddamned gun on the island started firing at the same time." Fearing the inexperienced gunners might shoot down their own planes, Air Command refused to let the 453rd take off.

The order to stay on the ground was particularly frustrating to three veteran Battle of Britain pilots, who contemplated taking off anyway, until threatened with court-martial if they did.

One of the men, Squadron Leader T.A. Vigors, later described the enemy flight as "the most perfect night-fighter target [he had] ever [seen]."

Greg Board never reached his fighter. "[Once] I saw the bombers heading for the airstrip," said the young Aussie, "I decided—very quickly— that this was no place for me."

Remembering a slit trench on top of a nearby hill, Board quickly spun around and headed for it, feeling, as he pedaled furiously, that he was losing the race with the Japanese bombers. Although he did not reach the trench in time, he survived by throwing himself into a shallow roadside ditch.

Board's observation about every gun on the island firing at once, wasn't far from wrong. According to another officer who witnessed the attack from Sembawang, everyone was shooting something.

"Every gun on the island, including rifles, machine guns, and anti-aircraft guns opened up," he said.

It was "a beautiful sight," but not a single Japanese plane was hit in the 20-minute attack.

Seven days earlier, on December 2, the British battleships *Prince of Wales* and *Repulse* and a six-destroyer escort, had arrived at the naval base at Singapore. The base, on the edge of the Straits of Johor on the northern-most tip of the island, could be seen from the slightly elevated Sembawang Air Base.

Like everything else, when the Japanese planes arrived, the super-structures of both ships were, as one man at Sembawang remembered, "lit up...as bright as day."

But not for long, as minutes later, the only lights that could be seen were from streaks of tracer bullets arcing fruitlessly from the ships toward the enemy formation.

Before the Japanese raid, most of the British, including many in the military, didn't believe there would be a war with Japan. One of those was the governor, Sir Shenton Thomas. Like many, the air raid and invasion of Kota Bharu that morning had made him eat his words. Words he no doubt remembered having said two days earlier when questioned by a woman staff member about the chances of Japanese bombs "falling on her head."

"You can take it from me," he said, "there will never be a Japanese bomb dropped in Singapore. There will never be a Japanese set foot in Malaya."

Curious residents inspected bomb damage near Raffles Square in downtown Singapore after December 8 bombing.

Reuters News Service

Ironically, by the time the enemy raiders had turned for home, several hundred Japanese had already "set foot in Malaya." But the struggle to stay there was proving difficult.

As skies began to lighten in the east, the three waves of Japanese who had struggled ashore at Kota Bharu found themselves facing a strong counterattack by Indian troops from General Key's crack Dogras Frontier Force Rifles. With two of their transports sunk, the third damaged, and the naval escort withdrawn out of artillery range, it looked for a while like Sir Shenton's comment, "I suppose you'll shove the little men off," might come true.

Even back in Singapore, the first war communique issued from General Headquarters made things look encouraging. It read, "All Japanese surface craft are retiring at high speed, and the few troops left on the beach are being heavily machine-gunned."

In reality, the dogged Japanese were far from through. As individually well-protected as the British pill-boxes were, they were placed 1,000 yards apart, and thus were not protected by interlocking fire from supporting positions. Once the Japanese penetrated the barbed wire and mine field, the issue was no longer in doubt.

British Lieutenant Peter Court of the Dogra regiment, said that in front of his position, "one Jap in each landing party ran in front of the troops and threw a mat made of bamboo slats over the barbed wire, allowing others to scramble over it. The mat carrier," he said, "was always killed, but others were able to get over."

Once the Japanese had moved past the wire and through the mine field, it was just a matter of time for the pill-boxes. "Suddenly," said Tsugi, "one of our men covered a loophole with his body, [allowing] a group of moles to rush the enemy's fortified position. Hand grenades and bayonets flashed, and...in a cloud of black smoke, the enemy's [position] was captured."

Cost to the Japanese in the bitter twenty-minute fight for the first pill-box was eighty men.

Further evidence of Japanese tenacity was noted by Colonel Tsugi, when they were faced with crossing one of the many forks of the Kelantan River in front of a well-fortified Indian position on the other side.

Men who still had their life jackets on were rounded up and ordered to lead the assault.

"Our men did not know the depth of the [river]," said Tsugi, "but...charged into the water, sending up clouds of spray and managed to cross...and capture the second line at bayonet point."

At dawn, after the enemy had overrun two pill-boxes, General Key ordered a counterattack against the expanding Japanese beachhead. Frontier Force units were ordered to attack from opposite ends of the beach, in a pincer movement designed to overrun and wipe out the Japanese invaders. In support of the attack, two field artillery batteries were placed in position near the airfield, directly in front of and less than two miles from the beach.

Although the obstacles presented by the terrain were the same for both, Key's Indian forces found it too much to overcome. The main culprit was the Kelantan River, whose main channel, as it meandered through the flat marshland near its mouth, forked at least half a dozen times, making it impossible to sustain an offensive thrust strong enough to dislodge the Japanese.

Ironically, it was not the failure of the counterattack or the success of the Japanese that would decide the outcome of the battle for Kota Bharu.

While the seesaw battle for Kota Bharu continued that morning, things were happening at the command level back in Singapore.

At 6:30 a.m., following the air raid and confirmation of the Japanese invasion of Kota Bharu, the Far East commander, Brooke-Popham, issued what was called the "Order of the Day." It was a message that had been drawn up seven months earlier in anticipation of such an occasion. To be distributed within his command, it read, in part:

> We are ready. We have had plenty of warning and our preparations are made and tested....We are confident. Our defenses are strong and our weapons efficient....What of our enemy? We see before us a Japan drained for years by the exhausting claims of her wanton onslaught on China....Confidence, resolution...and devotion to the cause must inspire everyone of us in the fighting services...

The reaction of one man, George Hammonds, assistant editor of the *Malayan Tribune* newspaper, summarized how those who knew felt, or would feel, after reading it.

"What a pack of bloody lies," he said. "I can't believe it. I can't believe anybody would deliberately tell so many lies."

8:00 a.m. (PH plus 6 hrs. 20 min.): On December 4, Brooke-Popham had cabled London for permission to violate Thailand's neutrality, by launching Operation Matador upon the likelihood of a Japanese invasion of that country. At 8:00 a.m., eight hours after the fact, and over 24 hours too late to effectively launch the operation, London okayed the request, subject to the Japanese landing at Kota Bharu.

Although it was too late for the entire operation to be fully effective, an order sending the 11th Division into Siam to establish a defensive position at what was called "the Ledge," a tactically important spot on the Patani to Kroh road just inside the Thai border, should have been sent immediately. However, in his response to General Percival's question about whether he should order the division to move out, Sir Robert told him to get ready, "but," he added, "do not act."

With the invasion of Kota Bharu already under way, it's difficult to understand Brooke-Popham's reason for hesitation, although some speculate it was because he was waiting for the results of the air reconnaissance mission he had ordered to Singora.

At the same time in another part of the city, word of a disaster of world-shattering significance, particularly for the British, had come through on the radio. It was word of the attack on Pearl Harbor, which, of course, meant the United States and Japan were at war.

George Hammonds, just about to take the first bite of his breakfast, dropped his knife and fork when he heard news of the attack over the radio.

The greatest fear the British had was that Japan would declare war on them and not on the United States. With America now at war with Japan, and soon, it was hoped, with Germany, their only chance for victory was at last realized.

Most local Americans, who didn't understand what the attack on Pearl Harbor meant to the British, were surprised by the sudden friendship and affection shown by the usually lukewarm English. They received a puzzling number of warm greetings and friendly handshakes.

"It's doubtful an American had to pay for a single drink," remembered George Hammonds, who had spent his lunchtime at the Cricket Club Bar toasting the U.S. entry.

It wasn't until 9:45 a.m., an hour and twenty-five minutes after he had ordered General Percival to stand by for orders to move into Thailand, that Brooke-Popham got word of the Japanese invasions of Singora and Patani. At 9:15, a badly damaged British Beaufort reconnaissance plane landed at Kota Bharu with news of enemy troops landing at the two locations.

Unknown to the Far East commander, it had been seven hours since the Japanese had violated Thailand's neutrality by landing at the two villages.

At Patani, a small market town on the Thai coast, 75 miles north of Kota Bharu, a regiment of Japanese 5th Division troops had hit the beach at 2:30 a.m.

True to their threat, the Thai Army was there to challenge the enemy as they left their landing craft. Finding themselves chest deep in mud and water, it was only the sheer weight of numbers that allowed the Japanese to finally get a foothold.

"At length, our troops fought their way ashore," wrote Colonel Tsugi of the battle later, but the assault was far from easy. "Once ashore, progress was slow, for determined [Thai Army] resistance had to be broken down. The results of [our] assault [were], however, remarkable; it drove a powerful wedge into the enemy's flank and made the operations on the main front [at Singora] much easier."

About the same time the regiment of 5th Division troops hit the beach at Patani, the enemy's main objective, Singora, was also being assaulted. The capture of Singora would give the Japanese immediate access to the main trunk road leading to the west coast of Malaya.

Ten transports carrying two regiments of 5th Division troops, tanks, artillery and enough supplies to carry what was to be the major Japanese offensive into Malaya, began disembarking at 2:30 a.m. But, like at Kota Bharu, it looked like high winds and rough seas might delay or even postpone the landing.

Colonel Masanobu Tsugi, who was involved in the landing at Singora, wrote that just as his transport, the *Ryojo Maru*, dropped anchor, "the northeast wind suddenly freshened. The question was, would it be possible to launch the boats in such heavy seas, and even if it were, could the troops laden with equipment climb down the rope ladders and transfer into the boats?"

"The seas," he wrote, "were at least three meters high—possibly higher....It seemed as if the boats would be swamped as they lay alongside."

There would be no delay or indecision from the Japanese at Singora like there had been at Kota Bharu, however. Come hell or high water, the invasion would proceed. To the surprise of those who had claimed it was useless to try to disembark in such heavy seas, the signal to "lower the boats" was soon flashed from the mastheads of the transports.

What Tsugi and the men on the *Ryojo Maru* went through getting into the landing craft, "tossing up and down on the waves like leaves of a tree in the wind," represented the difficulties encountered by the troops in the rest of the transports.

"The problem was to let go of the rope ladder at the right time," said Tsugi. "If [you] let go...as the boat commenced to fall from the top of a wave, [you] landed safely, but if [you] let go as the boat was rising, there was danger of breaking a leg."

It took almost an hour to load the little boats. Many of the men on board had become seasick while waiting. Heavy and light machine guns had to be passed down from hand to hand.

"We were getting worried about the time everything was taking," remembered Tsugi, "as we wanted all the boats landed before daylight.... Then, on the gunwale of the *Ryojo Maru*, three red lights appeared. It was the order to set out."

In the heavy seas, boats frequently lost sight of each other, making it impossible to maintain any semblance of formation.

"As we approached the beach...about a third of the boats were [either] tossed bodily ashore or smashed into each other before [they landed]," said Tsugi. "Everywhere soldiers could be seen holding up their weapons as they plunged into the sea."

With no opposition other than the sea, however, troops quickly scrambled ashore.

"It was exactly 4:00 a.m. on December 8, when my boat landed," wrote the 25th Army's director of operations.

Finding the Thai Army's beach defenses unoccupied, meant "our surprise attack had been successful."

Several weeks before the invasion, the Japanese had sent an army major, named Yoshikiko Osone, to Singora disguised as a civilian consulate worker. His job was to convince the Thai Army and police, one day prior to the landing, not to resist when the troops came ashore.

Since there had been no opposition, Tsugi figured Major Osone had successfully pulled off what was called the "Dream Plan." But, when the major failed to greet them on the beach, Tsugi suspected something had gone wrong.

He was right. Major Osone had inadvertently destroyed the cipher needed to decode the message he was sent informing him of the date and time of the landing.

Tsugi hurried off to the Japanese Consulate, where he awakened the consul, named Katsumo, and Major Osone. "Without a moment's delay," said Tsugi, "we had to make arrangements with the Thai police...and the Thailand troops."

With Consul Katsumo as a guide and 100,000 ticals in bribery money, they headed for the police station, where they were greeted with rifle fire as they reached the front gate.

"Suddenly, we heard a gunshot and our headlight exploded....Then came two or three more shots in quick succession," remembered Tsugi, taking cover in a nearby drainage ditch.

The only response he received from his interpreter's plea to cease fire, was "more and more bullets..."

Colonel Tsugi's main concern, however, was the Thai Army. After leaving the police station, he ran into a battalion of 5th Division troops who had hurried to the sound of gunfire. Tsugi sent them down the road with a large white flag toward what he hoped would be a friendly reception at the Thai Army camp.

He was wrong. "...suddenly, without warning," he said, "a machine gun opened up. We discovered they were deployed on a wide front and had ten machine guns and a number of other guns covering the road along which our troops were extended..."

As the battle with what turned out to be the Thai Military Police began, Tsugi returned to the beach, where he reported the incident to General Tomoyuki Yamashita, 25th Army commander, who had come ashore a few minutes earlier at 5:20 a.m.

"Without losing a minute," remembered Tsugi, "General Yamashita ordered that the resistance of the Thai Military Police was to be smashed immediately."

As he waited for units of the 5th Division to move out, Tsugi took a look at the landing beach. It was a mess. "...I saw thirteen or fourteen

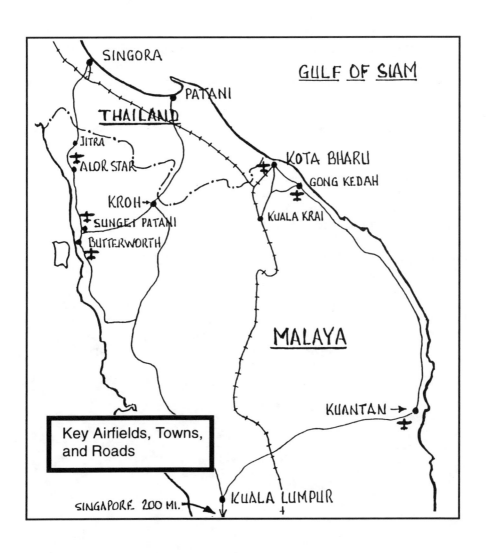

Key Airfields, Towns, and Roads

upturned motor boats floating on waves or washed ashore on the beach."
It was fortunate, he thought, that all the men had worn lifejackets.

In conjunction with Operation Matador, a few days before the war
started, the RAF had located two Blenheim bomber squadrons and a squadron of sixteen Brewster Buffalo fighters on their two main fields in northern Malaya, Alor Star and Sungei Patani.

Although they had been alerted of the Japanese invasion, the RAF
was not overly concerned about the immediate threat from the Japanese
Air Force. Since no aircraft carriers had been reported as part of the enemy
invasion force, there was little concern about a surprise attack.

Unknown to the British, however, the Japanese, in less than six weeks,
had constructed an airfield on Phu quoc Island off the western coast of
Indochina, that placed its long range bomber squadrons within easy striking distance of the two fields.

Although the reconnaissance plane that had reported the landings at
Singora and Patani, had also taken aerial photos of the field at Singora that
showed over fifty Japanese planes already on the ground there, they must
not have been processed in time to alert the two fields.

Whatever the reason, both air fields were struck almost simulta-
neously at 7:30 a.m. At Alor Star, twenty-seven Japanese bombers destroyed
all but six Blenheims of Number 62 Squadron.

At Sungei Patani, thirty-five miles south of Alor Star, radar had alerted
the field of approaching planes several minutes before they arrived. Only
two of the sixteen Buffalos of Number 21 Squadron got into the air, but malfunctioning guns forced them to land without firing a shot. Fortunately, there
were only five Japanese bombers in the group that hit the field, destroying

Sadly for the RAF, the inept American-made Brewster Buffalo was the only fighter
available to the British in Malaya.

US Navy

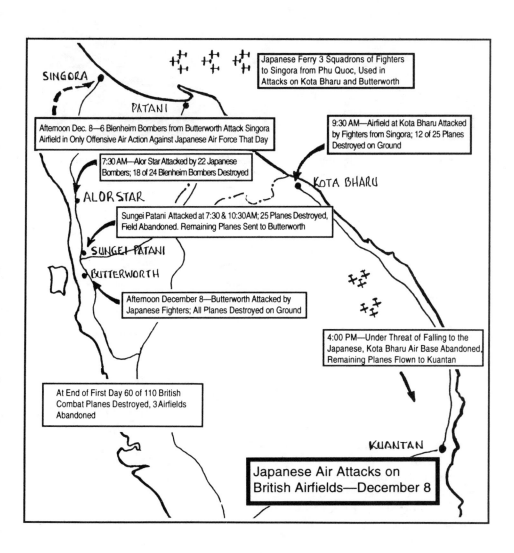

SINGORA

PATANI

Japanese Ferry 3 Squadrons of Fighters to Singora from Phu Quoc, Used in Attacks on Kota Bharu and Butterworth

Afternoon Dec. 8—6 Blenheim Bombers from Butterworth Attack Singora Airfield in Only Offensive Air Action Against Japanese Air Force That Day

9:30 AM—Airfield at Kota Bharu Attacked by Fighters from Singora; 12 of 25 Planes Destroyed on Ground

7:30 AM—Alor Star Attacked by 22 Japanese Bombers; 18 of 24 Blenheim Bombers Destroyed

ALOR STAR

KOTA BHARU

Sungei Patani Attacked at 7:30 & 10:30AM; 25 Planes Destroyed, Field Abandoned. Remaining Planes Sent to Butterworth

SUNGEI PATANI

BUTTERWORTH

Afternoon December 8—Butterworth Attacked by Japanese Fighters; All Planes Destroyed on Ground

4:00 PM—Under Threat of Falling to the Japanese, Kota Bharu Air Base Abandoned, Remaining Planes Flown to Kuantan

At End of First Day 60 of 110 British Combat Planes Destroyed, 3 Airfields Abandoned

KUANTAN

Japanese Air Attacks on British Airfields—December 8

Japanese Nakajima 96 fighter. Although obsolete at time of attack on Malaya, it easily drove off the more modern but inept Brewster Buffalo.

only seven of the thirty planes scattered about the base. Eighteen people were killed, including sixteen Chinese women.

Damage to the runways of both Alor Star and Sungei Patani was negligible, but not because of inaccurate bombing. The Japanese, anticipating the capture and immediate use of the two fields, had purposely stayed away from using heavy, high explosive bombs, which could render the runways unusable. Instead, smaller, 150-pound fragmentation bombs were used, whose grenade-like explosion on contact would avoid cratering the runways.

Not long after the raid on Sungei Patani, two Buffalo fighters, flown by Lieutenant J.R. Kinninmont and Sergeant N.R. Chapman, took off on a reconnaissance run to Singora. As they neared the coast, they ran into a dozen Japanese Type 96 "Claude" fighters. They were outnumbered six to one, but appearance of the slow, outmoded, open-cockpit, fixed-gear Mitsubishis erased any fear they had of taking on the enemy planes.

Kinninmont got only one quick burst at the lead plane before finding himself in trouble. "After spraying bullets in [the enemy's] general direction, I found somebody on my tail and tracers...whizzing past my wings."

Yelling at Chapman to return to base, he went into a vertical dive. Three Claudes followed him down, but two broke off the chase. "But one stuck like a leech," said the young lieutenant. "As I watched him, I saw his guns smoke and whipped into a tight turn. It was too late and a burst of bullets splattered into my plane."

Then, in a flash, it struck him. "This Jap was out to kill me." It's doubtful if a better description of man's fear of dying when exposed to hostile fire for the first time was ever written than by the young pilot. Of this experience he wrote, in part:

I broke into a cold sweat....A noise throbbed in my head and I suddenly felt...weak. My feet kept jumping on the pedals. My mouth was stone dry and I couldn't swallow. My mouth was open and I was panting as though I'd just finished a hundred yard dash and I felt cold. Then I was jibbering...He'll get you next burst. You'll flame into the trees. No, he can't get you—he mustn't get you. You're too smart. He'll get you next time. Watch him, watch his guns. Watch those trees. It's cold. My feet were still jumping on the pedals. I couldn't control them. Then I saw his attacks were missing me. I was watching his guns....And then my whole body tightened and I could think. I flew low and straight, only turning when he attacked. The Jap couldn't hit me again...

It was 10:30 a.m. when Kinninmont and Chapman, who had also outrun the enemy fighters, returned safely to Sungei Patani. They had no sooner parked their planes, however, when fifteen Japanese twin-engined bombers were spotted approaching out of the east. This time there was no warning. In less than fifteen minutes, Sungei Patani was finished as a function air base.

Two hundred thousand gallons of aviation fuel went up in flames during the attack. Every building on the base was destroyed. Of the twenty-six planes on the field, only four Buffalos and four Blenheim night fighters were still flyable after the attack. It was decided to transfer the eight remaining planes to the air strip at Butterworth, 45 miles to the south.

While preparing to transfer his remaining fighters, the squadron leader of the 21st was again ordered to send a plane to Singora to see what was happening there. A newly confident Kinninmont volunteered to take the reconnaissance run, and, although able to make only a single pass over the area before being chased away by Japanese fighters, he was able to return with a count of close to forty ships in Singora Harbor.

Japanese planes took the British by surprise again when they hit the air field at Kota Bharu. Like the pilots at Alor Star and Sungei Patani, no one was immediately concerned about being attacked by planes from the Imperial Air Force. Unknown to the British, as soon as Japanese troops secured the perimeter of the field at Singora, planes from their base at Phu quoc began flying in. They were supported by two transports carrying ground personnel, parts, and aviation fuel. As part of the invasion force, they had hurriedly set up shop the minute the field was captured.

At Kota Bharu, the pilots and crewmen of RAAF Squadron Number 1, whose actions against the enemy landings early that morning had forced the Japanese ships to withdraw, were feeling pretty good about their accomplishments. At the loss of only two Hudsons, they had sunk two Japanese transports and seriously damaged a third. Landing barges had also been attacked, and casualties had been estimated at 3,000.

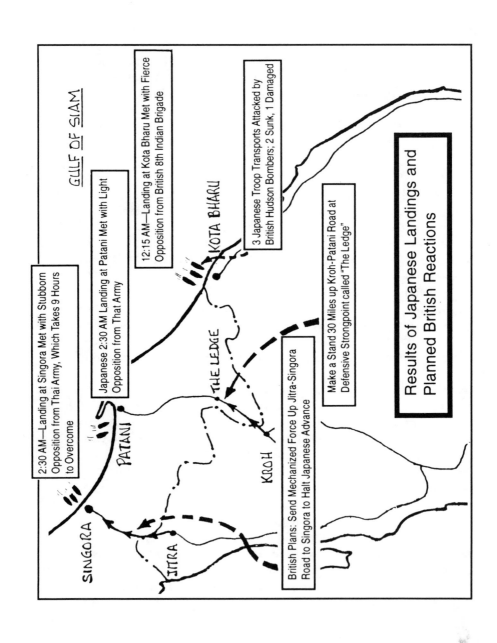

GULF OF SIAM

2:30 AM—Landing at Singora Met with Stubborn Opposition from Thai Army, Which Takes 9 Hours to Overcome

Japanese 2:30 AM Landing at Patani Met with Light Opposition from That Army

12:15 AM—Landing at Kota Bharu Met with Fierce Opposition from British 8th Indian Brigade

3 Japanese Troop Transports Attacked by British Hudson Bombers; 2 Sunk, 1 Damaged

British Plans: Send Mechanized Force Up Jitra-Singora Road to Singora to Halt Japanese Advance

Make a Stand 30 Miles up Kroh-Patani Road at Defensive Strongpoint called "The Ledge"

KOTA BHARU

THE LEDGE

PATANI

SINGORA

KROH

JITRA

Results of Japanese Landings and Planned British Reactions

It was 9:30 a.m. and it was raining. Gunfire could be heard from the beach less than two miles away, where the battle had become a stalemate since General Key's dawn counterattack.

Suddenly, out of the low rain clouds there approached what was described as "dozens of fighter aircraft." Thinking they were their own planes, men stood up and waved. Others ran out to see what all the commotion was. Moments later, they found out. The planes were Japanese and the targets were Britain's precious Hudsons and a squadron of Vildebeest torpedo planes from Gong Kedah, who had landed at the field after an aborted attack on an enemy cruiser earlier that morning.

After just ten minutes of uncontested strafing, only five Hudsons and seven Vildebeests out of twenty-five aircraft on the field remained flyable. Several men were killed, and most of the buildings were damaged.

At another air base on the other side of the Gulf of Siam, Japanese pilots on Phu quoc, like the Australian pilots had felt before the attack on Kota Bharu, were also feeling pretty good, but for different reasons.

As Lieutenant Sabao Takai later wrote, one of the reasons for rejoicing was because "by some miracle, the enemy had still not attacked our air bases [here]. It was inconceivable," he said, "that [they] would not [already have] launched a heavy attack against us."

The second reason involved word of the successful attack on the American fleet at Pearl Harbor.

Lieutenant Takai, of course, didn't realize that the reason their bases hadn't been bombed wasn't for the lack of trying. Realizing by the intensity and broad scale of attacks against his air bases, that it was impossible for the RAF to free themselves to retaliate against the Japanese, Brooke-Popham sent a message to General MacArthur in the Philippines asking for help. Indochina was within easy range of MacArthur's B-17s.

It is not known if MacArthur personally responded to Sir Robert's request, but by the time the Philippine commander got the message, it was impossible for his air force to respond. He had already lost eighteen B-17s at Clark Field, and was planning to use the remainder at Del Monte on Mindanao, to attack the Japanese at Formosa the next morning.

9:45 a.m. (PH plus 8 hrs. 5 min.): Back at Fort Canning in Singapore, it wasn't until 9:45 a.m., nine hours after the landing at Kota Bharu, seven hours after Singora and Patani, and following numerous air attacks on their key air bases in the north, that the British command finally committed the 11th Division to the fight. In this case, however, to commit was one thing, and to actually move out was another.

When Brooke-Popham received definite news of the landings at Singora and Patani at 9:45, he immediately notified his army commander, General Percival. Unfortunately, the general was not at his headquarters, but had left for the weekly routine meeting of the Straits Settlement Legislative Council, to which he gave "some first-hand information on what was really going on."

"Even in Singapore itself," Percival said, "apart from a few groups of people discussing the news, there was no outward sign that anything abnormal was happening."

After delivering this piece of questionably important information, at the cost of a precious hour and fifteen minutes, Percival returned at 11:00 a.m., where he immediately had orders cut directing General Lewis Heath to move up to Jitra on the Singora road. At the same time, another column was to cross the Siamese border at Kroh and move out to the Ledge position, thirty miles up the road to Patani.

For some unknown reason, Heath did not receive the orders until 1:10 p.m., upon which he called Percival for further clarification. Twenty minutes later, he called 11th Division headquarters and passed the orders on to its commander, General D.M. Murray-Lyon.

Finally, at 3:00 p.m., an hour and a half later, and an unbelievable twelve hours since the Japanese first set foot on the beaches at Singora and Patani, the British moved out against their new enemy. Obviously, it was too late.

General Murray-Lyon, upon receiving the order to move out, contacted Lieutenant Colonel H.D. Moorhead, commanding officer of what was called Krocol, an improvised column of 15th Indian Brigade troops, and told him to start immediately for the Ledge.

The hurriedly assembled column was forced to move out at less than half strength. Reaching the Thai border, they found the road blocked by a padlocked gate, and promptly smashed it open with axes. As the first Indian soldier started across, however, he was shot and killed by rifle fire from a force of 300 well-concealed and determined Thai constabulary.

Without armor or artillery support, Moorhead was unable to overcome the determined Siamese.

The British advance was consistently held up by roadblocks and snipers firing from trees or the dense jungle on either side of the road. On occasion, they would let the advance guard go by, then ambush the main body as it followed a few yards behind.

By nightfall, as the column dug in for the night, of the original 30 miles to there objective, they were still 27 away. In three hours, and at the cost of fifteen men, they had only been able to advance three miles against their surprising Thai adversaries.

Meanwhile, units of the 11th Indian Division, under the command of Brigadier General W.O. Lay, had started up the Jita-Singora road, and found the going relatively easy. Free from opposition, in less than four hours, the column, known as Laycol, had traveled ten miles into Thailand, where they halted to dig in for the night.

On the other end of the road at Singora, Japanese troops had successfully quelled all Thai Army resistance by noon. Despite intermittent shelling of the runways by Thai artillery, Japanese planes had been operating off the Singora airstrip since mid-morning, the effects of which have already been noted.

In case the Siamese refused to cooperate with Major Osone's Dream Plan, the Japanese had planned to dress soldiers in Thai Army and police uniforms. Colonel Tsugi, who had 1,000 uniforms made for the occasion, planned to use them to get his troops close enough to ambush their unsuspecting foes, and overcome what would be the only obstacle to crossing the frontier.

At noon, however, "white flags were hoisted along the entire front," said Tsugi, and it was announced that "resistance [from] the Thai Army [was] suspended for the time being."

"Casting aside the Thai uniforms...they changed back into their own Japanese dress," said the operational commander. "Our immediate need...was to launch the strongest possible attack on the frontier, so as not to give the enemy time for preparations."

Anticipating the British to launch a counterattack up the Jitra-Singora road, Tsugi personally rounded up a makeshift unit composed of three tanks, a field gun, and 300 men.

It wasn't long before his fears were realized, when the British force moving out of Jitra was spotted by a Japanese reconnaissance plane. It dropped a message that said, "Large enemy mechanized force this day at noon passed through Changlun moving north."

"Feeling uneasy," said Tsugi, "I hurried forward and before long overtook the leading troops of the 5th Division....They were under the command of Lieutenant Colonel Shizuo Saeki, who had been ordered to...protect the disembarkation of the main forces of the army."

Colonel Saeki, after hearing of the advancing enemy force, and "expressing willingness to attack [them]," voluntarily added two squadrons of mechanized cavalry and a light armored unit to Tsugi's force, and immediately moved out to meet the British.

4:00 p.m. (PH plus 14 hrs. 20 min.): As Saeki's makeshift column moved cautiously down the Singora-Jitra road, the situation at Kota Bharu, which had remained at a stalemate throughout the day, took a change for the worse; that is, it appeared to take a change for the worse.

The airfield, which was just two miles inland from the contested beachhead, although bombed and strafed several times during the day, was still functioning. At around four o'clock, rumor spread that the Japanese had broken through and were closing in on the field.

Even though General Key's counterattack had failed to gain the upper hand, the Japanese had not been successful at extricating themselves from their tenuous position on the beach. As Key later said, "We did pin the enemy that day, but it was impossible to throw him out."

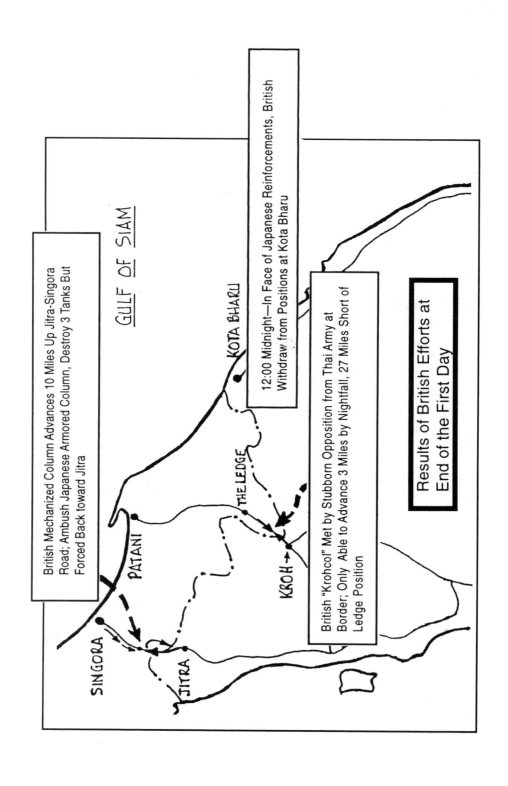

GULF OF SIAM

British Mechanized Column Advances 10 Miles Up Jitra-Singora Road; Ambush Japanese Armored Column, Destroy 3 Tanks But Forced Back toward Jitra

12:00 Midnight—In Face of Japanese Reinforcements, British Withdraw from Positions at Kota Bharu

British "Krohcol" Met by Stubborn Opposition from Thai Army at Border; Only Able to Advance 3 Miles by Nightfall, 27 Miles Short of Ledge Position

SINGORA

PATANI

JITRA

KROH→

THE LEDGE

KOTA BHARU

Results of British Efforts at
End of the First Day

Whether it was stray bullets from a firefight that had erupted on the beach or the onset of darkness that caused it, an unidentified officer at the field ordered that the pre-arranged evacuation plan, called the "Denial Plan," be put into effect immediately.

At the same time, a call was made to Air Marshal Pulford in Singapore, saying that the airfield was under attack by Japanese ground forces. Pulford ordered immediate withdrawal of all serviceable aircraft.

As air base personnel began setting fire to the buildings, as many as could be crammed into the few remaining Hudsons and Vildebeests took off for Kuantan, 160 miles south.

As soon as he got word of the evacuation, General Key, along with Base Wing Commander C.H. Noble, made a quick survey of the field to see if the rumored breakthrough was true. They found no Japanese or evidence that justified the ordering of the Denial Plan. But it was already too late. The last of the ground and maintenance personnel had already left by truck for the railhead at Kuala Krai, forty-two miles to the south.

In their haste, however, it was discovered that the most important part of the plan had not been carried out. It called for blowing up all unused bombs on the runways, making them unfit for use by the enemy. This had not been done.

By the time General Key returned to his command post, he was notified that several Japanese transports had again appeared off the beach. Knowing he would be unable to contest the landing of reinforcements without air support, nor contain the beachhead once they landed, he ordered his 8th Brigade troops to begin pulling back to Kota Bharu at midnight.

Masked by overcast skies and a heavy downpour, at twelve o'clock, Indian soldiers quietly gave up the positions they had so tenaciously held onto throughout the day. Sadly, by 1:00 a.m., twenty-four hours after the initial Japanese landing, enemy reinforcements were able to wade ashore uncontested on a beach over which a battle, that had taken the lives of over 320 of their comrades and had left them with 538 wounded, had been fought. As Colonel Tsugi would later write, "It was one of the most violent actions of the Malayan campaign."

About the time General Key's troops began their withdrawal, the makeshift 5th Division force, commanded by Colonel Saeki and accompanied by Colonel Tsugi, had reached the outskirts of the village of Ban Sadao, ten miles from the Thai-Malay border on the Singora-Jitra road.

"Approaching the village we heard rifle shots and gunfire at the head of the column," said Tsugi. "Our advance guard had come into collision with the British."

Collision was right. Headlights from the Japanese column had been spotted a few minutes earlier as it moved unsuspecting down the road through a heavy downpour.

Lieutenant May, in charge of the anti-tank Bren-carriers, held fire until the lead tank was less than 100 yards away. At that point, they opened fire, knocking out all three enemy tanks. Punjabi riflemen went to work on the vehicles behind the tanks, forcing Japanese soldiers to scatter on either side of the road.

Reacting to the ambush, "like hunting dogs," wrote Tsugi, "our men swiftly dispersed into the rubber plantation on both sides of the road and our field gun opened fire on the enemy front."

At that point, the Japanese, supported by artillery and mortar fire, began to do what everyone who would face them in the long war to come agreed they could do best—infiltrate. Before long, they had flanked the Punjabis, and, as Tsugi would later write, "...the British weakly crumbled to pieces and retreated to the south leaving a blood-stained armored car and a [motorcycle] sidecar."

As they soon found out, what had been left inside the armored car was worth far more than the vehicle itself. Not long after the shooting stopped, an excited Japanese officer ran back to Colonel Tsugi carrying a blood-smeared map that was found in the abandoned armored car.

"It was accurate and showed clearly in colored pencil the army fortifications and dispositions around Changlum and Jitra," said the 25th Army's Director of Operations. Since they were without a single accurate map of the area, "it was a gift for which we expressed our gratitude—especially for the penciled marks on it showing the [British troop] dispositions..."

Jumping into the captured sidecar, with map in hand, Tsugi headed back to Singora, where, stopping at 5th Division Headquarters, he heard news of the successful attack on Pearl Harbor.

"It was a good omen," he said, "a good omen."

Although the loss of the map appeared critical to the British, its effect was somewhat diminished when Laycol blew up three key bridges behind them as it withdrew back toward Jitra. They were bridges whose loss would give them time to reorganize and change troop dispositions before the Japanese arrived.

Colonel Tsugi, after delivering the prized British map to General Yamashita, routinely wrote in his diary that "six enemy bombing planes which had attacked Singora anchorage [that afternoon], were attacked by our fighters but escaped."

As already mentioned, when the British made the decision to abandon the airfield at Alor Star earlier that day, the remaining Blenheim bombers were withdrawn south to the air base at Butterworth.

It was the Blenheims who made the attack on Singora that Tsugi made reference to. Unknown to him, however, his Imperial Air Force comrades were quick to retaliate, catching all the Blenheims on the ground at Butterworth as they were preparing for a second raid on Singora; that is, all but one.

Squadron Leader Arthur Scarf, who had taxied his plane to the head of the runway when the Japanese struck, took off when he saw bombs beginning to fall on the far end of the field. As soon as the enemy raiders left, Scarf, who had circled at a distance, flew back over the damaged strip to see if anyone was able to join him. No one was. All five Blenheims had been destroyed.

Deciding to go it alone, Scarf headed for Singora. Although viciously attacked by Japanese fighters over the target, he was able to deliver his bombs. He was wounded during the attack, but was somehow able to escape, and force land the crippled bomber at Alor Star. His crew was unharmed, but Scarf's wounds would prove to be fatal.

Ironically, the young squadron leader's wife, who had recently joined the Malayan Government Nursing Service, was stationed at Alor Star.

In the struggle to save her husband, two pints of her blood were transfused into his body. But it was too late. Arthur Scarf died in his wife's arms later that night.

For his heroism and gallantry under fire, Squadron Leader Arthur S.K. Scarf was awarded his country's highest medal, the Victoria Cross. It was the first such medal given in the war with Japan.

Back at Naval Headquarters in Singapore, Admiral Thomas "Tom Thumb" Phillips, commander in chief of the Eastern Fleet, called a noon meeting of all his senior officers on the *Prince of Wales*. He told them of the Japanese landings at Singora and Kota Bharu, and said that he believed with fighter protection and the element of surprise, the *Prince of Wales* and *Repulse*, supported by destroyers *Vampire*, *Electra*, *Tenedos* and *Express*, had a good chance of "smashing the Japanese [invasion] forces" at Singora. It had already been decided that it was impossible for the fleet to remain at Singapore, so the plan was accepted.

Phillips had discussed the air support situation with Air Marshal Pulford earlier. The admiral told him that in order for the attack to succeed, he had to have reconnaissance reports of enemy ship movements throughout the ninth and before dawn on the tenth, as well as fighter protection to support his attack on enemy transports at Singora that same morning.

Unaware at that moment of the overwhelming success the Japanese air force would have against the RAF that day, Pulford tentatively agreed to Phillips' plan. The air support problem would have already been taken care of had the carrier *Indomitable,* originally ordered to the Far East with the two battleships, had not run aground in the course of training exercises in the Caribbean.

Britain's confidence in Force Z, as it was called, was demonstrated by their anxiousness to have members of the press on board to witness the "smashing [of] the Japanese..."

The first newsman to be invited aboard was Associated Press correspondent Yates McDaniel, who got a call at the AP (Associated Press) newsroom in the Cathay Building from his good friend, Vice Admiral Sir Geoffrey Layton.

"We're sending out two capital ships under Tom Thumb Philipps," said Layton. "Would you like to go along?"

McDaniel asked him how long they'd be gone.

"Five or six days," he replied. They were going up the east coast of Malaya to attack the Japanese invasion convoys landing at Singora.

Being the only Associated Press correspondent *in* Singapore, McDaniel thought for a minute, then turned Layton down.

Around 1:30, the phone rang at the Raffles Hotel dining room. The man on the other end of the line asked the manager if Mr. Cecil Brown of CBS was there. He was.

Brown, who was lunching with O.D. Gallagher, of the *London Daily Express,* went to the phone. It was Major Charles Fisher, assistant director of public relations for the military in Singapore.

"Do you want to go on a four-day assignment?" he asked.

"What is it?"

"I can't tell you what it is or where you're going, but I must have an immediate yes or no answer and you must leave at once."

"All right, I'll take it," said Brown, who changed his mind by the time he returned to the table.

"I agree with you," said Gallagher, "I wouldn't go either."

A few minutes later the manager came back and called Gallagher to the phone. It was Major Fisher again.

"Do you want to go on a jaunt?" he asked. "Can't tell you what it is. You must say yes or no at once. You'll be away four of five days. Do you want to go?"

"...has it anything to do with those 'new boys' [*Prince of Wales* and *Repulse*] we saw?"

"Yes. Two can go—one American and one British reporter."

Gallagher rushed up to the table and grabbed Brown's arm.

"Cec," he panted, "it's the *Prince of Wales*! We're going on the *Prince of Wales*. We've got to pull out right away. They're on the way for us now."

"I thought you said you wouldn't go," said Brown.

"Oh, Christ, I don't know what to do. What are you going to do?"

"It's a chance," said Brown, "but why don't we take it? When we get back we'll probably be fired and then we'll start a newspaper or radio station of our own."

"Fine," said Gallagher. "They're coming for us right away to go to the naval base."

The debate over whether to go or not still wasn't over. When the two men arrived at the naval base, they were told that they were going on the *Repulse,* not the *Prince of Wales,* as they were led to believe.

"It makes a hell of a lot of difference if you can begin your story by saying, 'I stood on the bridge of the *Prince of Wales* when we sank four Jap battleships,' rather than 'I stood on the bridge of the *Repulse*,' " said Brown, appealing to Captain Leach of the *Prince of Wales*.

"I'm terribly sorry," said Leach, "there just isn't room."

Particularly angered when told that the *Prince of Wales* was the only ship the censors would allow mentioned in their reports, the two men again wrestled with the decision of whether to go or not.

"If we went in the *Repulse,* all we would be able to say would be, 'with the Eastern Fleet,' " complained Gallagher. "From a story point of view the whole thing's a washout..."

"Well, since we've come this far," said Brown, "why don't we go on with it? We'll have a [four-day] sea trip and get fired when we get back anyhow."

Since there wasn't time to send other correspondents to replace them, Gallagher agreed to go.

"At 6:20, the *Repulse* drew out into the Straits of Johor," remembered Brown. "Within minutes, the *Prince of Wales* drew up alongside and started past."

The decks of both ships were lined with men. As the *Prince of Wales* slid by, the crew of the *Repulse* saluted.

Brown glanced over at Gallagher, who at that moment had prophetically written in his notebook, "The Prince slipped past us to death or glory..."

Whether it would be "death or glory" was in the hands of Admiral Phillips. Just before sailing, he had received word from Air Vice Marshal Pulford that fighter protection off Singora on the tenth was doubtful.

As final preparations were being made before sailing, Phillips asked one of his officers, Captain Arthur Bell, to come down to his cabin. Filling him in with what had transpired during his meeting with Pulford, he told Bell, "I'm [still] not sure that [Pulford] realizes the importance I attach to fighter cover over Singora." Picking up his pen, he said, "I'm therefore going to send a letter stressing this point again and asking him to let me know as soon as possible what he can do for certain."

Signing it, he handed it to Bell, who took it to the admiral's driver for immediate delivery to Pulford.

An hour or so later, as the big ship slid past the harbor entrance for open water, Changi signal station flashed the following message from Pulford: "To Fleet commander. Regret fighter protection impossible."

"Well," said Phillips, shrugging his shoulders, "we must get on without it."

Around midnight, armed with news of the heavy attacks and abandonment of Sungei Patani and Alor Star along with word of the loss of Kota Bharu, Pulford immediately contacted Rear Admiral A.F.E. Palliser, Phillips' chief of staff, who had remained behind in Singapore and was in touch with the force commander.

As soon as he was briefed on the situation in the north, Palliser sent the following message to Phillips: "Fighter protection on Wednesday 10 will not, repeat not, be possible." The signal, received at 1:25 a.m. on the ninth, said that reconnaissance scheduled for that day and dawn of the tenth was still possible, however.

Despite the warnings, Phillips continued on, unworried as long as he was able to maintain the element of surprise, and unconcerned about the Japanese Air Force. Although his biggest fear from the air was enemy torpedo planes, based on intelligence reports, he figured as long as he stayed outside of 200 miles from the nearest Japanese air base, he couldn't be reached. He expected to encounter high-level bombers, but figured that high speed maneuvering would neutralize that threat.

"...to death or glory."

At 11:07 a.m., December 10, the two ships were attacked by both Japanese high-level bombers and torpedo planes, who had flown 600 miles from Saigon to reach their targets. Outside of underestimating their range, Tom Phillips was right about the effectiveness of both bombs and torpedoes. Although only three of fifty-seven bombs dropped hit either of the two ships, torpedoes from fifty-one planes were responsible for sinking both battleships and killing 840 officers and men, including Admiral Phillips and Captain Leach of the *Prince of Wales*. Cecil Brown and O.D. Gallagher both survived and were rescued. They were not fired when they returned.

By the end of Malaya's first 24 hours of war, the outcome was already foreordained. With no Matador to oppose them, the Japanese successfully landed in force at three key locations on the east coast. Equally important, as they had done in the Philippines, before the sun had set that first day, they had gained complete control of the air, destroying 60 of 110 British combat aircraft and forcing the abandonment of three key airfields in northern Malaya.

CHAPTER 2

"LAST NIGHT JAPANESE FORCES
ATTACKED HONG KONG..."

TIME DIFFERENCE: 5 HOURS 30 MINUTES.

4:45 a.m. (PH plus 2 hrs. 15 min.): The anticipation of war between Great Britain and Japan in the Far East had been building for several weeks. The political situation between the two countries had all but deteriorated, and with news of the large Japanese invasion force just hours away from the coast of Malaya, the feeling that it was near was never stronger than it was on Sunday, December 7, in Hong Kong.

Major General C.M. Maltby, commander of the colonial forces on the island and the New Territories, just across Victoria Harbor on the China mainland, had placed his small 11,319-man force on alert.

Without an air force, and, like Singapore, with all his fixed guns pointing toward the sea, Maltby's only hope was that an attack would come from that direction. But, with the Japanese occupying the city of Canton, less than 100 miles to the north, the likelihood of an assault from the sea had long since been discounted. Without a major offensive by the Chinese against Canton, which wasn't likely, an attack against Hong Kong and the New Territories would be from China's mainland, and the British wouldn't be able to stop it.

In fact, stopping it was never planned. The main objective was to hold up the enemy long enough to evacuate Europeans from the mainland city of Kowloon and the island of Hong Kong.

Parts of that plan had already been initiated weeks before. With the exception of the mile-long Sha Tin Tunnel, it began with the destruction of many of the tunnels and bridges inside the New Territories on the Canton to Kowloon railroad. This was followed by an order to evacuate British women and children from the Colony.

It appeared that the Japanese "balloon" was poised to "go up," as the British wryly referred to the war starting. For several days, army intelligence had been monitoring Radio Tokyo for leads that might give them a hint as to when it might occur.

Two of their most skilled linguists, Major Charles Boxer and James "Monkey" Giles, had been assigned around-the-clock duty of listening to the broadcasts from the army's main military complex in Hong Kong.

At 4:45 a.m., Boxer, who had the duty between midnight and 6:00 a.m., suddenly sat up in his chair. The routine Radio Tokyo broadcast he had been sleepily listening to, was suddenly interrupted.

The Army and Navy divisions of Imperial Headquarters jointly announced at 3:30 this morning, December 8, that the Imperial Army and Navy forces began hostilities against the American and British forces in the Pacific at dawn today.

3:30 a.m. Tokyo time was eight o'clock Hawaii time, and 4:30 in Hong Kong.

Boxer tore off his headset and went over and shook Giles. "Wake up, Monkey!" he said. "It's started. You don't want to miss it, do you?"

Dashing back to his desk, he quickly phoned General Maltby's aide, Lieutenant Ian MacGregor, who woke up the British commander with the news.

As he pulled on his clothes, Maltby told MacGregor to alert all the forward outpost units in the New Territories, so they could begin preplanned delaying action demolition of all the bridges and tunnels on the Canton-Kowloon road.

The British plan, which was, of course, defensive, had been in place for months. The only hope they had of holding the Japanese came from knowing exactly which route the enemy assault would take. That was easy.

The Japanese attack would be launched from the northern boundary of the New Territories, fifteen miles above Kowloon. From there, the only way the Japanese could be successful, was for the main assault to come through a narrow, four-mile wide opening between Gindrinkers Bay on the west and Tolo Harbor on the east. It was here, on what was variously called the Bottle Neck, Inner Line, or Gindrinkers Line, that the British planned to make their stand.

Anchored by the Shing Mun Redoubt, according to British operations officer, Captain Freddie Guest, the line "was unquestionably the strongest position, as it was flanked on each side by water...and was well studded with pill-boxes and concrete shelters."

"Yet at no time," he added, "could it be thought...that [it] could be held indefinitely against a strong force. The most it could [do] was to sufficiently hold up the enemy, and allow a complete evacuation of Europeans from Kowloon and the island of Hong Kong."

Therefore, that first morning, outside of small groups of Royal Engineers blowing up bridges, and dynamiting huge craters in the roads to slow the enemy advance, nothing was seen of the British Army. In fact, not a single colonial soldier was seen for the first two hours, nor a shot fired by either side until just before noon.

Japanese commander, Lieutenant General Takashi Sakai, anticipating that the first British opposition would come from the main road and railway junction at Fan Ling, six miles into the New Territories, was shocked to learn his lead elements had reached the outskirts of the village without running into any opposition.

"Tell them to keep going," he told his aide to signal to the officer in charge. "The English must be someplace. Where can they go?"

The war was less .than two hours old, he thought. Maybe his orders to mop up the Hong Kong operation in ten days could be fulfilled. And maybe his division would be fighting in the Dutch East Indies before Christmas as the Imperial General Staff had predicted.

7:57 a.m. (PH plus 5 hrs. 53 min.): Back in Hong Kong, outside of the military and the press, few were aware that the war had started.

Because of the impending crisis, on Sunday, Pan American Airways officials had decided to move the Monday morning takeoff time of the Manila-bound *Hong Kong Clipper* up one hour.

As the shuttle taking passengers from the Pan Am offices in front of the Peninsula Hotel to the airport was just ready to leave, an excited Chinese employee ran out and stopped the bus. "Everyone get off," he said. "The flight has been delayed."

Jan Marsman, one of the passengers, remembered someone saying they'd heard war with Japan had started. "He was considered an alarmist and a rumor-monger," said Marsman, "and subsided under the weight of general disapproval."

With time on his hands, Marsman, a Dutch-born businessman, scouted up his old friend, T.B. Wilson, of the American President Steamship Lines, who was staying at the Peninsula Hotel.

The *Hong Kong Clipper*, seen here at Pearl Harbor in 1937, was strafed and destroyed on the morning of December 8, Hong Kong harbor.

National Archives

The two were enjoying a cup of coffee together in Wilson's room, when Marsman "looked out of the window and saw airplanes circling and diving over the [Kai Tak] airport."

From three miles away, it was hard to tell. "What do you think those planes are?" he asked Wilson.

"Aw hell, just maneuvers, Jan," he said.

"But what about all the smoke?"

"Don't you know they use smoke screens in maneuvers?" said Wilson, as he walked back and sat down in his chair.

It was exactly 7:57 a.m. What Wilson had guessed to be British planes on maneuvers, were really the first of a squadron of thirty-six Japanese bombers and twelve Zero fighters attacking the airfield. The "smoke screen" was created by burning British planes.

The five planes representing the entire RAF presence at Kai Tak, three Vildebeest biplane torpedo bombers and two target-towing Walrus amphibians, were destroyed in the first five minutes of the attack, as were seven civilian aircraft on the field.

The Japanese then turned to the big *Hong Kong Clipper*, tied up at the end of Kai Tak dock on the edge of Kowloon Bay. At the moment of the attack, Clipper pilot, Fred Ralph, and his six-man crew were standing on the dock, contemplating whether they would be allowed to take off for Manila. Departure time, which had been moved up an hour, had now been indefinitely delayed.

"I was...standing beside the *Clipper* when the attack came," said Ralph. "The alarm sounded almost immediately, then planes appeared and began diving toward the field. The crew and [I] managed to scramble to safety behind a concrete dock pillar."

"There were at least a dozen different strafing attacks on the *Clipper* before she finally caught fire and started to burn."

Although Ralph thought no one was on board the big plane when the attack came, he was apparently unaware that a Filipino cabin boy was inside at the time. The boy saved himself by diving into the water and swimming into the opening of a large sewer pipe, where he remained until the attack was over.

When it ended, Ralph and his crew, with the shaking and unpleasant smelling Filipino steward, walked across the field to catch a bus back to the Peninsula Hotel.

"There were craters on the runways, and one bomb had gone right through the center of the hangar roof," remembered Ralph.

When the crew arrived back at the hotel, they ran into Jan Marsman, who had decided "to go down to the lobby and chase down a little information [about what had happened at Kai Tak]."

"I didn't have to chase far," said Jan. "The *Clipper* crew burst into the lobby at that moment. Words tumbled over one another as they told how thirty-five Japanese dive bombers had set their plane ablaze."

He also saw the Filipino mess boy, who he said was "still trembling violently, [and] scarcely able to talk."

Had the Japanese hit Kai Tak a few minutes earlier, they would have caught a DC-2 airliner on the ground, and perhaps killed the sister of Madam Chiang Kai-shek, Madam H.H. Kung. She had flown in from Chunking on a China National Aviation Corporation plane, and was met by her other sister, Madam Sun Yat Sen. Fortunately, the American-piloted plane had taken off on its return flight to Chunking minutes before the Japanese raid.

Luck was not only with Madam Kung, however. In order to inform all thirty-two of their passengers of the new schedule, Pan Am Airways officials advised all hotels to inform everyone of the one-hour change that had been made. The night clerk at the Hong Kong Hotel on the island neglected to tell Jan Marsman.

"When I was finally awakened," said Marsman, "amid a lot of confused accusations among the clerks, I was told that the bus [to the airport] was being held for me across the harbor..."

Unknown to everyone on the bus, who were obviously irked for having to wait an hour for one passenger, and thus delay the takeoff time of the *Clipper*, their lives were probably saved because of it.

"We probably owed our lives to [the clerk's] inefficiency," remembered Marsman, "since otherwise we would have been in the *Clipper* about to take off at the moment the Japs dive-bombed.

"On our return to the Hong Kong side, [we] all decided we ought to chip in on a life pension for the clerk who failed to wake me up."

Anti-aircraft defense for the airfield amounted to only four machine guns. Not a single Japanese plane was hit or damaged in the 7:57 attack, or on the second 10:00 a.m. raid.

Across Victoria Harbor on the island, an Englishman, after noting the results of the attack from the veranda of his flat, in typical British fashion, said, "That's it. The Japs have just committed suicide."

Had he been able to see the string of Japanese warships that had moved into position to block the entrance to Hong Kong Harbor, it's likely his comment would have been tempered a bit.

The British United Press correspondent who sent the story of the raid that appeared in the *London Times* the next night, like the gentleman who claimed the "Japs just committed suicide," also must have been quite a distance away when the raid occurred. It read, in part:

> Two Japanese raids have been made on the Colony, the first of which twenty-seven planes took part. Enemy aeroplanes dropped a few bombs, but scattered in the face of AA fire. A German pilot is claimed to have been piloting one of these enemy machines.

Realistically, though, it also said:

> Battle positions had also been manned at dawn. Parties which were already in position blew up demolitions in the forward areas.

The Japanese are putting field bridges across the frontier in two places and are expected to cross shortly.

Parties of between 300 and 400 Japanese could be seen on the other side of the frontier, but the garrison at Hong Kong is in a confident mood.

Demolitions had indeed taken place. The bridge over the Shum Chun River at Lo Wu was the first to go, cutting the main road into the New Territories at the Chinese border. The only sounds of war that were heard throughout most of the morning were those of demolition charges going off, as colonial troops began their systematic withdrawal back towards the confines of the Gindrinkers Line.

The *London Times* had also accurately reported that the Japanese were seen "putting field bridges across the frontier..."

Correctly anticipating the destruction of every bridge along the Canton-Kowloon road and railroad, well-organized Japanese engineers were seen erecting temporary crossings just minutes after the dust had settled from the blast that destroyed the original structure. Where huge craters had been blasted in narrow spots along the roads, they too were quickly filled in.

Because of the ability of their engineers to all but neutralize the British delaying tactics, on three occasions, lead elements of Japanese 38th Division troops caught up with demolition crews as they were preparing to blow up a bridge. Coming under enemy small arms fire, all three times they were able to set off their charges before successfully extricating themselves from the situation.

On one occasion, the engineers were driven off a bridge when they were surprised by a detachment who had suddenly appeared from around the bend of the road. As the demolition team headed for cover on the other side, a Japanese officer quickly ran onto the bridge and cut the wire leading to the detonator.

Smiling, he confidently waved his troops forward onto the bridge, where, seconds later, they, along with the bridge they were standing on, blew up. The engineers had planted a second line that he had overlooked.

2:00 p.m. (PH plus 11 hrs. 30 min.): By mid-afternoon, the Japanese had advanced eight miles into the New Territories. Outside of being delayed by downed bridges and cratered roads, they had met no opposition. Except for retreating demolition engineers, the Japanese had not seen an enemy soldier or had any shots fired at them in anger. Because of the easy time they'd had, it was not surprising they got careless.

Around two o'clock, on the Canton-Kowloon road above the village of Tai Po, a column of Japanese 229th Regiment troops were ambushed by a company of Indian troops of the 2/14 Punjabi Regiment, who were in position to protect a demolition crew setting charges on a bridge below the town.

When Major George Grey, commanding officer of the Punjabi company, first spotted the Japanese, he couldn't believe what he saw. "You'd think they were on a victory march through Trafalgar Square," he said.

The unsuspecting enemy, leading pack mules carrying dismantled field pieces, were moving at a rout-step pace, with apparently no concern that they were about to enter a village that they had not even bothered to reconnoiter. They would pay a price for their carelessness.

When the enemy column reached a point 200 yards away, Grey ordered his anxious Punjabis to open fire. Although it was eight hours in coming, the first shots fired by Colonial troops at the Japanese that day were effective.

The Indian fire was so accurate and surprising that not a single shot was fired in return. There wasn't a Japanese soldier who was not dead or wounded left in the road. All but the 50 who had been shot, had run back over the hill, leaving the mules and the wounded behind.

About an hour later, a second incident involving the same Punjabi company occurred. Although not present at the time, the decision to open fire on the Japanese was also made Major Grey. It was a much more difficult decision than the first one.

The situation was similar to the first one. The Punjabis were protecting a demolition crew setting charges on a nearby bridge, when a small enemy detachment was spotted preparing to cross an open field, 500 yards from their position.

Anticipating opposition from the defenders, with fixed bayonets, the Japanese started across the field behind a human shield of a dozen Chinese peasant women they had rounded up from a nearby village.

The Indian commander called Major Grey on the field telephone, asking him whether he should fall back or open fire.

Grey hesitated for a minute, then said, "Do your job. Stop the enemy advance, blow the bridge, and fall back to Gindrinkers."

Although the thought of carrying out the major's order was revolting to the young officer, he ordered his men to prepare to open fire on his command. When the Japanese and their begging and weeping captives reached a point less than 150 yards away, the Punjabis opened fire. It was slaughter. No one left the field alive.

3:00 p.m. (PH plus 12 hrs. 30 min.): Back in Hong Kong, the fact that the war with Japan had at last broken out had finally hit home.

"Japanese bombs had blown off the lid of complacency, said Jan Marsman, on his return from Kowloon, "with feverish activity boiling over in all directions. Trucks, cars, buses, carts and 'rickshas' [were] churning through the streets to the tune of an...international chorus of expletives.

"Some of the wealthy householders, with the specter of looting ahead, were rushing from their homes in the hills into the confines of Victoria

City, [while] others were doing the exact opposite. Polyglot Hong Kong, with 35 different nationalities included in its population, looked and sounded like a World's Fair gone crazy."

Preparations for the inevitable siege were also under way. Since the movement of troops and equipment was vital to the defense of the island, Canadian soldiers spent most of the day commandeering vehicles. By three o'clock, they had rounded up eighty-five trucks of various types and over twenty cars. They were so desperate that when the Canadian officer in charge of the operation called headquarters to ask if he should include the ten trucks used to carry sewage on the island, he was told, "Yes!"

Until the battle for the island began, the biggest threat to British security became Chinese saboteurs. Although army intelligence was aware that the colony had been infiltrated by Japanese agents, as the day wore on, it became powerfully evident how successful they had been in enticing local, and, in many cases, trusted Chinese to work for them.

Fifth column activity also began, and would remain persistent until the island fell. Sniping, in particular, was the most disturbing. That day, several military vehicles came under fire from Chinese and Japanese snipers on isolated roads and from windows of tall buildings. That night, telephone lines were cut, grenades were tossed out from the darkness, and fires were set.

Things on the Kowloon side were also happening. Most of the efforts were directed toward getting everything that would be needed to ride out a prolonged siege, across mile-wide Victoria Harbor to the island.

The primary effort involved securing transportation. Over 300 trucks and drivers were rounded up by the Traffic Office to haul rice and food supplies to the docks, where it could be towed across to the island.

Although the spoils of war are usually reserved for victorious armies, one item the Japanese would be denied when they entered Kowloon was Irish whiskey, and all other liquor for that matter. Instead of attempting to bring their stores of alcohol with them when they evacuated to the island, the managers of several English clubs in Kowloon decided to give it away. It wasn't long before lines of cars were seen queuing up in front of club entrances, and individuals with bottles under each arm were spotted walking along narrow side streets.

Captain Freddie Guest was in Kowloon when he got orders to report to British headquarters in Victoria. Before heading for the waterfront, he stopped at the Kowloon Hospital. It had already taken in over 100 patients who had been wounded in the two bombings of Kai Tak and the surrounding area that morning.

Doctor Isaac Newton, who had rushed to the hospital in his pajamas and slippers after the first bombing, would be in the same clothes when he operated on his last patient twelve hours later.

Guest, who had been a patient at the hospital a few weeks before with a polo injury, was recognized by several of the sisters.

"They were hungry for news," said Guest. "Any kind of news."

"We've lost contact with everyone since the balloon went up," said one. "What's happening?"

"There's nothing from the frontier," Guest told them, trying to sound reassuring.

"But little did any of us dream," said the young officer, "that within 48 hours the hospital would be overflowing with wounded from the Indian and British battalions from the frontier."

It was late in the afternoon when he started for the ferry. What he saw on the way surprised him.

"The streets," he said, "were exactly the same. I glanced up and down the many side streets, and everywhere the busy Chinese gave no hint of the tragedy that was rushing down on all of us."

On one street, he caught a glimpse of the tail-end of a Chinese dragon.

"Great Heavens," he thought. "What on earth have the poor devils to celebrate? There they were, following the dragon, a laughing, chattering, happy crowd, [like] a party of school children on an outing."

It was dark when he got to the ferry, where he found the pier jammed with people waiting to cross.

"Things had changed quickly in the few hours I'd been away," remembered Guest. "Thousands were fleeing to the island, and a large queue had formed for the next ferry."

Although General Maltby had ordered that the island be blacked out, it hadn't happened. "The view of the island of Hong Kong from Kowloon was as magnificent as ever," recalled Guest. "Any idea of a blackout...was almost out of the question. There were the myriad of lights as usual from quayside...up the side of Mount Victoria.

"You can't get a blackout in China merely by saying 'You mustn't show any lights,' " he said. "[It's] just not done that way in this teeming land."

Waiting for the ferry, Guest heard a plane take off from Kai Tak aerodrome. It was one of several China National Aviation Corporation planes that had begun airlifting refugees out of Hong Kong that night.

With Japanese warships blocking any attempt to escape from Hong Kong by sea, it wasn't long before word of the flights out of Kai Tak reached three men who had been scheduled to take the *Clipper* to Manila that morning. Having explored every other avenue of possible escape, Jan Marsman, Richard Wilson, and George Dankworth were on the next ferry to Kowloon.

All hopes of getting on a plane were dashed when they got to the airfield, however. By then, "hundreds of Europeans and Chinese refugees who wanted to get to China [had already] encircled Corporation headquarters," said a disappointed Marsman.

"Through the blackout, planes of the CNAC were taking off, overloaded with refugees, and returning empty to get more," said the Dutch businessman.

"So that they could transport a maximum number of refugees—many with high Jap price tags on their heads—the American pilots, [instead of flying all the way] to Chunking, were setting down [in unoccupied China] as close to the Japanese rear as possible." Before they were through, they would make sixteen trips into China and back.

By midnight, the three men were back at the Hong Kong Hotel, disheartened by losing out on what might have been their only chance to escape the obvious fate of the surrounded island.

When Freddie Guest finally got on the ferry to the island that night, he ran into a fellow operations officer, Captain Peter MacMillan.

"I asked eagerly for news from the New Territories," said Guest.

Peter looked serious. "They're moving. The Japs crossed the boundary this morning and are advancing on a very broad front towards Kowloon."

"Great Scott!" gasped Guest. "That's faster than I thought."

"Too damn fast, Freddie. The general's damned worried already."

6:00 p.m. (PH plus 15 hrs. 30 min.): Despite the fact that the Japanese were moving "too damn fast," the closer they got to the Gindrinkers Line, the more opposition they met.

Since their main advance was down the Canton-Kowloon road, most of the opposition came from Major George Grey's Punjabis. Along with the early afternoon ambush at Tai Po, the Japanese were jumped twice more by Grey's men before nightfall. The last, coming at 6:00 p.m., resulted in a rout similar to the one at Tai Po. Surviving enemy soldiers fled to the rear, and pack mules ran wildly in all directions.

The story of the incident that was released by British headquarters in Hong Kong that night, and seen later in the *London Times*, said:

"By means of a Bren-carrier patrol, we engineered a highly successful ambush of a Japanese platoon, which was practically annihilated on the Castle Peak road."

Despite the delaying tactics of the demolition crews, and the moderate success of Grey's unit and others, efforts to slow down the enemy advance had not succeeded. By midnight, the Japanese had closed to within two miles of the illusionary Gindrinkers Line.

Within the first twenty-four hours of the war, lead elements of the Japanese 38th Division had advanced some fifteen miles into the New Territories without help from the main body, whose troops would move into the line that night. Less than 10,000 men would be facing them on a line whose dubious existence, outside of the Shing Mun Redoubt, left no one with any doubt of the outcome.

This included British Prime Minister Winston Churchill, who, a month earlier, wrote, that "If Japan goes to war with us, there is not the slightest chance of holding Hong Kong."

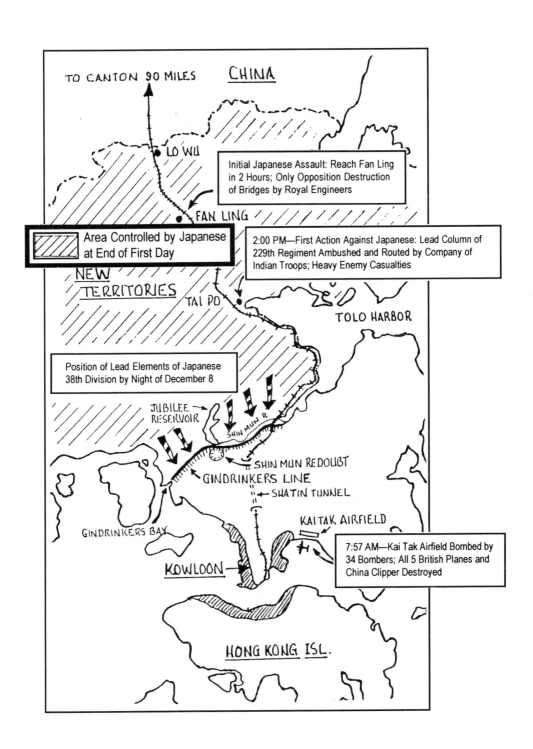

That night, he repeated that he had no illusions about the fate of the colony. "The garrison," he said, "[was] faced with a task that from the outset was beyond their powers."

The prime minister was, of course, right. The Japanese captured the Shin Mun Redoubt, despite its complex of reinforced pill boxes and underground tunnels, the next night, forcing the complete collapse of Gindrinkers and the evacuation of Kowloon twelve hours later. The island of Hong Kong lasted another fourteen days, surrendering on Christmas Day, 1941.

CHAPTER 3

"LAST NIGHT JAPANESE FORCES
ATTACKED GUAM..."

TIME DIFFERENCE: 3 HOURS 30 MINUTES.

5:27 a.m. (PH plus 53 min.): On the morning of Monday, December 8, 1941, the teletype machine in the Navy Communications Office on Guam received the following communique from Admiral Thomas Hart in Manila:

0325 08DEC41

FROM: CINCAF
TO: ASIATIC STATIONS; ASIATIC FLEET
JAPAN STARTED HOSTILITIES. GOVERN
YOURSELVES ACCORDINGLY

The operator tore the message from the teletype machine and quickly notified the navy base and island governor, Captain George McMillan, and the commander of the Marine garrison, Lieutenant Colonel William McNulty.

It was no surprise to anyone. For several weeks, things had been happening to indicate that war with Japan was close. On October 17, dependent families of U.S. military personnel on the island had been sent home. On December 4, the Navy Department in Washington ordered Guam to "...destroy all secret and confidential [papers] and other classified matter [relating to] special intelligence." They were also told to be prepared to instantly destroy "all classified matter...in event of [an] emergency."

When Radioman First Class George Tweed arrived at the Navy Communications office after receiving a call from headquarters that the war had started, the "classified matter" mentioned in the Navy Department's order was already being fed into the fire. Someone asked the chief on duty what were they supposed to do? His only response was, "I don't know."

"Everyone in the office realized that there was nothing we could do," said Tweed.

Ensign Leona Jackson, one of five navy nurses not ordered out by the government in October, said she wasn't surprised by the Japanese attack.

"...I think for many it didn't come as a surprise....Our first reaction was one of relief that we didn't have the women and children on the island."

Nurse Jackson wasn't entirely correct, however. The wife of navy Chief Petty Officer J.A. Hellmers, was too far along in her pregnancy to be evacuated. She and her newborn baby daughter were still on the island at the time.

Although a navy base under the jurisdiction of Admiral Thomas Hart's Asiatic Fleet in Manila, Guam functioned only as a refueling base for navy ships crossing the Pacific, and was the site of a naval radio station. It was also a refueling stop for Pan American Clippers on the way to and from the Far East.

Under the War Department's "RAINBOW FIVE" plan for the defense of the Pacific in the event of war with Japan, Guam was on the expendable list. Sitting alone 145 miles from Saipan, considered Japan's Truk of the Central Pacific, it had no coastal defenses, no airfield and no planes. Outside of a token force of 153 Marines, twenty-nine of which were spread around the 209-square-mile island on police duty, and 246 Insular Force Guards—native Chamorros officered by Marine NCOs—there were no combat troops to defend it. The largest guns on the island were about half a dozen .30 caliber machine guns, with only one ancient Lewis Gun mounted against air attack. Of the World War I Springfield rifles issued to the Insular Guardsmen, eighty-five were stamped, "Do Not Shoot: for training purposes only."

As for the navy, there were 230 enlisted men, 30 officers, 5 nurses and 6 warrant officers. Outside of the crew of the minesweeper *Penguin*, almost all were specialists and hospital personnel, and none were trained for combat.

The "Guam Navy" was made up of four ships: two patrol craft, YP-16 and YP-17, each carrying a crew of five; an old harbor oiler, the *R. L. Barnes*, used primarily for training of new mess attendants and local Insular Guards; and the USS *Penguin*. The 840-ton *Penguin* was crewed by 75 officers and men, carried one three-inch anti-aircraft gun, two .50 and several .30 caliber machine guns.

Despite the fact that the helpless island's fate was foreordained, as long as there were Marines, there would be no surrender without a fight. As quickly as they could assemble, the Marines moved out to positions on Orote Point on the southern edge of Apra Harbor, ready to make a stand with their 1903 Springfield rifles, two .30 caliber machine guns, and a few .45 pistols.

7:30 a.m. (PH plus 3 hrs.): About 7:30, Marine lookouts on Orote Point spotted a ship north of Cabras Island heading in their direction. A few minutes later, it was identified by its single smokestack as the *Penguin*, forced to cut short its routine island-circling patrol because of a boiler leak.

A little after eight o'clock, as the old minesweeper pulled in to tie up to its usual buoy in Apra Harbor, a small boat left Piti Naval Yard and headed for the *Penguin*. On the way, it passed one of the sweeper's lifeboats jammed with a few dozen crewmen, on their way to prepare for the ship's annual December picnic.

When the boat reached the *Penguin* a sailor yelled up to one of the crewmen, "Where's the captain? I've got an important message for him." He was directed to the bridge, where moments later the General Quarters alarm sounded.

The message, of course, was that the war with Japan had started. The *Penguin* had not been notified of Admiral Hart's "JAPAN STARTED HOSTILITIES..." message because the ship's radio had gone dead just after midnight. The last message radioman Alan Livingston received was permission to return to Apra because the boiler leak had forced the ship to cut her speed to only five knots.

Captain J. W. Haviland, realizing the *Penguin* was a sitting duck while moored inside the harbor, ordered the ship to get under way immediately. With a leaky boiler, the twenty-three-year-old veteran began moving at an agonizingly slow pace back toward the harbor entrance.

At 8:15, she had just cleared the harbor when three twin-engined Japanese bombers dove on the old ship out of the north. Although none of the bombs dropped by the enemy planes hit the *Penguin*, the concussion from several near misses violently shook the little ship. Moments later, the engines stopped, and the old girl went dead in the water.

As the attack progressed, because of erratic return fire from the *Penguin*'s three-inch anti-aircraft gun, it wasn't long before the Japanese figured out that the Americans were firing without the benefit of a range finder.

After expending their bombs, they returned to strafe the helpless little ship. Closer and closer they came, machine-gunning her from bow to stern, killing Ensign Robert White, who was manning the three-inch gun. Three men were wounded, including Captain Haviland, whose left arm was nearly blown off. One of the other wounded men, Seaman Earl Ratzman, who had been hit in the stomach by shrapnel, had to cradle his intestines in his hands for two hours until he reached the Naval Hospital in Agana.

Despite the inaccurate fire, from what the Marines could tell from their positions on Orote Point, it appeared that *Penguin* was making a pretty good fight of it. In fact, one of the Japanese planes was hit, causing it to "swirl downward, as if in trouble," witnessed Chief George O'Brien, from the *Penguin*, "but we didn't see it go down." The Marines did though, and it brought them to their feet, cheering and shaking their fists in defiance.

As the Japanese bombers ended their attack less than twenty minutes after it had started, the fate of the old minesweeper had been decided. Unknown to those watching, Captain Haviland had decided to abandon ship and to scuttle the *Penguin,* rather than take a chance of it falling into enemy hands.

As the crew made ready to leave the ship, it was discovered that the remaining 30-foot lifeboat was unseaworthy, having been riddled with shrapnel and bullet holes during the Japanese attack. It was decided that the body of Ensign White, the two wounded men and any nonswimmers amongst the remaining crewmen would go ashore in the two remaining six-man life rafts on board. For everyone else it was on with the life jackets and into the water for the two-mile swim to shore.

Unknown to those busy on deck, someone had forgotten to pass the abandon ship order on to the six-man boiler room crew, who had been frantically working to get the engines working again.

When things quieted down after the bombing, Eddie Howard, one of the crewmen, whistled into the voice tube leading to the engine room. There was no response. He did it again, but there still was no answer. A couple of the crewmen picked up wrenches and banged on the bulkhead separating the two rooms. Still nothing.

Convinced that everyone was dead, the six men were plotting what to do next when someone opened the hatch above them and yelled, "Everybody out down there!"

Imagining that the voice belonged to a Japanese, they decided the ship had been captured. "...we've been boarded," said Howard, as he started up the ladder.

When they reached the main deck they found that it was the executive officer, and not a Japanese, who fortunately had remembered that they hadn't been notified of the abandon ship order.

After scrounging through several storage lockers for life jackets, the six men jumped over the side and began swimming for shore.

The last man off the ship was Captain Haviland, who, despite his badly shot up arm, had refused to go in one of the lifeboats. Donning a life jacket, and with the aid of a mop handle to cradle his nearly shredded limb, Haviland made the two-mile swim to shore with one arm.

By the time the *Penguin*'s skipper reached the beach, his ship had disappeared into the murky waters off Orote Point.

While the three enemy planes were working over the *Penguin,* another fifteen were busy attacking the facilities on the island itself. With a single .30-caliber machine gun on the hill above Agana representing the island's only air defense, the Japanese had a field day, bombing and strafing at will.

For the Japanese, outside of Piti Naval Yard, most of their targets were confined to Orote Peninsula, a rocky promontory facing the southern edge of Apra Harbor. There, adjacent to the town of Sumay and the Marine Barracks, was the wooden-framed, twenty-room Pan American Hotel, airways office and maintenance facility.

Simultaneous to the attack on *Penguin*, nine enemy bombers, engines feathered to avoid detection, began a glide-bomb attack on the Marine Barracks and Pan Am facility. Three Marines were seriously wounded, Corporals Albert Legato and Harry Anderson, and PFC James Babbs.

The Pan Am buildings took a beating. First to go was the company's huge Standard Oil fuel tank, which instantly burst into flame, and sent billows of black smoke into the morning sky.

Another bomb hit the hotel kitchen, killing two Chamorro kitchen workers, Larry Pangelian and Teddy Cruz.

Juan Wesley, a 40-year-old Pan Am maintenance man, was hit in the stomach by shrapnel from a bomb that exploded near the office, opening a wound large enough for his intestines to protrude through. Using his T-shirt to hold them in, he was able to make it to his house in nearby Sumay, where he was picked up and driven to the hospital in Agana.

With most of Guam's civilian population "headed for the hills" after the bombing, by the time Wesley reached home, Sumay had become a ghost town.

Regarding the attack, the following message was sent to Admiral Hart in Manila:

> Guam being attacked by air by two Jap squadrons. Casualties four Chamorros on Pan Am dock while securing radio station. Hotel destroyed. Gas tanks aflame. Offices and shops machine-gunned.

Next to be hit was the Piti Naval Yard at the eastern edge of the harbor. Despite damaging a warehouse in the bombing, the most serious threat to human life came when several hundred workers rushed the yard gate in an attempt to escape the enemy attack. Fortunately, cooler heads prevailed, and no one was injured. As at Sumay, within a few minutes, the entire yard was void of human inhabitants.

Like the reactions at Sumay and Piti, as soon as word reached Agana of the bombings at Apra, almost every one of the town's 10,000 inhabitants took to the hills. Within an hour after the announcement was made, the island's capital was little more than a ghost town.

Outside of the staffs at the Naval Hospital and the governor's office, most of those who remained in the city were Japanese nationals, who had been arrested and detained by order of the governor within an hour of the attack on Sumay. Of the thirty-eight families living on the island at the time, twenty—all Japanese men—were detained.

One of those arrested was the owner of the most popular saloon on the island, that happened to be the one most frequented by American sailors and Marines.

Two other men held, a Japanese named Shinohara and a German named Scharff, were both arrested after prematurely displaying flags of their respective countries in front of their homes.

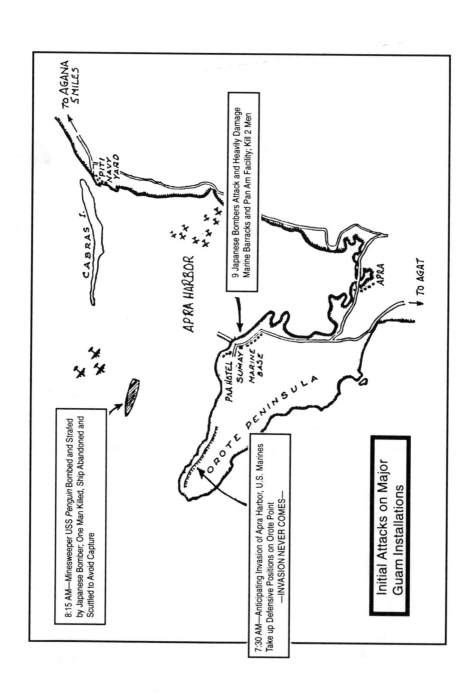

To AGANA
5 MILES

CABRAS I.

PITI
NAVY
YARD

APRA HARBOR

APRA

To AGAT

PAA HOTEL
SUMAY
MARINE
BASE

OROTE PENINSULA

8:15 AM—Minesweeper USS *Penguin* Bombed and Strafed by Japanese Bomber; One Man Killed, Ship Abandoned and Scuttled to Avoid Capture

9 Japanese Bombers Attack and Heavily Damage Marine Barracks and Pan Am Facility; Kill 2 Men

7:30 AM—Anticipating Invasion of Apra Harbor, U.S. Marines Take up Defensive Positions on Orote Point
—INVASION NEVER COMES—

Initial Attacks on Major Guam Installations

When word of the attack reached the governor's office, two of his staff members soberly went about the pre-arranged task of burning all confidential papers and documents.

Another man, Navy Yeoman First Class Lyle Eads, who had spent the week before taking copious notes at a court-martial trial, and was facing the unpleasant prospect of having to transcribe what he had written, actually appeared relieved at news of the attack. Because of the Japanese, his job was finished.

2:40 p.m. (PH plus 10 hrs. 10 min.): At 2:40 that afternoon, the following brief message was sent from the communications office on Guam to Asiatic Fleet headquarters in Manila: "GUAM BEING ATTACKED BY SIX SEAPLANES."

The west coast villages of Merizo, Umatac, Agat, Tepugan, and Asan were the focal point of the enemy planes. It was a softening up of those towns lying in the path of the anticipated Japanese invasion. They also attacked and cut the important phone lines on Libugan Hill behind Agana.

With telephone communications out, navy radioman George Tweed was ordered to Libugan with a portable radio transmitter, from which he could view the coast and warn if an enemy landing was attempted.

"I hardly got there when the Japanese planes came in again," said Tweed. "A fighter headed for me, machine guns sputtering. I was in the middle of an open field [and] all I could do was hit the dirt. [Fortunately] my khaki uniform blended in with the dead grass [and] the Jap stopped shooting."

But that was only the beginning for the young sailor. "[Now] a Jap bomber came toward my hill," he said. "Then I saw that [a] bomb was careening...in my direction. It seemed to be making a beeline right for me. It grew bigger and bigger...[but] in the last second it passed over me and struck the earth." The concussion bounced him off the ground, and made his head feel "like it was bursting."

Soon, more planes arrived. As they dove, "I would look up, thinking each bomb was going to hit me," Tweed said, "[but] they all passed over my head, landing 50 or 75 feet beyond."

The target, which appeared to be a steel beacon tower near the top of the hill, remained untouched. "The Japs [were] damn poor shots," he said.

Shaken from having dodged Japanese bombs for over an hour, the young radioman was back in Agana later, where he and another navy buddy had rented a small house.

"A native came up and [told me] only one bomb fell on the city."

"What did it hit?"

"Your house," said the young Chamorro.

"I raced home," said Tweed, "and there it was, practically demolished. The first day of the war, the only bomb dropped on Agana, and it

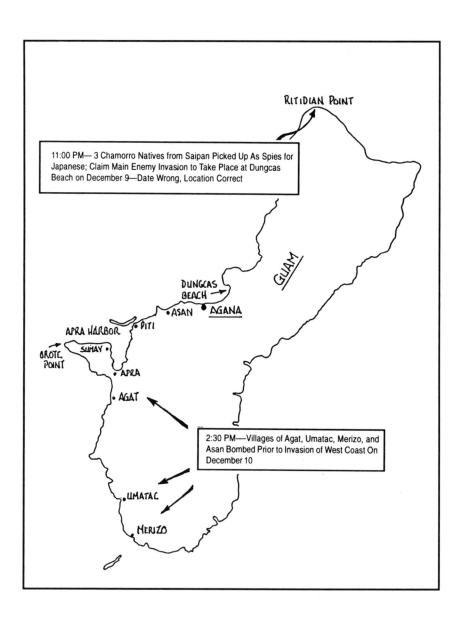

RITIDIAN POINT

11:00 PM— 3 Chamorro Natives from Saipan Picked Up As Spies for Japanese; Claim Main Enemy Invasion to Take Place at Dungcas Beach on December 9—Date Wrong, Location Correct

GUAM

DUNGCAS BEACH

• ASAN   ● AGANA

APRA HARBOR   • PITI

BROTE POINT   SUMAY •

• APRA

• AGAT

2:30 PM—Villages of Agat, Umatac, Merizo, and Asan Bombed Prior to Invasion of West Coast On December 10

• UMATAC

MERIZO

had to hit my house. I didn't [even] have to open the front door—it [had been] blasted out. The bomb had gone clear through the roof and exploded on the front porch [and] the [whole] roof had been blown off."

Actually, half a dozen bombs had been dropped on Agana that afternoon. Aside from Tweed's house, one of them took out part of the jail, but not enough to make it unsafe.

The bombs that fell on Agana were dropped by Japanese fighters, who were around for target-of-opportunity shooting throughout most of the day. On one occasion, Harrison Chuck and Richard Ballinger, two Marine PFCs attached to Agana's 28-man Insular Military Police Patrol, thought they had been spotted by a marauding Japanese fighter.

Thinking they might be strafed, they ran into the basement of a nearby building, where a debate occurred between the two men. Ballinger wanted to take his chances outside, fearing their hiding place would invite a bomb rather than bullets. Chuck refused to leave for the same reason Ballinger wanted to go. In the end, the debate remained unresolved. The enemy pilot apparently hadn't seen them after all.

6:00 p.m. (PH plus 13 hrs. 30 min.): Later that afternoon as he drove through the town on the way back to headquarters, Tweed glanced up at the marquee of the Gaiety Theater, where he had watched the movie *Flight Command,* starring Robert Taylor, a few nights before.

"Sure wish we had some of those planes used in the movie," he thought to himself. "Hollywood has more priority than we do."

When the young radioman arrived at the Communications Office, he was surprised to find "sledge hammers lying on the tables." Asking what they were for, he was told they were "to wreck the radio transmitters and generators if the Japs came ashore."

Under what circumstances they would come ashore had also been decided. "They say we're going to put up a fight," said one man.

"What do you mean?" asked Tweed.

He was told that Governor and Navy Captain McMillan had received permission from Admiral Hart in Manila to surrender the island without a fight, but was overruled by the Marines.

"Colonel McNulty told him no, that the Marine Corps [wouldn't] give up without a fight."

McMillan agreed to go along with it only if the fight would maintain the character of a "token resistance."

"We sure had to hand it to the Marines," said Tweed. "At all costs they were going to uphold their tradition of honor."

11:00 p.m. (PH plus 18 hrs. 30 min.): As darkness settled about the island on the first night of war, the question was not if the Japanese would come, but where they would land when they did.

Around eleven o'clock, on distant Ritidian Point, on the northern-most tip of the island, three men disembarked from a small native dugout. The minute they reached shore, they were taken into custody by Insular Force Guards, who had been patrolling that section of beach.

The three men, who claimed they were Saipan natives, were driven to Marine Headquarters, where they were questioned as to where they had come from and what they were doing there. All three supported the claim that they were an advance party sent to act as interpreters for the Japanese when they landed on the island.

"When will this landing take place?" they were asked.

"At dawn, tomorrow morning," they said.

"Where will it take place?"

They said it would take place on a popular recreation beach north-east of Agana, known locally as Dungcas Beach.

Captain McMillan was skeptical. Of the information volunteered by the three Saipanese, he later wrote:

> I was not inclined to accept the story at the time, since I thought it might be a trick to have the Marines moved from Sumay to the Beach during the night in order that they might make a landing in the Apra Harbor area without opposition.

Colonel McNulty suspected it was a trick to get him to weaken his Orote Point defenses, and, outside of moving the Insular Force Guards and a few *Penguin* sailors into Agana, no changes were made in Marine defenses.

Unknown to the sailors and Marines as they awaited their anticipated fate that night, the outside world had been told that the island was already in enemy hands.

Tokyo Radio, soon to become famous throughout the war for its ex-aggerations and lies, didn't waste any time in getting started. That night, in a broadcast monitored by CBS, radio Shanghai reported that Guam was already "under the Japanese flag." A Japanese broadcast from Formosa claimed the island had been "taken without resistance."

The Saipan natives, probably to the best of their knowledge, did tell the truth. The invasion was originally scheduled for the ninth, but was changed at the last minute to December 10. As for the invasion beach, they were correct. Dungcas Beach was invaded before dawn on the tenth by a crack, 400-man Special Landing Force. A second, larger invasion force that came ashore on a beach between Merizo and Facpi Point on the southwest-ern part of the island, found that there was no road connecting Merizo and their objective at Sumay. The entire 5,000-man force was forced to re-em-bark and move two miles west to Facpi Point where the road started. Al-though it was bombed again, no invasion of Apra Harbor occurred, nor were the Marine positions ever challenged by the Japanese. The only opposition to the enemy landing came from a few determined *Penguin* sailors and a handful of Insular Force Guards, who tangled with the Japanese as they moved up from Dungcas Beach toward Agana. In the brief fire fight, twelve Americans, three Insular Guards, and three Chamorros died. Captain McMillan officially surrendered the island to the Japanese naval commander shortly after 6:00 a.m.

CHAPTER 4

"LAST NIGHT JAPANESE FORCES ATTACKED
THE PHILIPPINE ISLANDS..."

TIME DIFFERENCE: 5 HOURS 30 MINUTES.

2:53 a.m. (PH plus 23 min.): When the teletype machine began clattering early in the morning at Asiatic Fleet Headquarters in Manila, the half-asleep radio operator pushed himself across the floor on his four-castor swivel chair to see what the fool message was that had disturbed him. The text of it amounted to only eight words. They were eight words that would not only startle the navy radioman awake, but eight words that would startle the entire Pacific awake: "AIR RAID PEARL HARBOR THIS IS NO DRILL."

A couple of minutes later the excited operator burst in on the duty officer, Marine Lieutenant Colonel William Clement.

"What's ya got?" asked Clement, realizing by the look on the man's face that whatever brought him into the room without knocking was important.

Clement looked at the message. "Good God! Is this true? Are you sure this is not a hoax?"

The radioman said that it had been repeated twice and was sent in the clear, not in code. He also recognized the technique of the sender, since each man had his own signature, so to speak.

Clement immediately picked up the phone and called Admiral Thomas Hart, Asiatic Fleet commander, at the nearby Manila Hotel.

The meaning of Admiral Thomas C. Hart's "Japan Has Started Hostilities. Govern Yourselves Accordingly" message baffled some who received it.

US Navy

"Sir, splash some cold water on your face. I'm coming over with an important message."

Admiral Hart was sitting on the edge of his bed when Clement arrived less than ten minutes later. Rear Admiral William Purnell, the admiral's chief of staff was also in the room.

Clement showed his boss the message. "Are you sure this is authentic?" asked Hart, passing it to Purnell.

"Yes sir, it is," said Clement, explaining how his operator had identified the sender and that it had been repeated twice.

Taking a piece of paper off the night stand, Hart wrote, "Japan has started hostilities. Govern yourselves accordingly," and handed it to Clement. "Have communications send this to every ship and naval station within the command." "You go with him and get this thing started," he told Purnell. "I'll be over as soon as I can get some clothes on."

By the time the two men reached Naval Headquarters a few minutes later, a second message had been picked up that left no doubt that the first was the real thing. It was from the Pacific Fleet commander himself, Admiral E. Husband Kimmel. "...TO PACIFIC FLEET: HOSTILITIES WITH JAPAN COMMENCED WITH AIR RAID ON PEARL." It had come in just two minutes after the first message.

3:30 a.m. (PH plus 1 hr.): Like the navy, the first the army heard about the attack on Pearl Harbor was from an enlisted signalman listening to shortwave radio station KGEI from California. He too, rushed to tell his duty officer, who immediately phoned Brigadier General Spencer B. Akin, Army Signal Corps commander. Akin personally went to USAFFE (U.S. Armed Forces Far East) headquarters at old Fort Santiago in the Walled City, where Major General Richard Sutherland, General MacArthur's chief of staff; Brigadier General Richard Marshall, Sutherland's deputy; and chief of engineers, Colonel Hugh "Pat" Casey, were sleeping on cots.

"Wake up, Pat," said Akin, shaking Casey. "The Japs just bombed Pearl Harbor!"

General Richard Sutherland kept General Brereton from speaking directly to General MacArthur in the crucial early morning hours of December 8.

US Army

All three men sat up at the same time. Sutherland went over and picked up the phone. "Has this been authenticated?" he asked Akin.

It hadn't, so Sutherland called General MacArthur, asleep in his penthouse at the Manila Hotel, and told him what they had heard.

"What was the general's response when you told him?" asked Akin.

"He said that if it were true, he didn't see how it could happen; that it should be our 'strongest point.' "

Ten minutes later, the Philippine commander knew it was true, when a call came through from Brigadier General Leonard T. Gerow, army chief of war plans in Washington. Gerow told him that the ships and aircraft in Hawaii had suffered "considerable damage," and that there was a good chance the Philippines would be attacked "in the near future."

After notifying MacArthur, Sutherland called Major General Lewis Brereton, Philippine air commander, at his headquarters at Nielson Field. Lieutenant Colonel Charles Caldwell, Brereton's G-3, picked up the phone.

"What is it, Charley?" asked Brereton.

"It's General Sutherland. He says Pearl Harbor's been bombed. He wants to talk to you."

Sutherland informed Brereton that "the Japs had bombed Pearl Harbor at 7:55 a.m., Hawaii time...and that a state of war existed."

While slipping into his uniform, Brereton told Caldwell and his chief of staff, Colonel Frances Brady, to alert all air units of the attack on Pearl Harbor and have them prepare for action. He also told them to phone Colonel Eugene Eubank, his bomber commander at Clark Field.

It was a little after 4:00 a.m. when Caldwell got through to Eubank at Clark. After their conversation, Eubank hung up the phone, then turned and said to the three officers who shared the room with him, "Well boys, here it is. It's what we've been waiting for. The Japs have just bombed Pearl Harbor. Brereton wants me to fly down to Nielson as soon as I can."

Eubank hurriedly assembled his staff and, after breaking the news, told them to get the planes ready for an attack on Takao Harbor on Formosa. It was an order that needed no further explanation, as it already had been planned to the last detail. It was decided not to arm the B-17s with bombs, however, in the event there would be a last minute change of target. They decided it would also be safer if they happened to be caught on the ground in a surprise attack.

General Lewis Brereton. The 10-hour delay in okaying his raid on Formosa resulted in the loss of all 18 B-17s at Clark Field.

USAAF

4:45 a.m. (PH plus 2 hrs. 15 min.): Meanwhile, the attack against the Philippines that Gerow had warned MacArthur was likely to happen "in the near future," appeared to be under way. At that moment, the huge map in the Air Warning Service room at Nielson Field was showing a flight of unidentified aircraft approaching the northern coast of Luzon.

A couple of minutes later there was a bang on the door of the officers' living quarters at Nichols Field, where pilots of the 21st Pursuit Squadron were sleeping. It was the duty officer, Lieutenant Lloyd Coleman.

"Wake up, wake up," he shouted, "get dressed. Pearl Harbor has been bombed."

It was the second time in less than three hours that Coleman had rousted them. The first time, at 2:30, was a false alarm. This one sounded like the real thing.

"He ordered us into our new P-40E pursuit planes," said one of the pilots, Lieutenant Sam Grashio, "and directed us to start our engines and stand by on the radio." A few minutes later, as the plot on the approaching planes apparently dried up, "...we cut our engines, got out of the cockpit, sat under the wings and waited."

Unknown to them, however, at that very moment, the three Japanese planes that had disappeared off the screen, were dropping the first bombs of the two hour and 15 minute-old Pacific war on the Philippine Army radio station at Aparri, on the northernmost tip of Luzon.

(As mentioned, this was the second time the stillness of the warm Philippine night had been broken by the roar of P-40 engines. The first had come at 2:30 a.m., when the radar screen at Iba Field, 90 miles north on the Luzon west coast, notified Air Warning Service at Nielson of an approaching flight of Japanese planes. Iba immediately scrambled all 18 3rd Pursuit Squadron P-40s, and vectored them straight at the closing enemy bombers.

Back at the AWS room at Nielson, the air was filled with apprehension as the two converging lines on the big plotting table map grew closer and closer, then finally touched. It looked like an intercept. But was it?

Unknown to everyone, including the pilots of the 3rd Pursuit, since radar was unable to judge altitude, at the moment of anticipated contact, the Japanese planes unknowingly passed several thousand feet above Lieutenant Hank Thorne's P-40s, neither flight aware of the other. At that point, the AWS map showed the Japanese planes turning north back toward Formosa.)

Colonel Harold George, commanding officer of the Fifth Interceptor Command, whose fighters had just missed tangling with the flight of Japanese bombers 20 miles outside his "20-mile-shoot-on sight" limit two hours before, was not informed of the attack on Pearl Harbor until the phone rang at 4:45 a.m.

"Jesus Christ!" exclaimed George after listening to the voice on the other end. "All right...thanks, Bud," he said, hanging up the phone.

"Japan has commenced hostilities," he told Captain Harold "Lefty" Eads and Allison Ind, his G-3, who were sharing the room with him.

Ind and Eads looked at each other. What did he mean, and where?

"Army radio—Pearl Harbor," said George, as he climbed back into bed again and turned out the lights.

Ind looked at the luminous dial on his watch. It was 4:17 a.m., Philippine time, Monday, December 8, 1941.

Ten minutes later, the phone rang again. It was United Press correspondent Frank Hewlett wanting to know if anything official had come in yet.

Ind told him they had less information than he had. "What do you know?" he asked.

Hewlett told him all hell had broken loose in Hawaii. "There's been a heavy attack on all army and navy installations...it's very bad," he said.

At 4:25, the phone rang in the quarters of Major General Jonathan Wainwright, asleep in his room at Fort Stotsenberg, located a few hundred yards from Clark Field. It was Colonel Pete Erwin, General MacArthur's operations officer.

"Admiral Hart has just received a radio message from Admiral Kimmel, Pacific Fleet commander at Pearl Harbor, informing him that Japan has initiated hostilities," said Irwin.

It was 4:30 a.m. Wainwright jiggled the phone and got his aide, Lieutenant Colonel John Pugh. "Johnny," he said, "the cat has jumped! Get over here."

Ten minutes later, while Wainwright was dressing, Irwin called again with more detailed information. He told him that the battleship row at Pearl Harbor and the big Hickam Field air base had been heavily bombed.

As soon as he learned Hickam had been bombed, Wainwright called Colonel Eubank at Clark Field, but they had already been informed.

5:00 a.m. (PH plus 2 hrs. 30 min.): Believing, since the attack on Pearl Harbor, that getting permission to bomb Formosa would now just be a matter of routine, General Brereton was in USAFFE headquarters an hour before dawn asking to see General MacArthur. General Sutherland told him the Philippine commander was in conference with Admiral Hart, and couldn't be disturbed.

Brereton told Sutherland, a man often allowed to speak for the general on routine matters, that he wanted to attack Takao Harbor on Formosa with the B-17s at Clark Field. He told him it was an attack they had long prepared for and were well-prepared to carry out.

Sutherland told him to go ahead and make the necessary preparations, but not to issue orders for the attack until they were approved by MacArthur. Brereton drove back to Nielson to await the okay, which he was sure would come soon.

Meanwhile, three things were about to happen within the next two and a half hours, that should have influenced the high command to give Brereton the okay he was waiting for.

The first one came at 5:30 a.m., when General MacArthur got a radio message from his boss in Washington, Chief of Staff General George C. Marshall. It was an order to initiate RAINBOW FIVE, the basic war plan designed just for such circumstances. Three weeks earlier, MacArthur had requested that the plan be revised to allow him to attack Japanese installations if they were within the operating radius of his bombers. It was approved by Marshall. Clark Field was well within that "operating radius."

The second one came at dawn, at approximately 6:15 a.m., when tiny Batan Island, one of the northernmost islands in the Philippines, was invaded by 500 Japanese naval combat troops. Their objective, the partially finished air field that the Americans had ironically planned to use someday as a refueling base for bombers en route to the Japanese homeland, was taken without opposition.

The third thing that occurred happened at 7:10 a.m. in Malalag Bay, 630 miles south on the lower tip of Mindanao.

The minute the seaplane tender USS *William B. Preston*, anchored inside the bay, got Admiral Hart's "JAPAN STARTED HOSTILITIES. GOVERN YOURSELVES ACCORDINGLY" message at 3:40 a.m., plans were made to send one of the three PBYs moored nearby, on patrol. At 5:15,

Converted 4-stacker, USS *William B. Preston*, was first US ship attacked by Japanese planes at 7:10 a.m. on morning of December 8.

US Navy

plane number six of Patrol Wing Ten (Patwing 10), lifted off the smooth waters of the bay to scout the entrance to the thirty-mile-wide Gulf of Davao.

Unknown to the Americans, however, twenty Japanese planes had taken off from the carrier *Ryujo* at dawn for Malalag Bay, where intelligence believed a U.S. carrier was located.

At exactly 7:10, the six lead fighters from the *Ryujo*, flying low under an early morning overcast, dove on the surprised Americans. Their target was the two moored PBYs. It was over in a hurry, as in seconds, both planes were engulfed in flames, then blew up.

A man on board one of the planes, Ensign Robert Tills, was killed instantly in the attack. Ironically, had the Japanese hit ten minutes later, Tills would probably have lived, because he was about to be relieved from his all-night onboard plane watch when the enemy attacked.

Meanwhile, the *Preston*, making a run toward open waters of the bay, was jumped by a formation of Japanese bombers. For nearly 30 minutes the running battle with enemy planes and the old converted World War I four-stacker went on. In the end, not a single bomb found its mark.

The moment the attack began, the radioman on board the *Preston* radioed in plain language to whomever was listening, that they were under attack. It was picked up by communications at Nielson Field, who quickly notified naval headquarters at the Marsman Building in Manila. The message read, "THE PRESTON IS BEING ATTACKED BY BOMBERS AT DAVAO NOW."

Within the first five hours of war in the Pacific, the Philippines had been both invaded by land and attacked from the air by the Japanese. Although General MacArthur was hamstrung until then by the War Department war warning he received on November 27, which said that "If hostilities cannot...be avoided, the United States desires that Japan commit the first overt act," being ordered to initiate Rainbow 5 by General Marshall that morning, even if he was aware of only one of the two "overt acts" that had already occurred, would lead one to believe that the afore planned air attack on Formosa would be routinely granted.

While waiting for what he was sure would be the okay of his Formosa attack request, General Brereton had called a meeting of his staff to mastermind the plans for the mission. By 7:00 a.m., Brereton's office was crawling with brass. Among others, Colonel Eubank and his operations officer, Major Birrell Walsh, were there, having flown down from Clark in a B-18. So was Colonel George who, despite what had transpired that morning, had slept clear up to 5:30 and enjoyed a big breakfast before coming over. The only one missing, General Brereton himself, had driven back to USAFFE headquarters to see what was holding up the order.

He was back at Nielson a little before eight o'clock. The news was disappointing simply because there was no news, other than Sutherland

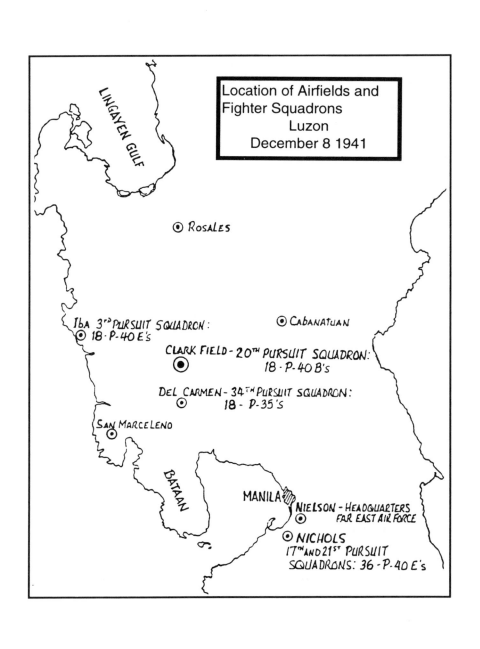

Location of Airfields and
Fighter Squadrons
Luzon
December 8 1941

LINGAYEN GULF

⊙ ROSALES

IbA 3ʳᵈ PURSUIT SQUADRON:
⊙ 18 · P-40 E's

⊙ CABANATUAN

CLARK FIELD - 20ᵀᴴ PURSUIT SQUADRON:
◉ 18 · P-40 B's

DEL CARMEN - 34ᵀᴴ PURSUIT SQUADRON:
⊙ 18 · P-35's

SAN MARCELENO
⊙

BATAAN

MANILA
NIELSON - HEADQUARTERS
⊙ FAR EAST AIR FORCE

⊙ NICHOLS
17ᵀᴴ AND 21ˢᵀ PURSUIT
SQUADRONS: 36 · P-40 E's

telling him that MacArthur had said that they couldn't attack "until fired upon."

It's too bad Brereton didn't know about the attack on the *Preston*, which Nielson radio had received and passed on to the navy while he was away, or been more aware of the latest Rainbow 5 revisions. He would have appreciated anything that could have been used to convince or remind the Philippine commander that there was no longer any reason to delay the attack on Formosa. Anticipating that orders for the attack would still come through, Brereton told his disappointed staff to go ahead and finalize the plans. Although objective folders on Formosa targets had long since been prepared, they lacked both maps and aerial photographs, prompting Brereton to order a photo reconnaissance mission over the planned target.

Captain Allison Ind, Colonel George's intelligence officer, entered Brereton's office in time to hear Colonel Eubank ask his chief of staff about the decision. "Well, do I go, or don't I?"

"You go, Gene," said Colonel Frances Brady, "reconnaissance."

"All right then. I'll get 'em off the ground," said Eubank, "and stand by to get others up if necessary."

At that point, Colonel George told Eubank that Air Warning Service had just picked up a large flight of enemy planes heading for Lingayan Gulf and possibly Manila. "I hope it doesn't take long, Gene," said George. "They're headed this way."

Under the "combat alert" status Brereton had ordered be put into effect at daylight, it could take the B-17s close to an hour to get into the air. Aware of this, Eubank phoned Clark, but was told Major David Gibbs, group operations officer and senior officer at the base in Eubank's absence, had already ordered the big bombers into the air when Nielson informed him of the approaching enemy flight a few minutes earlier.

When Chief of the Air Force, General Hap Arnold, got word of the Pearl Harbor attack, he was outside the town of Bakersfield, California, dove hunting with Donald Douglas of the Douglas Aircraft Corporation. He immediately flew to March Field, outside of San Bernardino and, after getting the details of what happened to his air force in Hawaii, called Brereton. Arnold told him that his entire force was "caught napping," and had been destroyed on the ground. He warned him not to let that happen there. Brereton guaranteed that it wouldn't.

Up to the time the order to get the B-17s off the ground came, things had also been happening up at Clark Field.

First news of Pearl Harbor had come at 3:30 a.m., when an army enlisted man, listening to short-wave station KGEI in San Francisco, heard the same announcement that had alerted General MacArthur in Manila.

Although the news remained unofficial until close to eight o'clock, several men heard about the attack over Manila radio KZRH. One of those was Captain Frank Kurtz, a B-17 pilot, who heard it while shaving.

"I got up at seven as usual," said Kurtz, "and stumbling in sleepily to shave, snapped on my portable to get the early morning news broadcast by Don Bell in Manila. In even more rapid-fire style than usual, he told the big news—that the Japs had hit Hawaii.

"The other guys gathered around, and it stunned us all....It sounded like they'd split the place wide open."

Another officer, Lieutenant Edgar Whitcomb, a B-17 navigator, got the news while walking to the officers' mess, but didn't believe it.

The first most of the men at Clark Field heard of the attack on Pearl Harbor on December 8, was from Don Bell's radio broadcast from Manila.

AP

"Did you hear about the Japs attacking Pearl Harbor?" said a friend walking up behind him.

"Yeah, sure, we heard about that yesterday," joked another man walking next to him.

"No kidding. A bunch of Jap planes bombed hell out of Pearl Harbor and Hickam Field."

"The conversation continued over breakfast," said Whitcomb. "Some people at our table had heard rumor of the attack. Others had not. In general, we concluded that it was just a rumor and changed the subject...It did not make sense to us that the Japanese should attack Pearl Harbor and leave Clark Field unbombed."

Little did they know or suspect that Clark Field wouldn't remain "unbombed." Nor did they know that they had eaten the last meal they would ever eat in that mess hall, and that they had slept for the last time in the quarters they had just left. In less than six hours, they would both be gone; blasted to pieces by Japanese bombs.

After breakfast, as "we strolled back toward the headquarters building,." remembered Whitcomb, "everyone stopped suddenly as a radio from a nearby hangar blared out the excited voice of KZRH news commentator Don Bell: 'Japanese aircraft have attacked Pearl Harbor. There is no report of damage at this time. Further information will be broadcast as soon as it is available.' "

"Then the rumor was true," lamented Whitcomb, "it was true."

Fifteen minutes later, all the pilots were in the operations tent listening to Major Gibbs.

"Well, gentlemen, this is it. If they've hit Hawaii," he said prophetically, "they can't miss hitting us. I can't tell you when it will come, but it will come."

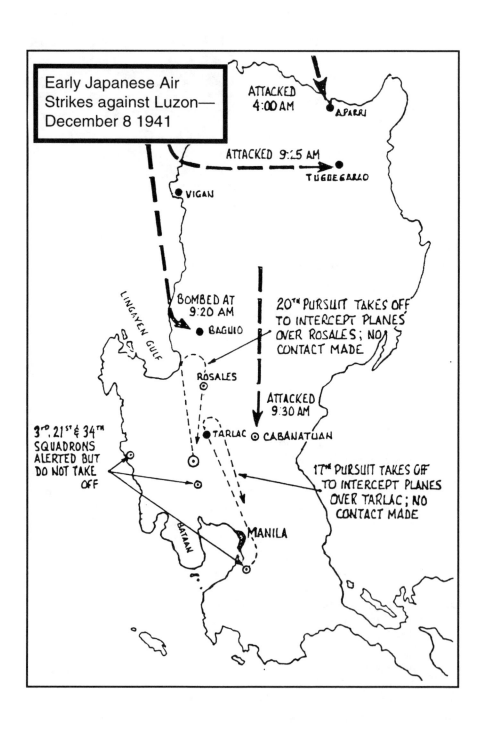

Early Japanese Air
Strikes against Luzon—
December 8 1941

ATTACKED
4:00 AM
APARRI

ATTACKED 9:15 AM
TUGUEGARAO

VIGAN

LINGAYEN GULF

BOMBED AT
9:20 AM
BAGUIO

20ᵀᴴ PURSUIT TAKES OFF
TO INTERCEPT PLANES
OVER ROSALES; NO
CONTACT MADE

ROSALES

ATTACKED
9:30 AM

TARLAC   CABANATUAN

3ᴿᴰ, 21ˢᵀ & 34ᵀᴴ
SQUADRONS
ALERTED BUT
DO NOT TAKE
OFF

17ᵀᴴ PURSUIT TAKES OFF
TO INTERCEPT PLANES
OVER TARLAC; NO
CONTACT MADE

BATAAN

MANILA

Of course, everyone was anxious for the attack on Formosa. Gibbs told them it would come, but it had been decided to send three planes on a photo reconnaissance of anticipated targets in "Sector 32" first. Their objective was to locate and photograph Japanese airfields, but the enemy shipping in Takao Harbor would be attacked first.

As the meeting ended, Gibbs ordered the pilots to get their crews together, go out to their planes, and warm up their engines for a few minutes. He told them to make sure everything was combat-ready in case an emergency arose and they had to take off in a hurry.

"And stay close to your ships," he said. "If you have to take off before we get the order to bomb, I want every plane off this field in 20 minutes."

It wasn't long after that Gibbs got the call from Air Warning Service at Nielson of approaching Japanese planes, prompting him to immediately order the tower to fire the green signal flare. It was a signal everyone knew meant take off in a hurry.

One by one, the giant fortresses took off. Down below, tractors began towing carts loaded with 100- and 300-pound bombs, that had been lined up near the parked planes, back to the dumps.

It wasn't until half the planes were off the ground that they were told where to go. "Climb to 20,000 feet and circle Mr. Arayat until further notice." Arayat, the 3,400-foot ancient volcano that dominated the central Luzon plain, was just 20 miles east of Clark Field.

Back at Clark, there were still three B-17s on the ground. One, piloted by Lieutenant John W. Carpenter, had last-minute carburetor trouble, and did not get off until after ten o'clock. When he did, he was told to fly reconnaissance over the east coast of Luzon.

The other two planes were scheduled for camouflaging that morning. One belonged to Captain Frank Kurtz. He had been told by Major Gibbs earlier that he was on standby. "Orders will be coming through fast all morning," said Gibbs.

"Only the orders that came seemed conflicting," said Kurtz. "First came one countermanding the camouflaging. Instead we were to load bombs, so we taxied over toward the ammunition dump."

A few minutes later another change in orders. "Take her back to the hangar; they want the camouflaging finished..."

"Presently came another order for me and two other planes of the 30th Squadron to unload bombs and insert cameras. It was clear they were preparing us for reconnaissance over Formosa."

One of the other planes being prepared for the same mission was that of Lieutenant Ed Green. His navigator, Lieutenant Edgar Whitcomb, was told to check the cameras in the plane for film.

Finding them empty, "...I proceeded back to the tent about 25 yards behind the plane to get the necessary film," said Whitcomb.

When he returned with it a few minutes later, the plane was gone. "I shouted at a soldier nearby, 'What happened to that ship?' "

He gestured toward where the plane had gone, shouting, "Took off. Dangdest thing I ever saw, took off with only three engines turning. Never saw anything like it."

Dashing back to headquarters to find out what had happened, he was told that enemy planes were heading this way, and that all the planes had been ordered off the ground.

8:50 a.m. (PH plus 6 hrs. 20 min.): By 8:50, the flight of Japanese planes reported heading toward Lingayen Gulf that triggered Major Gibbs to order the B-17s into the air 40 minutes earlier, brought Colonel George to scramble the 20th Pursuit at Clark Field to intercept. In case the target turned out to be Clark itself, he ordered the 17th Pursuit Squadron at Nichols to cover it.

By the time the 20th reached the anticipated point of intercept at Rosales, 60 miles to the north, the Japanese planes, consisting of 32 twin-engined army bombers, were nowhere to be seen. In fact, one-third of them had turned east near Vigan, some 120 miles north of Rosales, and attacked the airfield near the town of Tuguegaro in northern Luzon. The remaining 18 planes, continuing south, also turned east when they reached Lingayen Gulf, striking the summer capital at Baguio and the airfield at Cabanatuan before returning unchallenged to Formosa.

Three B-10s were destroyed at Cabanatuan. At Baguio, it was different. Three miles from the town of Baguio itself was Camp John Hay, site of an army command and staff school for American and senior Philippine Army officers, and a rest area for U.S. servicemen. It was also the summer capital of President Manuel Quezon, who happened to be convalescing there from a bout with tuberculosis when the Japanese struck.

An hour or so earlier, his Chinese valet, Ah Dong, had awakened the Philippine president with a long distance call from Secretary Jorge Vargas in Manila.

"George," said Quezon, "what is it?"

"Mr. President, Pearl Harbor has been bombed by the Japanese, and war has been declared!"

"You're crazy, George," replied Quezon, "the Japanese would never dare attack Hawaii. Pearl Harbor is the best defended naval station in the world. Where did you get that nonsense?"

"Both the United and Associated Press phoned me, and General MacArthur confirmed it."

In less than an hour, the 18 Japanese bombers bearing down on Baguio would erase any doubt in the president's mind.

Natalie Crouter, an American housewife, and her husband, Jerry, owner of a Shell station and insurance agency in Baguio City, heard of the attack on Hawaii over the radio at their home, a mile or so outside of town.

While listening to Don Bell's broadcast from Manila, they heard planes and went out to take a look. Thinking they were American, Natalie made the prophetic remark, "...we probably won't be standing here looking up at planes like this much longer."

A few seconds later, amidst the explosions of bombs falling on nearby Camp John Hay, Jerry gasped, "My God, those are Japanese planes!"

At a nearby Maryknoll Convent, several nuns were watching the same formation of planes as the Crouters. They too, had just heard about Pearl Harbor and couldn't imagine the planes were anything but American. Seconds later, they were both shocked and horrified when they realized the tiny objects falling from the bellies of the planes were bombs being dropped on Camp John Hay.

The Crouters, meanwhile, had decided to drive into Baguio City. When they got there, everything was normal. It was obvious that no one knew what had happened. It was so normal, in fact, that despite the insistence by Jerry that the planes everyone had seen were Japanese, and that they had dropped bombs on Camp John Hay, no one believed him.

Meanwhile, after a fruitless two and a half hour search for the Japanese, the 17th and 20th Pursuit Squadrons landed at Clark Field to refuel. It was 11:15. When 20th Squadron commander, Lieutenant Joe Moore, was asked about the results, his remarks, listed under "comments" in the Fifth Interceptor Command diary for that day, were, "No interception, Japs feinting. Instead of proceeding south from Lingayen gulf, turned northeast. 20th Squadron then out of gas, landed at Clark Field to refuel."

Twenty of the 23 P-40Bs of the 20th Pursuit Squadron, shown here in this pre-war photo, were destroyed on the ground at Clark Field on December 8.

USAAF

Back at the Air Warning Room at Nielson, however, everyone knew it hadn't been a "feint," as reports of the bombing of both Baguio and Tuguegaro had been received by 9:25. Information on the attack on the airfield at Cabanatuan had also been recorded.

Although the exact context of the message Nielson received about the attack on Baguio is not recorded, the information they forwarded later to the navy read, "Baguio bombed with 27 bombs. 7 killed, wounded unknown. Bombed area Camp John Hay. 17 planes in attacking formation."

Armed with irrefutable evidence that the Philippines had now been "fired upon," General Brereton immediately phoned MacArthur's headquarters. Again, the chief of staff intervened on behalf of the general; and again, even after informing General Sutherland of the attacks on Baguio and Tuguegaro, his request to raid Formosa was denied.

Brereton was beside himself. Outside of Del Monte Field in Mindanao, Clark was the only other airfield in the Philippines that was equipped to fuel, arm, and perform maintenance on the big bombers. "If the Japs beat us to the punch and hit Clark first," he thought, "there was no way Formosa could ever be attacked."

"If Clark Field is attacked," he warned Sutherland, "we won't be able to operate off of it." Brereton listened to the answer from the other end of the line, then slammed the phone down.

"Permission still not granted." he told his anxious bomber commander, Colonel Eubank.

There's little doubt that Sutherland's refusal was because he was not authorized to give permission until he conferred with MacArthur. Despite the confidence the Philippine commander had in his chief of staff, a decision of that magnitude would have to come from MacArthur himself.

Evidence of this came ten minutes later at 10:10 a.m., when Brereton got a call back from Sutherland, officially okaying the photo reconnaissance mission. At this, Eubank, convinced that there was a good chance the raid would get the green light, headed back to Clark Field.

10:14 a.m. (PH plus 7 hrs. 44 min.): No sooner had Eubank left, than the phone rang again. According to the entry for 10:14 on December 8, 1941, found in the "Summary of Activities of the HQFEAF, 8 Dec 41 to Feb 42," it was from General MacArthur himself. It said, in part, "General Brereton received telephone call from General MacArthur....The decision for offensive action...left to General Brereton. All bombers are ordered to arm and be on alert for immediate orders."

The entry at 10:20 confirmed the call. "The staff was called in and informed of General Brereton's telephone conversation with General MacArthur. General Brereton directed that a plan of employment of our Air Force against known aerodromes in southern Formosa be prepared."

Following this meeting, Major David Gibbs, in command at Clark Field during Eubank's absence, was told to order the B-17s down for refueling; that the raid on Formosa was on. By the time Eubank arrived at 10:45, 2 of the 14 Fortresses that had been monotonously circling Mr. Arayat for two hours were already down. It would be an hour before the rest could land.

By the time the last plane taxied on to its assigned bay at 11:30, the order everyone had been waiting for was coming through on the teletype machine from Air Force Headquarters at Nielson.

FIELD ORDER NO. ONE: Two (2) heavy bombardment squadrons to attack known airdromes .on Southern Formosa at the latest daylight hour today that visibility will permit. Forces to be two (2) two squadrons of B-17's...two (2) squadrons of pursuits to be on alert to cover operation of bombardment...pursuits to be used to fullest extent to insure safety of bombardment...

It went on to detail the 100- and 300-pound bomb loads, and said that the two squadrons of B-17s that had been transferred to Del Monte Field a few days earlier, were to fly back to Luzon late that afternoon, and land at San Marcelino, the only other field capable of handling the weight of the Fortresses, then make the short, 30-mile hop over to Clark during the night. The plan was for them to attack Formosa at daybreak the next day.

As soon as the planes got down, their crews were ordered to the mess halls for an early lunch. Briefing of the pilots, navigators, and radio operators was scheduled for 12:20. While the ground crews began refueling the half-empty tanks of the planes that had been clustered together to simplify their preparation, armament personnel got ready to tow the already loaded bomb carts out to the ships.

Meanwhile, back at Fifth Interceptor Command Headquarters at Nielson, reports of enemy activity had been filtering in steadily all morning from many different sources, including the navy, a dozen postmasters trained as coast watchers, and telephone and telegraph reports from up and down the Luzon west coast.

As early as 6:25 a.m., eight warships were reported in the vicinity of Batan Island. At 7:15, two Japanese planes reportedly "landed at Calayan Island, north of Luzon...and departed at 7:45." Three Japanese flying boats were also seen "soaring slowly" over the same two islands, and unidentified ships were reported "steaming at a high speed off the north coast." Enemy battleships had also been spotted "off the coast of Ilocos Norte," and it was also reported that a Japanese flying boat had crashed off Babuyan Island. The crew, armed with revolvers and "hiding in the reedy shallows," were permitting "no one to come close."

Allison Ind, 5th Interceptor intelligence officer, had been working at the temporary "situation map" in the communications center all morning, helping plot each new message as it came in.

By nine o'clock, they had become so overwhelmed by the number of messages that, according to Ind, "Our modest equipment and restricted staff were threatened with submergence almost at once. Just when our need was mounting in geometric leaps, the order came [to] evacuate...all civilian secretaries. It was paralyzing..."

Ind was right. From that time on, the number of messages would increase, and so would their significance to the events of the next four hours.

It started at 9:15, when he was handed a message. "My gaze swept [it]," he said, "then froze on the words...Baguio bombed."

Minutes later, two more messages and two more bombings, at Tuguegaro and Cabanatuan were reported. Next, Tarlac, only 30 miles north of Clark Field was bombed. A couple of minutes later, at 9:23, the navy reported that Clark Field itself was under attack.

At 10:20, 24 enemy bombers were reported "in Cagayan Valley proceeding south in direction Manila." The towns of Vigan and La Union were reportedly attacked, and leaflets dropped on San Fernando and La Union, saying that "...to end this war, we [the Japanese and Filipinos] should cooperate fully."

At 11:10, much to the relief of Captain Ind, Clark Field reported that it hadn't been attacked.

11:27 a.m. (PH plus 8 hrs. 53 min.): At 11:27, as the B-17 crews and pilots of the 17th and 20th Pursuits were at mess as Clark Field, Iba radar notified Air Warning Service at Nielson of another formation of planes heading across the South China Sea toward Manila. Nielson was also warned that the flight was a big one; much larger than the one that had hit Baguio and Tuguegaro.

They were right. It was larger, ninety-eight planes, to be exact. When they were detected, they'd already been in the air for an hour, and were another hour away from their main targets, Clark and Iba Fields.

Had things gone the way the Japanese had planned, Iba radar would have picked up the same planes six hours earlier. Anticipating a quick retaliatory strike from the Americans as quick as they could react to the news about Pearl Harbor, the Japanese had planned to beat the U.S. to the punch with a dawn attack on Clark and Iba Fields. At the originally scheduled takeoff time at 4:00 a.m., however, a rare, dense fog had drifted in over the field, cutting visibility to less than 15 feet.

Feeling that the delay would rob them of the element of surprise, for a time it looked like the Americans would "beat them to the punch." When the order for the B-17s to take off from Clark Field was issued earlier that morning, it was apparently monitored by the Japanese, who interpreted it as the launching of a raid on Formosa. With news of Pearl Harbor five and a half hours old by then, they braced for an attack.

At 9:30, the fog that had unexpectedly blanketed Tainan Field on Formosa, had lifted, and, despite the threat of an American raid, by ten o'clock, the first of 54 Japanese twin-engined bombers took off. As the seventh plane sped down the runway, its right landing gear gave way, and it ground-looped near the end of the runway, blowing up moments later. None of the crew survived.

Within 20 minutes, repair crews had cleared the field of debris and filled the crater created by the exploding bombs. By 10:45, all remaining 53 bombers and 45 Zero fighters were off the ground.

After passing the southernmost tip of Formosa, one of the Zero pilots, Saburo Sakai, spotted a nine-plane bomber formation flying directly toward Formosa, to "apparently attack our field," he said. "We dropped out of the formation and dove for the [American] bombers. In seconds I was in firing position and closed to take the lead plane [when]...I suddenly realized that these were Japanese Army planes."

Thinking they were out on an unannounced training flight, Sakai thought to himself, "Those fools in the bombers! [Why hadn't someone] taken the trouble to coordinate their flight with [us]?"

Actually, the army bombers they had dived on were part of those involved in the attacks on Baguio and Tuguegaro. Although avoiding being shot down at the last minute by their own planes, at 10:10, the formation was again identified as an incoming flight of American B-17s. This time, southern Formosa sounded air raid alarms and passed out gas masks.

In the meantime, at the Air Warning Room at Nielson, three officers were closely monitoring the progress of the enemy flight since it first appeared on the big Plotting Table map at 11:30. At 11:40, the three men, Colonel George, his operations officer, Lieutenant Bud Sprague, and Colonel Alexander Campbell, aircraft warning officer, all agreed that its objective was either Clark Field, or Manila, or both.

Campbell quickly wrote out a message alerting Clark Field, and handed it to communications NCO, Sergeant Alfred Eckles, and told him to send it by teletype. When Eckles returned, Campbell asked him if it had been acknowledged. Eckles said it had. Campbell looked at his watch. It was 11:45 a.m.

Colonel George, meanwhile, had scrambled all 90 of his fighters. Anticipating that the enemy flight might split before they reached Clark, the 18 P-40s of the 17th Pursuit, who had finished refueling at Clark, were ordered to patrol over Bataan peninsula and the entrance to Manila Bay. The 3rd Squadron at Iba, under Lieutenant Hank Thorne, was to orbit near Point Iba, and tie into the hostile formation as it came in from the South China Sea. Captain Ed Dyess was to fly a standing patrol between Cavite and Corregidor with his 21st Squadron from Nichols.

This left 36 fighters to handle whatever came over Clark, the 34th Squadron of slow, obsolete P-35s, whose field at Del Carmen was just 14 minutes south of Clark, and the 20th Pursuit at Clark Field itself, whose planes were just then completing refueling.

Unfortunately, if George guessed wrong and the entire formation went after Clark, all three squadrons covering the anticipated attack on Manila would be over 45 miles away. It was too far to visibly be aware of the attack, and at least 20 minutes flying time away from being able to help if they were called.

The first squadron to reach its patrol area was the 17th from Clark, ordered up by 24th Pursuit Group commander, Major Orrin Grover. In less than 15 minutes after they took off, the lead P-40 of Lieutenant Boyd Wagner's 18-plane formation was over Manila Bay. Ironically, of the five squadrons of 24th Pursuit planes that were ordered to their respective patrol areas in the face of the oncoming Japanese, only one squadron, the 17th, was able to fulfill its assigned task without incident.

Like the pilots of the other two squadrons that had yet to be ordered into the air that morning—the 21st and 34th—Lieutenant Hank Thorne's 3rd Pursuit boys at Iba had been sitting in their planes since daylight, waiting for orders that never came. When Iba radar reported a large formation of incoming planes from its crude, half-buried hut at the end of the runway at 11:27, Thorne had his men start their engines. But again, the takeoff was delayed until orders from Group Headquarters came down, directing them to fly a standby patrol in the vicinity of Point Iba.

At this point, as the most critical moments of the first day of the war in the Philippines neared, one of the greatest contributors to the outcome of not only this, but of other military battles throughout history, reared its ugly head—the breakdown of communications. Whether through poorly functioning equipment, confusion, the excitement of battle, sabotage, or just hard luck, the Japanese would probably never know to what degree this breakdown added to their success that day. The Americans would though, and it started with the planes at Iba.

At 11:30, squadron leader Hank Thorne received a radio message from 24th Pursuit Group Headquarters at Clark, ordering him to take off immediately. A Flight was under Thorne, B Flight under Ed Woolery, and C Flight was under Lieutenant Herb Ellis. The six planes of Thorne's A Flight took off first, and headed for their assigned patrol area over Mt. Iba. Next off was Woolery's B Flight, who, taking off in the opposite direction of Thorne, was unable to locate A Flight. Nor could four of the C Flight fighters, who decided to join up with Woolery's B Flight.

With his radio apparently on the blink, young Woolery did not know what to do. He decided to head for Nielson Field, where he hoped to get some instructions, once they got within radio range.

Reaching Nielson 20 minutes later, Woolery tried unsuccessfully to get a response from anyone there or at nearby Nichols Field. Suddenly,

Andy Krieger, Woolery's wingman, heard a voice through the crackle of static on his radio transmitter. It sounded like "Tally-ho, Clark Field! All pursuits to Clark." That was good enough.

As Woolery's ten-plane B Flight banked away towards Clark Field, the last of Captain Ed Dyess' 21st Pursuit Squadron was taking off from Nichols Field. Like the 3rd Pursuit at Iba, the 21st pilots too, had remained close to their planes all morning in anticipation of having to take off. When the order came at 11:30, Dyess, leading A Flight, took off, with instructions to the leaders of B and C Flights to "Follow me!"

A and B Flights successfully joined up, but C Flight had trouble. "...a couple of our planes developed minor engine difficulties," said Lieutenant Sam Grashio, one of the pilots, "that delayed us just enough that we lost contact with A and B Flights. Only at about 11:50 did we get into the air."

At that point, unable to make radio contact with Dyess, and with no orders other than to follow him, flight leader Bob Clark turned south for giant Laguna de Bay, where they could make a quick check of their guns.

"[There] for the first time," said Grashio, "[we] tested our .50 caliber machine guns by firing short bursts into the water....Our P-40s were so new that [they had just] been taken out of their crates and had their...guns divested of cosmoline."

A few minutes later, remembered Grashio, two pilots in the flight, one of them Bob Clark, radioed that their engines were "throwing so much oil on the windshields that they couldn't see," and had to return to Nichols Field. The flight was turned over to Grashio.

"This left four of us," said the young lieutenant. "Since I had to do something, I radioed Joe Cole [one of the pilots] that we should fly towards Clark Field....It seemed a logical target for Japanese planes flying in from the north."

Ironically, that's exactly what Dyess had done. Apparently hearing the same "Tally-ho, Clark Field" message that sent Ed Woolery's 3rd Squadron flight racing north, Dyess reported to air force headquarters that he too, was responding to Clark's call for help.

"But," said the 21st Squadron leader, "we were just north of Manila when we were ordered back to a point midway between Corregidor and Cavite to intercept Jap bombers."

Meanwhile, as B Flight of the 3rd, and Grashio's four C Flight planes roared on toward Clark Field, tension was mounting at Air Force Headquarters at Nielson.

Spotters along the northwest coast of Luzon had begun reporting on the progress of the large flight of enemy planes as soon as they came into view over the China Sea. Although each tally on the number of fighters varied, the count on the bombers consistently came up 100-plus. Later reports also indicated that the formation had split. It was with this information that Colonel George ordered Dyess back to Manila Bay to "intercept [the] Jap bombers."

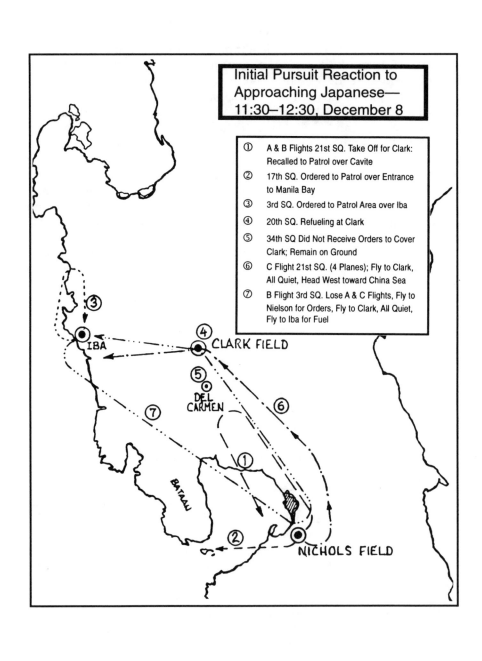

Initial Pursuit Reaction to Approaching Japanese—11:30–12:30, December 8

① A & B Flights 21st SQ. Take Off for Clark: Recalled to Patrol over Cavite

② 17th SQ. Ordered to Patrol over Entrance to Manila Bay

③ 3rd SQ. Ordered to Patrol Area over Iba

④ 20th SQ. Refueling at Clark

⑤ 34th SQ Did Not Receive Orders to Cover Clark; Remain on Ground

⑥ C Flight 21st SQ. (4 Planes); Fly to Clark, All Quiet, Head West toward China Sea

⑦ B Flight 3rd SQ. Lose A & C Flights, Fly to Nielson for Orders, Fly to Clark, All Quiet, Fly to Iba for Fuel

③
IBA
④ CLARK FIELD
⑤
DEL CARMEN
⑥
⑦
①
BATAAN
②
NICHOLS FIELD

As George and Colonel Alexander Campbell watched the picture begin to take shape on the Plotting Board in the Air Warning Room, both men began to panic, particularly after following the progress of the flight that appeared headed for Clark Field.

"[We] watched this particular flight for a considerable length of time," wrote Campbell in his notebook later. "I kept urging them to do something about it, but they insisted on waiting until [it] reached a certain distance from the field."

The "certain distance" was reached the minute George was positive Clark Field was the target. When that moment arrived, he was on the phone to Clark, "begging and begging," as he described it later, to get the B-17s off the ground. It was impossible. The pilots were at the Formosa briefing, and the planes were in the process of being refueled and "bombed up" for the raid.

In the meantime, when the two flights of 3rd and 21st Pursuit P-40s reached Clark Field between 12:10 and 12:20, both found everything looking normal. Ed Woolery, exhausted from the 210-mile wild goose chase to Nielson Field and back, directed his B Flight Kittyhawks west over the Zambales Mountains to Iba for fuel.

Sam Grashio, arriving about ten minutes later with the four remaining C Flight fighters, and "observing nothing unusual at Clark," also turned west toward the China Sea.

12:20 p.m. (PH plus 9 hrs. 50 min.): As the enemy formation continued to bear down on Clark Field, fear had set in back at Nielson. Colonel Alexander Campbell, rightfully nervous about whether or not the big airbase had received the 11:45 teletype warning, got a call through to an unknown junior officer at about 12:20. The man, probably lunch relief for the regular operator, told Campbell that he would give the message about the rapidly approaching enemy formation to "the base commander or operations officer...at the earliest opportunity." Apparently the "opportunity" did not come in time, as neither that nor the 11:45 teletype message was ever delivered.

Colonel George, who had held up ordering the 20th Pursuit Squadron at Clark Field into the air until they were finished refueling, at 12:20 sent Lieutenant Bud Sprague to the teletype room with the one-word message "Kickapoo."

"I asked what 'Kickapoo' meant," wrote Colonel Campbell later in his notebook, "and was told it meant 'Go get 'em.'"

At this point, George felt he had done everything that could be done to protect Clark Field and Manila against attack. It was out of his hands now. Both the 17th and 21st Pursuit Squadrons from Nichols—less one flight—were in position to take on the Japanese when they reached Manila Bay. The 3rd Pursuit from Iba—less ten planes—was also waiting to take on the enemy flight before it reached Manila; if Manila was the target. But what of the eighteen 34th Squadron P-35s and the 20th Squadron P-40Bs, the least combat-efficient fighters in the Philippines, whose job it was to protect Clark Field?

Communications with the 34th at Del Carmen had been shaky all morning. While the 3rd, 17th, 20th, and 21st Squadrons had been on the alert since 4:30 that morning, the Del Carmen pilots did not even hear of the attack on Pearl Harbor until 8:00 a.m. Outside of sitting in their planes awaiting orders to take off, like pilots of the other squadrons had done all morning, Sprague's "Kickapoo" message never got through, nor did anything else.

That left it up to Lieutenant Joe Moore's Tomahawks at Clark Field. When "Kickapoo" came through to the 24th Pursuit Group communications center at Clark at 12:20, for some unknown reason, Major Orrin Grover, Group CO, refused to let the 20th take off. All 18 of its pilots were sitting in their planes watching and waiting for the red takeoff flag to be run up. When it was run up 15 minutes later at 12:35, it was too late. The order to take off came, not from Grover, but in response to the huge formation of Japanese bombers seen approaching from the north. Fate and Grover's hesitation cost the 20th 23 of the squadron's 26 fighters, none of which ever left the ground, and the lives of four of its pilots.

As luck or fate would have it, not a single American fighter of the 90 ordered into the air that day would play the role it was designed for. Not one Fifth Interceptor Command plane would intercept a single enemy aircraft.

When examining what went on at Clark Field before the attack, there's little doubt that, outside of Sprague's last-minute "Kickapoo" message, warning of the raid did not get through. The only concern anyone had when General Brereton gave the green light on the Formosa raid at 10:30, was to be ready for it.

As soon as the crews of the returning B-17s stepped out of their planes, the pilots and navigators were off to the mess halls for early lunch and a 12:20 briefing. The remainder of the crews ate in shifts and stood by to help with the refueling and bomb loading.

By 12:30, "the operations tent was crowded with about forty pilots and navigators waiting for the briefing to begin," said Captain Frank Kurtz, one of the pilots. "As we waited, I snapped on my radio and we all listened to Manila....Don Bell was really packing it across in his excited delivery. Suddenly he said 'This is an unconfirmed report that they're bombing Clark Field.' "

"We all smiled at this," said Kurtz, "and were listening for whatever crazy thing [he] would say next."

The operations tent wasn't the only place men laughed or smiled in disbelief at his comments. Radios all around the field—in barracks, mess halls and hangars—had been tuned in all morning to Bell. His report was so ridiculous that no one even bothered to question where he got his information. Frank Kurtz unknowingly came the closest. "...broadcasting from the top of one of Manila's tallest buildings...[if there was any] he could [probably] see big plumes of smoke rising from Clark Field."

Although it wouldn't be long before Bell would see "big plumes of smoke" rising from Clark Field, had he been able to, he would also see it rising from Iba as well.

Unknown, of course, to Colonel George back at Nielson, the target of the 106 Japanese planes that he had anticipated were heading for Manila, was actually Iba. Aside from being one of the most important fighter fields on Luzon, it had the only working radar unit in the Philippines. Without it, Interceptor Command would be completely blind.

As the first bombs were falling on Iba, Lieutenant Ed Woolery was leading four of his B Flight planes on their final approach to the field. The sixth fighter, piloted by Second Lieutenant Andy Krieger, who had stayed up to cover the landing, was watching Woolery's plane touch down when the entire strip went up in a single blinding explosion.

Before the bombs actually hit the ground, Krieger was totally unaware of the presence of Japanese bombers flying 15,000 feet above him.

Unlike the startled young lieutenant, many of the men on the ground at Iba had seen both planes and bombs falling. Until the bombs began to all, many thought the planes were B-17s.

"Wow, look at that formation," one said.

"Didn't know there were that many B-17s," said another.

"There aren't. Those are Jap planes!" exclaimed a young pilot officer who had wandered over to watch B Flight come in. "They're dropping bombs!" With those words, everyone headed for shelter wherever they could find it.

Meanwhile, Andy Krieger had gone after the Japanese. Without oxygen and the odds 53 to one against him, it was impossible. After a few minutes, he broke off the chase and returned to Iba.

Coming in he saw what he first thought was a squadron of P-35s circling the field. When he got closer, he noticed that they were all white with big red dots on their wings. They were Japanese, in the process of strafing everything in sight.

"I was about to call 'All pursuits to Iba,'" remembered Krieger, "when 'All pursuits to Clark' cracked in over the R.T."

It was the second time he had been beckoned to Clark Field, but this time the great columns of smoke rising high over the Zambales Mountains, told him it was real.

Deciding that there would soon be enough planes to handle the Clark Field attackers without him, he called "All 3rd Pursuits to Iba," then banked his Kittyhawk toward the circling Japanese fighters. Unable to get below them because they were flying so low, Krieger decided his best bet was to join their circle. After firing a burst at the first plane he saw, he spotted three Zeros closing in on his tail. With tracers whizzing over his canopy, Krieger shoved the throttle as far forward as it would go and began to climb. Fortunately, the Zeros chose not to follow, staying instead on their strafing run.

After making his escape, the needle on his fuel gauge told him he had better find a place to land pretty quick.

"I asked for landing instructions to anyone listening," said Krieger, "and was surprised to hear Hank Thorne's voice. He told me to try for Rosales, a small auxiliary field 60 miles southeast. It would be close."

It was close. In fact, his P-40 actually ran out of gas as he was taxiing toward five other members of his squadron who had also flown into Rosales with dry fuel tanks. One of them was squadron leader Thorne, who, unknown to Krieger, had responded with A Flight to his "3rd Pursuits to Iba" call in time to get in on the tail end of the battle. They too had to abandon the fight because of fuel problems.

Thinking that he might be the only survivor from B Flight, Krieger told Thorne that he saw Woolery land right in the middle of the first stick of Japanese bombs.

Unknown, of course, to the young lieutenant, only two of the six-plane flight were lost. Woolery, who had the tail of his plane blown off by one of the Japanese 132-pounders, jumped out with his prop still turning, making it safely to a nearby gun position. The third fighter behind Woolery, flown by Lieutenant Richard Root, crashed after being hit by shrapnel attempting to climb out of his landing pattern. Root was killed.

Andy Krieger wasn't the only 3rd Pursuit pilot to give futile chase to the Japanese bombers, and then fly into circling enemy fighters over Iba. Herb Ellis, leader of C Flight, who had become separated from the rest of his flight after takeoff, mirrored Krieger's action, and downed two Japanese Zeros in the process. Unlike Krieger, however, Ellis was shot down over Clark Field, but safely bailed out.

Of the eighteen 3rd Pursuit fighters that had taken off that morning, and the six that were on the field when the Japanese attacked, only seven were flyable at the end of the day. Three pilots were killed.

Back at Iba, little was left of the once picturesque little field, whose single grass strip bordered the very edge of the South China Sea. Considering the number of attackers, 53 bombers and 53 fighters, it was second only to Clark Field on their priority list. If destruction of the radar unit was one of their main objectives, then it had been accomplished, because little was found of either the radar or its heroic crew, who had died at their posts.

As a functioning airfield, it was finished. With all buildings destroyed, all methods of communication knocked out, and the strip itself pockmarked with a dozen craters, for all practical purposes, it had to be abandoned within three hours after the first bombs were dropped on the Philippines.

A few minutes before the Japanese high level bombers began bombing Iba, the lead formation of planes heading for Clark, for the first time, spotted their target.

"The sight which met us was unbelievable," remembered Saburo Sakai, one of the escorting fighter pilots. "Instead of encountering a swarm of American fighters diving at us...we looked down and saw 60 enemy bombers and fighters neatly parked along the airfield runway....There like sitting ducks."

On the ground at Clark, the reaction was different. When the enemy planes were initially spotted, at first no one thought they were Japanese. Although some described them as B-18s, the navy got most of the votes.

"Here comes the navy," most exclaimed when they first saw them. "It's about time they came to help."

In the operations tent, pilots and navigators were waiting for the briefing to start, when an army private standing outside said, "...gee! Look at the pretty navy formation."

It got a different reaction from some inside. "It froze me," said Frank Kurtz, one of the pilots. "I think it froze all of us. The next second, Lieutenant Lee Coats stepped to the opening [and looked]. 'Navy hell!' he yelled, 'here they come.' "

"We turned over tables in the confusion of piling out of [the] tent," recalled Kurtz. "There they came...in an enormous V of V's, three in all and about 25 Mitsubishi bombers in each V...coming right at us!"

In the nearby Headquarters Building, Colonel Eubank was interrupted while briefing the crews on the photo reconnaissance mission. "He was just pointing out our objective...when someone came running in," remembered one of the pilots. [He] shouted 'the Japs will be here in 20 minutes.' We started to get out and get to our planes. Two minutes later, the bombs crashed down all around us."

To one person, at least, the sight of bombs falling was at first interpreted as something else. "Why are they dropping tin foil?" asked a puzzled member of the 200th Coast Artillery, who had their 37mm and 3-inch anti-aircraft guns set up around the perimeter of the field.

"That's not tin foil, those are goddamn Japs!" responded one of the gunners as he took off towards his battery.

Back outside the operations tent, Frank Kurtz watched the formation of enemy planes at it approached. Everyone else had taken cover in a nearby drainage ditch.

"I stood there because I thought it would be five or ten seconds before they came to their bomb-release line," said Kurtz. "I hadn't long to wait because now came the first unmistakable whistle and then the dull cr-r-ump. The first bombs of their pattern hit way up the field, three thousand yards away. I didn't know then it had hit the mess hall I had just left...and killed our group engineer officer."

A mile or so west of where Kurtz was standing, General Jonathan Wainwright had just walked out on the porch of his quarters at Fort Stotsenberg, when, he said, "the thunder of a flight of approaching planes hit my ears."

"They swept over Stotsenberg, shaking the ground, and let their bombs go on Clark Field....The very air [around us] rattled with concussion."

While standing on his front lawn watching the bombs fall, Wainwright saw his Filipino house boy run out of his quarters wearing the general's own steel helmet.

"Mother of God, General, what shall I do?" he shouted.

"Go get me a bottle of beer," Wainwright said calmly.

"I know it helped me," he explained later.

Reacting earlier to a warning from MacArthur's USAFFE headquarters of a possible paratroop attack on Clark Field, Wainwright had deployed a battery of 26th Cavalry pack howitzers at the west end of the Stotsenberg parade ground.

He had gone over near one of the guns when the attack started, "...watching the black bursts of our modest anti-aircraft fire trying to follow the Jap bombers...when I heard the moist impact of metal against flesh and bone.

"I turned and saw one of [the Scout] gunners fall near me," said Wainwright. "His face was a bloody blob. A bomb splinter...from Clark Field, twelve hundred yards [away had] hit him in the lower forehead, just below the helmet."

"Get this man to a doctor," ordered Wainwright.

"No," said the boy. "Staying by my gun...staying by my gun."

Before the last Japanese plane had unloaded its bombs on Clark Field, Wainwright had written out the order which gave the young Philippine Scout the first Silver Star of the hours-old Pacific War.

Over at Clark Field, Lieutenant Edgar Whitcomb was standing outside the door of the Headquarters Building catching as much of Colonel Eubank's photo-reconnaissance briefing as he could, when he heard someone yell from the other side of the building, "Here they come!"

"...I rushed to the back steps and made a wild dive for a trench about 20 feet away," said Whitcomb. "...as I hit the bottom...there was a terrible explosion followed by another, another, and another."

Not far away, Frank Kurtz and another officer had jumped into the same one-man fox hole.

"We could think of nothing except this earthquake roar...and the whistling of a mighty storm moving down the field," remembered Kurtz.

"[Then] it began. Not so much the thunderous roar as the shaking...[which] at its worst bucked and pitched like a bronco. And then quite suddenly [it] was gone, and the Japanese formation was moving off."

It was not until the two men stood up that either realized they had been lying on top of another man. Three men in the one-man fox hole.

It was the same in the trench Ed Whitcomb had jumped into, except he was the one on the bottom. "[After] the roaring and rumbling subsided," he said, "I realized I was on the bottom of a trench...that a large number of persons [also jumped] into..."

When Whitcomb was able to get to his feet, he ran around the end of the Headquarters Building to get a look at the field. It was a nightmarish scene.

"There across the field, [I] could see our beautiful silver Flying Fortresses burning and exploding right before [my] eyes, [and was] powerless to do anything about it."

The Japanese had come in from the northeast, and dropped their bombs in a diagonal pattern across the field. Hit by over 600 bombs that had been dropped were the row of officers' quarters, the shop and hangar areas, the communication center, the infirmary, both the officers' mess and 20th Pursuit Squadron's mess tent, and an oil storage area. Five P-40s waiting to take off were also destroyed, along with several parked on the edge of the field.

From the sky, according to Saburo Sakai, flying cover for the bombers, the attack was perfect. "Their accuracy was phenomenal," remembered the young Zero pilot "...the most accurate bombing I ever witnessed by our own planes throughout the war. The entire air base seemed to be rising into the air with explosions. Pieces of airplanes, hangars, and other ground installations scattered wildly. Great fires erupted and smoke boiled upward."

Unobserved by either the Japanese or the Americans, at the exact moment the first string of enemy bombs hit the northeast corner of the field, a lone B-17 was crossing, wheels down, over the far end of the runway on its way to land. The plane, piloted by Lieutenant Earl Tash, had taken off from Del Monte Field on Mindanao at 9:45 that morning for Clark Field, to have a damaged wing repaired.

It's strange the commander at Del Monte would let Tash fly all the way to Clark for a repair job that was obviously minor, particularly since they had been alerted to the opening of hostilities with Japan at 6:30 a.m., and had sent two B-17s on a reconnaissance flight in anticipation of being attacked themselves.

Stupefied by the sight of bombs falling in front of him, Tash ordered wheels up, and, at full throttle, banked away to the right to escape being hit.

Lieutenant Earl Tash. Twice attempted to land his B-17 on Clark Field during the height of the Japanese attack.
USAAF

After spotting the formation of enemy planes above, Tash headed east for the backside of Mt. Arayat, where he circled, trying to figure out what to do. They still had enough gas to get back to Del Monte with 25 minutes to spare. On the other hand, if they waited that 25 minutes, maybe they'd be able to get into Clark after all.

But what of the B-17s already on the ground at Clark Field? A quick check by Colonel Eubank indicated that only few had been damaged in the bombing. Among others, the two planes in the hangars for camouflaging had been taxied out onto the field and were both untouched.

He wondered if some miracle had saved most of the big bombers. Thinking the raid was over, he felt better. At that moment, however, another formation of planes was seen heading toward Clark from the north. Frank Kurtz and Lieutenant Glenn Rice followed their approach.

"They were coming around beautiful Mr. Arayat in a long string like geese flying north in the fall," said Kurtz. He concluded that the planes he had seen "must be our P-40s."

"If they'd been only a little earlier and higher," he thought, "they could have knocked hell out of [the] Jap [bombers]."

The string of fighters came on and had started to circle the field, when Rice, excitingly pointing in their direction, yelled, "Look! For God's sake, look at that red circle—they're Japs," They were, 36 "Japs" to be exact, who would soon be joined by 40 more fighters from the Iba raid.

All over the field, men had come out of their fox holes and slit trenches when the bombers left. "But now," said Kurtz, "we ran back, looking over our shoulders to be sure there wasn't a Nakajima coming, spitting guns at our backs!"

One man who refused to move was Gene Eubank. "Through all of this, a lone figure stood on top of a mound near my trench...looking [numbly] across the field," remembered Ed Whitcomb.

"You'd better take cover, sir," said the young lieutenant. Sensing that the final destruction of his bombers was about to occur, and like a captain ready to go down with his ships, the colonel refused to move.

Eubank had sensed correctly. The primary target of the strafers were the B-17s. Saburo Sakai, diving with his two wingmen, had selected two of the undamaged Fortresses for their first target, all three pouring "a fusillade of bullets into the big bombers."

When Major David Gibbs ordered the B-17s off the field earlier that morning in anticipation of a Japanese attack, the plane piloted by Lieutenant John Carpenter, it will be remembered, failed to take off because of carburetor trouble. When he did get up some 20 minutes later, he was ordered to fly reconnaissance along Luzon's east coast.

Carpenter was 200 miles northeast of Clark Field when he got a call to return to the big base. Unbelievably, as with Earl Tash's B-17 a few minutes earlier, it's doubtful anyone on the ground was aware that for the second time during the attack, the pilot of a lone Fortress was approaching the field completely oblivious to what was going on.

Misinterpreting the smoke and poor visibility over the field as a thunderstorm, it wasn't until Carpenter was jumped by enemy fighters on his way in, that he realized what he was flying into. Like Tash, he too poured the coal to the big bomber, making good his escape toward Mt. Arayat.

Unbeknownst to each other, there were now two B-17s in the sky over Mt. Arayat, whose pilots were trying to figure what to do next. At one time, when they had actually seen each other, Tash decided to join up with the other bomber. But Carpenter, who wasn't sure the plane approaching him wasn't Japanese, ducked into a nearby cloud bank, which he would fly in and out of for over three hours, landing at Clark at 4:00 p.m.

By then, Tash's fuel gauge told him it was time to make a decision. Seeing that the sky was clear of enemy bombers as he cautiously approached the big base for a second time, and, mistaking the string of fighters circling the field as returning American pursuit planes, he once again lowered his wheels and started in.

Suddenly, at almost the identical spot as when they first came in, they were again shocked into reality, this time when a burning Japanese fighter flashed in front of them in a vertical dive straight into the ground. They had done it again, only this time it wasn't bombs they had to avoid, it was enemy fighters and their own anti-aircraft guns. At full throttle and at tree-top level, Tash banked away again, but this time, he was not alone. Three Japanese fighters had spotted the big silver B-17, and were closing in. Without a tail gun, Tash's D-model Fortress was a sitting duck for the first Zero, whose .25 caliber machine guns and 20mm cannon chewed up his aileron and flap cables and nicked one of the propellers. Bombardier, Sergeant Mike Bibin, voluntarily firing one of the waist guns, was wounded, but survived.

As the first Zero sped by, the second and third took turns blasting at the big bomber, but to no avail. When the third enemy fighter broke away, Private First Class Al Norgaard, firing the top radio guns, hit the Japanese plane, which was last seen fighting to stay in the air. Staying low, Tash turned for Mindanao, landing there safely four hours and 35 bullet holes later.

Back on the ground, the only hope of disrupting the systematic destruction of the B-17s came from the anti-aircraft guns of the 200th Coast Artillery, who, according to Kurtz, "were thumping away at the enemy, but, because of the dense smoke, [not] doing much good.

"So in our ditch we start a little war of our own," he said. "Forty of us [who have .45s] versus the Imperial Japanese Air Force. Every time a Jap strafer comes over, we bang away at him."

In a revetment not far from where the forty men were standing, a B-17 was being worked over by a single Japanese plane.

"The Jap pilot with [a] yellow scarf, who [had been] working on the Fortress in the revetment, [was] coming in lower and closer each time," said Kurtz. Finally, on the eighth pass, his tracers found their mark, the already riddled Fortress bursting into flames.

Possibly to admire what he had accomplished, "he made the mistake of coming back just one more time," remembered Kurtz. "But for whatever reason, at [that] point the anti-aircraft opened up on him through a hole in the smoke....'Look!' somebody said, 'he's been hit.' We held our breath as he wobbled and wavered off like a wounded bird, [disappearing over] the horizon, never to rise again."

It's true, it never would "rise again." Sadly, of the seven Japanese planes lost that day, it would be the only one shot down by ground fire.

"This seemed to signal the end of the attack," said Kurtz, "for now the Nakajimas and Zeroes rose from the field like crows from a well-picked carcass [and] disappeared around Mt. Arayat."

All through the attack, men could be heard saying, "Where the hell are our fighters?" Not counting the momentary presence of a dozen P-35s from the 34th Pursuit at Del Carmen, who, in a matter of minutes were chased away by half their number of Zeroes, only nine P-40s actually took part in the fight. But not all at once, and certainly not as the "swarm of American fighters" Saburo Sakai had anticipated.

The main reason the thirty 17th and 21st Pursuit fighters, fruitlessly patrolling over Manila Bay in anticipation of an attack on Manila and Cavite, weren't called to help over Clark, is because its communication center took a direct hit, cutting off the field from all contact with fighter operations at Nielson. From approximately 12:30 that afternoon until sometime after 2:00 p.m., Colonel George at Fifth Interceptor Command Headquarters at Nielson was completely in the dark as to what was going on at Clark Field.

The first of the nine planes to arrive on the scene at Clark Field were two stragglers from the 3rd Pursuit Squadron, piloted by Lieutenants Don Steel and Ship Daniel. Originally members of Ed Woolery's B Flight, they had become separated on the long flight to Nielson, and were about five minutes out from Clark when they heard the "All pursuits to Clark..." call for help.

When they arrived, both dove on the Japanese strafers working over the field. Steel, with only one of his six .50 caliber guns working, was able to shoot down a Zero before he and Daniel were forced to break off the fight and head for Iba for fuel.

Arriving at Clark about a minute behind Daniel and Steel were three 21st Squadron fighters, piloted by Sam Grashio, Gus Williams, and Johnny McCown. Fifteen minutes earlier, it will be recalled, they, along with a fourth plane piloted by Joe Cole, had found everything quiet and peaceful over the big base before heading west toward the South China Sea. Flying at 10,000 feet, they had just spotted Woolery's flight of P-40s heading south, when the call, "All pursuits to Clark. Enemy bombers overhead," came in.

"Right at this crucial juncture," remembered Grashio, "Joe Cole radioed that his engine was throwing oil so badly that he couldn't see out of his windshield." Leaving Grashio, Williams, and McCown to go it alone, the three turned back towards Clark. A few minutes later, as the field came into view, they got their first glimpse of what was left of the big air base. It was startling.

"Where the airfield should have been, the whole area was boiling with smoke, dust, and flames," said Grashio. "In the middle was a huge column of greasy black smoke from the top of which ugly red flames billowed intermittently."

Grashio and Williams, who had momentarily lost McCown, went in first. After a single burst by Grashio at a lone Zero, they were jumped by a pair of the quick-maneuvering enemy fighters. Both were able to escape, although Grashio's Kittyhawk was hit in the left wing by a 20mm cannon shell, that, as he said later, "[made] my plane shudder...and blew a hole big enough to throw a hat through.

"I ...remember what Ed [Dyess] had told us," said the young lieutenant, "...never try to outmaneuver a Zero; go into a steep dive and try to outrace it."

With two Zeroes still on his tail, Grashio "...pushed the throttle wide open and roared for the ground....My luck held," he said. "[After pulling] out of the dive at treetop level just west of Clark...I was overjoyed to see [them] falling steadily behind. Midway between Clark and Nichols they gave up and turned back."

Williams, meanwhile, also dove his P-40 and escaped his pursuer, and, like Grashio and McCown, decided to return to Nichols.

As Sam Grashio approached Nichols Field after successfully escaping the two pursuing enemy fighters, he wondered if he would be able to land his damaged Kittyhawk with the huge hole in the left wing.

"I radioed Nichols tower for advice, [and] was told to climb to 8,000 feet...and simulate a [wheels and flaps down] landing. " He did. "The hole in the wing presented no problems, "he said later. Arriving over the field at 1:30, "[I was] the first pilot to make it back from combat."

In the confusion caused by the planes of the 3rd Pursuit taking off from Iba in different directions, it will be remembered that four lost C Flight fighters joined Ed Woolery's B Flight to Nielson. On the return, two of those planes, piloted by Fred Roberts and Bill Powell, who had dropped well behind the rest, spotted a huge column of smoke rising from Clark Field. Arriving over the field at 12:45, both dove on the Japanese. As they lined up to fire on two Zeroes, whose pilots were preoccupied with strafing the field, Powell found his guns wouldn't fire. Roberts' luck wasn't much better, as only one of his was functioning.

Over before it started, both were able to escape from the Japanese beehive they had dived into, but Roberts' plane was hit and he was nicked in the leg.

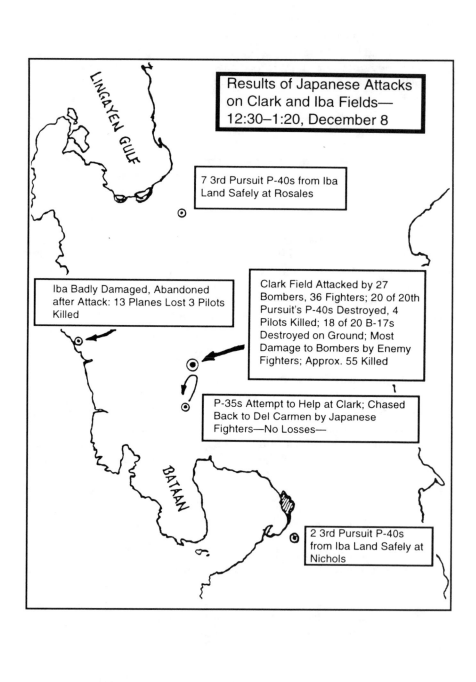

Results of Japanese Attacks on Clark and Iba Fields— 12:30–1:20, December 8

7 3rd Pursuit P-40s from Iba Land Safely at Rosales

Iba Badly Damaged, Abandoned after Attack: 13 Planes Lost 3 Pilots Killed

Clark Field Attacked by 27 Bombers, 36 Fighters; 20 of 20th Pursuit's P-40s Destroyed, 4 Pilots Killed; 18 of 20 B-17s Destroyed on Ground; Most Damage to Bombers by Enemy Fighters; Approx. 55 Killed

P-35s Attempt to Help at Clark; Chased Back to Del Carmen by Japanese Fighters—No Losses—

LINGAYEN GULF

BATAAN

2 3rd Pursuit P-40s from Iba Land Safely at Nichols

All 18 pilots of the 20th Pursuit Squadron at Clark Field were in their planes, engines running, waiting for orders to take off, when the Japanese bombers were spotted less than three minutes from starting their bomb run.

The first three planes, piloted by squadron leader Joe Moore, Randy Keator, and Edwin Gilmore, were able to get off, while literally being chased down the runway by the first stick of Japanese bombs. None of the remaining planes of the squadron would be so lucky. Two took direct hits, killing both pilots. Three were disabled from shrapnel hits, forcing their pilots to abandon their damaged ships and run for cover. Three others that were hit burst into flames, all three pilots suffering from severe burns.

What was to be the fifth plane to take off behind Moore, piloted by Max Loux, amidst the confusion caused by smoke and falling bombs, slammed blindly into a cart loaded with incendiary bombs, that had been left on the edge of the field when the attack started. Those who witnessed the collision were transfixed by the explosion and fireball that followed. Along with the precious fighter and its young pilot, several ancient P-26s that were parked nearby, were also destroyed in the explosion.

A fourth pilot, Lieutenant Jim Drake, was strafed and killed by Japanese fighters while attempting to take off after the bombing.

In the end, not a single 20th Pursuit fighter got up to do battle with their Japanese counterparts over Clark. The three that did get up, piloted by Moore, Randy Keator, and Ed Gilmore, were several miles west of Clark in pursuit of enemy bombers when they ran into a flock of nine escorting Zeroes.

Apparently oblivious to Moore, all nine of the nimble fighters immediately went after Keator and Gilmore, who were strung out several hundred yards behind and well below their squadron leader.

Randy Keator, who had banked his Tomahawk toward the Japanese, found the lead plane of the diving formation dead in his sights. He fired. The Zero exploded.

Like Keator, Gilmore too, had initially turned toward the enemy formation, but soon found himself the object of a Zero which had gotten in behind him. Taking the only evasive action available to the slower American fighter, Gilmore dove for the ground. It worked. It also worked for Moore and Keator, who, before it was over, found themselves in similar predicaments.

When it was over, each man, unaware of what had happened to the other two, headed east toward Clark Field. About halfway to Clark, Keator spotted a lone enemy fighter 1,200 feet below him flying south. Diving out of the sun, the Tomahawk's guns caught the unsuspecting Zero, that, when last seen, was burning as it disappeared into a cloud bank.

1:30 p.m. (PH plus 11 hrs.): Exactly ten hours and 37 minutes after they were notified of the attack on Pearl Harbor, the skies over the Philippines were at last clear of Japanese planes.

Before the enemy attack, there had been approximately 118 operational fighters available for use on Luzon. By 1:30, that number had been cut in half.

Although the skies over the Philippines had seen the last of the Japanese for the day, it was not over for the several American pilots who had survived the battle. Outside of the thirty 17th and 21st Squadron planes, which, after patrolling without incident over Manila Bay, had all landed safely at Nichols, and the 34th's P-35s, who had somehow managed to return safely to Del Carmen, it was a mess.

The 20th Pursuit at Clark was hit the hardest. It lost 20 planes and four pilots killed. The 3rd at Iba didn't fare much better, losing 13 planes and three pilots.

For those pilots of the 3rd Pursuit who had survived the battle, but were without a field to land on because Iba's runway had been cratered from end to end by Japanese bombs, it was catch as catch can.

Seven landed at Rosales, and two made it all the way to Nichols. One of those pilots was Ed Woolery, who had the back of his plane blown off as he landed at Iba when the first Japanese bombs hit. Finding another flyable P-40 on the field, he jumped in and was able to take off for a second time.

Two other pilots, Don Steel and Gordon Benson, had coincidentally chosen the same dried-up river bed near San Marcelino to land on, neither aware of the other's presence when they landed

Of the 18 P-40s that were airborne that day, only one attempted a landing on the bombed-out field they had taken off from. Ship Daniel, who had flown to Iba from Clark to refuel, had to come in, despite the condition of the field. He somehow made it, becoming the last pilot to ever land on the little field.

He was also the last to take off from it, as well. Of the four spare P-40s at Iba before the attack, Daniel took off in the only undamaged one left, later becoming one of the seven to end up at Rosales.

Although Daniel was the only pilot to land on Iba, he wasn't the only one to contemplate it. Fred Roberts had arrived over the field while the enemy strafing attack was still in progress. Although only one of his guns would fire, the young lieutenant quickly dove on one of the circling enemy fighters, but soon found himself in the sights of a second Zero, who immediately scored. As his plane started to burn, Roberts looked down at what was left of the field. Deciding it was out of the question, he chose to land in the water, as close to the beach as possible. Here he was rescued after a rough landing by three ground crewmen who had seen him crash.

Bill Powell, who had flown over from Clark to gas up at Iba, quickly picked up a Zero on his tail when he arrived over the field.

With all guns malfunctioning, he decided to try to outrun the Japanese, who chased him for 50 miles before giving up. Sixty miles north of

Iba, with fuel tanks nearly empty, Powell picked out what looked like an auxiliary air strip near the gulf town of Lingayan to land on. It turned out to be a Philippine Army parade ground, but he was able to bring his Kittyhawk in, using his last ounce of fuel to do it.

Iba wasn't the only field that was damaged so badly that landing on it was almost impossible. Of the three 20th Pursuit fighters from Clark Field who were able to get up, two, flown by Joe Moore and Randy Keator, returned from their run-in with nine enemy fighters, to find the base smoke-covered and in shambles. It took Keator, who arrived first, no less than three passes to size up the field before he was able to negotiate a landing on the fourth. Moore made it on the third attempt. Ed Gilmore, the third 20th pilot, had opted for Del Carmen, where he landed safely.

What faced Moore and Keator and the men on the ground as they walked amongst the burning and smashed rubble of what two hours before had been the base for the "mightiest fleet of four-motored bombers in the world," as Frank Kurtz put it, "made [them] sick...and you wanted to look the other way."

The hangars, one of the prime targets of the bombers, were in shambles. Bombs had ripped through corrugated metal roofs and detonated on concrete floors, blowing everything outward, including windows, and the sides of the buildings. Walls and roofs were perforated by hundreds of shrapnel holes.

Unfortunately, both the officers mess and 20th Pursuit Squadron mess tent were located next to the hangars. Both took direct hits, and so did the kitchens. Over 50 men were in the officers mess when bombs fell. Although the exact number of casualties caused by the hits on the mess halls and hangars will never be known, it is estimated that approximately 55 were killed and 110 were wounded at Clark that day.

The Field Infirmary was also hit, forcing its staff to continue working on the front lawn. Over at the 19th Bomb Group Dispensary, which was forced to take most of the infirmary's wounded, smoke from the fiercely burning oil storage area fire covered the area. But the Flight Surgeon, Major Heidger, remembered Colonel Eubank "didn't mind. He remarked how lucky he was to have a smoke screen provided courtesy of the Japanese."

Among those "quiet heroes" on the field that day was a 32-year-old first lieutenant, Joseph La Fluer—Chaplain Joseph La Fluer—who was seen moving from wounded man to wounded man, calmly reassuring them, and, in some cases, delivering last rites. Even for those who were not wounded, his very presence helped reduce the fear and anxiety of the moment and restore confidence.

Another "quiet hero" was Private Robert Andres, who appropriated an abandoned truck to transport the wounded from different parts of the field back to the infirmary. How many wounded men he delivered in the seven or eight trips he made was not recorded.

Two or three B-17 gunners, who were near their undamaged planes when the strafing started, manned their guns and began firing at the diving enemy planes. One man, Private First Class Greely Williams, refused to leave his position even when his plane was on fire, and died at his gun.

5:30 p.m. (PH plus 15 hrs.): That afternoon, Colonel George ordered his 17th and 21st Squadrons at Nichols to Clark Field, in fear of Nichols being the next Japanese objective.

The 21st was off first. Ed Dyess, leading his squadron, remembered that they could see "towering pillars of smoke" rising from Clark Field as they got close. Once over the field, they found it "was a mess. Oil dumps and hangars blazing fiercely. Planes...burning on the ground. Runways...bombed so systematically we could use only the auxiliary landing strip [which] was little better than a country road."

Dusty country road would have been more accurate, as "each landing stirred up [such] blinding clouds of dust," said Dyess, that "we could only go down at intervals of several minutes....It was [also] a difficult job weaving the planes in and out among the bomb craters."

Circling over the field waiting for the last of Dyess' eighteen 21st Squadron Kittyhawks to land, Buzz Wagner and his 17th pursuit pilots were beginning to worry. With darkness coming on, and having to wait several minutes for the "blinding clouds of dust" to settle after each landing, Wagner ordered the 17th to nearby Del Carmen. Although the dust there was even worse, by seven o'clock all seventeen had landed safely.

The eighteenth 17th Squadron fighter, flown by Lieutenant John Posten, had missed Wagner's order, and landed at Clark. Walking by one of the burned-out B-17s, Posten came across a heart-rending scene. What appeared to be the plane's entire crew was lying dead in a line leading from the plane to some nearby woods. It appeared that they had been killed by a Japanese bomb while making a run for the woods.

The plane itself, christened "Old 99" by her crew because of the last two digits of her official serial number, was piloted by Captain Frank Kurtz. One of the three planes scheduled to fly the photo-reconnaissance mission over Formosa, her eight-man crew was waiting by the plane when the Japanese bombers came.

Kurtz, who had sweated out both the bombing and strafing in a fox hole near the operations tent, had no idea of the fate of his plane or its crew until it was over.

After the strafing ended, he climbed out of his fox hole and started back toward the operations tent to report. "...we had to walk around the wreckage of [a] poor old Fortress, still burning in her revetment," he said. "We walked wide...because...we could hardly bear to watch."

Finding the operations tent by some miracle still standing, Kurtz ran into Major Bill Gibbs, who told him to check on his plane and see if it was still okay for the reconnaissance mission.

"I jumped on my bike and rode down the runway through the smoke of other burning Fortresses, to see what happened to Old 99," remembered the captain.

"...for a minute I was afraid of what I would see....But my heart suddenly gave a big pound, because there was Old 99's [tail], gleaming above the runway."

But then he saw her. "...all that [was] left [was] that tall silver tail. Everything else was still there, only melted and bent and ruined and her back [was] sagging and broken."

There was something else, too, he said. "...I couldn't make out what it was, [but] as I got closer I couldn't deny to myself [that] it was one of my crew. And...beside him another."

Only after walking to the other side of the plane did he discover that his entire crew was there, "eight in a row. There they were, lying so very still...my eight boys of Old 99's crew in a senseless, irregular line towards the woods..."

At the very end of the line, Kurtz found his close friend and co-pilot, "Tex." His clothes had been torn off in the blast that killed all eight men. He was identified by his Texas A & M class ring.

On another part of the field, Lieutenant Edgar Whitcomb, like Kurtz, had climbed out of his trench after the strafing "to have a look at the wreckage. Across the field there did not seem to be a plane that had not been hit," he said.

When he found his own plane, number 87, he was confronted by a scene similar to the one Kurtz had found, but there were four bodies lying on the ground instead of eight. "Four bodies...beside our own ship, all charred beyond recognition." Ironically, one of those lost was a close friend of Whitcomb, who was also nicknamed "Tex."

A survey of the number of flyable aircraft on Clark Field after the enemy raid turned out to be zero. Every plane, whether B-17, B-18, A-27, P-40 or P-26, had been destroyed or knocked out of commission, although one shot-up B-18 was able to get off the ground in the middle of the attack, and fly over to Del Carmen. The anxious pilot, with a radio operator in the co-pilot seat, had never flown a B-18 before.

The most damaging to the air force in the Philippines, of course, was the loss of every B-17 at Clark, amounting to exactly half of the Flying Fortresses in the islands.

The only two B-17s that were flyable at the end of the day were on patrol when the raid came. One of those, flown by Lieutenant John Carpenter, it will be remembered, had attempted a landing right in the middle of the attack. On his second attempt, three and a half hours later, he was successful, bringing the big plane to a bumpy but safe landing on a narrow, hastily repaired strip, precariously surrounded on both sides by bomb craters.

An hour later, the second B-17, flown by Lieutenant Hewitt "Shorty" Wheless, touched down. Earlier that morning, Wheless had been ordered to patrol the 300-mile stretch of ocean between Luzon and Formosa. Unaware of the results of the enemy raid, the shocked look on the faces of the young pilot and his eight crewmen when they landed, no doubt resembled the look of shock and disbelief on the faces of every American man, woman, soldier and sailor, when they heard what had happened across the Pacific that fateful December day.

CHAPTER 5

"LAST NIGHT JAPANESE FORCES
ATTACKED WAKE ISLAND..."

TIME DIFFERENCE: 2 HOURS 30 MINUTES.

6:50 a.m. (PH plus 1 hr. 20 min.): Reveille for the three islands that collectively make up Wake Island (Wake, Peale, and Wilkes), sounded, as usual, at 6:00 a.m. Monday, December 8, was supposed to be a regular work and duty day for the garrison of 449 Marines, 1,200 civilian construction workers, and two dozen Pan American Airways employees on the islands.

Despite the November 27 "war warning," and the obvious threat of war, the Marines and construction workers had been given Sunday off. It was the last day off many of them would ever get for the rest of their lives. The results of this rare day of rest were reflected in the renewed vigor of the entire island that morning. By 6:50, the place was bustling with activity.

As construction workers moved out to their assigned job sites, and Marines squared away their tents before reporting to their various work details, the roar of the engines of the Pan American *Philippine Clipper* were heard, as Captain John Hamilton started the big four-engined flying boat in its takeoff run across Wake's two-mile wide lagoon—destination Guam. Over on the island's small runway, ground crewmen were preparing two new Grumman F4F fighters for their morning patrol, due to take off shortly after 7:00 a.m.

In a small communications trailer at Camp One, one mile from the end of the runway, Sergeant James Rex, a radio operator from the army's six-man signal detachment, sent to the island to guide the anticipated large number of B-17s into Wake and onto the Philippines, decided to tune in to Hickam Field, to see what was going on in Hawaii. It was just after 9:00 a.m. in Hawaii, on Sunday morning. Probably not much happening, he thought.

A few minutes later, Captain Harry Wilson, commander of the small detachment, was frantically called to the trailer.

"Sir," said the excited signalman, "Hickam radio says they're being attacked by Jap planes. Look at this."

Wilson looked at the message Rex had written down. "Hickam Field has been attacked by Jap dive bombers. This is the real thing."

Wilson stared at the message for a moment, then darted from the trailer for Major James Devereaux's tent a few yards away.

Devereaux, Marine commander on Wake, had just finished shaving when Wilson burst in, message in hand. After reading it, he picked up the phone and called Commander Winfield Cunningham, island commander, at his office at Camp Two across the lagoon. There was no answer.

At that moment, Cunningham, who had just left the mess hall for his office, was being flagged down by a man running toward him. He was waving his arms and shouting something that could not be heard over the incessant roar of the surf against the island's surrounding reef.

"As he came nearer," said Cunningham, "I could see his face was flushed and he clutched a piece of paper in his right hand.

"'Commander, Commander!' he yelled...pushing the paper toward me....'[This] just came in.' "

Cunningham looked at it. "AIR RAID ON PEAL HARBOR THIS IS NO DRILL," it said.

Running for the phone in his office, "I realize[d] what had been uppermost in my mind from the moment I read the message," remembered the island commander. "[It was] our planes. I must get word to [Major] Paul Putnam at once, and get our planes in the air."

Meanwhile, back at Camp One, Major Devereaux had called navy communications at Camp Two for verification of the attack on Hawaii.

"Yes sir," Devereaux was told, "it's being decoded now."

On the way to his office, Devereaux yelled into the guard tent to send him the bugler. When he arrived, the Marine commander said, "I ordered [him] to sound 'Call to Arms.' "

When the bugle sounded, nobody believed it at first. "They took it for just another dummy run...laughing [and] skylarking as they went for their rifles."

"This is no drill! Pass the word," Devereaux shouted to them.

As the "word" was passed, Marines began to move. It made no difference if they were fully dressed or not. "They were moving now," said Devereaux. "They were piling into the trucks and the trucks were moving....This is what we'd been waiting for. Now it was here. The chips were down.

"It seemed to me," he remembered, "as though an electric current had passed through the island." Within 45 minutes, every Marine battery and defense position on the island had reported that they were "manned and ready."

On the other side of the island, Commander Cunningham had also been busy. After talking to Major Putnam, it was decided that four instead of two planes should be used to patrol the island, since they were restricted to a maximum range of only 50 miles.

Both lamented the absence of the twelve PBYs that had been there to escort Putnam's squadron in from the carrier *Enterprise* five days earlier. They had a range of over 600 miles.

It was also decided that, since the field was without revetments for the remaining planes, they should be dispersed as far apart as possible. If the Japanese would hold off the attack until after two o'clock, construction crews had promised to have revetments for six planes finished by that afternoon.

In the meantime, because of the narrow landing strip and rough terrain surrounding the field, the remaining eight fighters would be dispersed on a small 100 by 250 yard parking apron, leaving a space of less than forty yards between planes.

Navy Commander Winfield Scott Cunningham, overall commander of Wake Island.

US Navy

"What about the *Clipper*?" someone asked Cunningham.

"I...called Mr. [John] Cook at the Pan American office, and suggested that the big plane be recalled," said Cunningham. Cook agreed.

When the radio message from the island came through, the plane was about eight minutes out from Wake.

"[We were] outbound for Singapore and starting the Wake-Guam sector of the schedule," said pilot John Hamilton, "when we were advised that hostilities had begun, and it was suggested we return to Wake.

"We circled, dumped about 3,000 pounds of gasoline to get to our landing weight of 80,000 pounds, and returned to Wake....We landed about 20 minutes after taking off, [which] was approximately 7:20."

As Hamilton taxied the big *Clipper* up to the Pan Am loading dock on Peale, a big man wearing a construction hat burst into Commander Cunningham's office at Camp Two.

"I'm Dan Teters," he said. "What can I do to help?" Teters, civilian superintendent of construction on Wake, had been on the island for eleven months, but the two men had never met.

"[Word was that] Teters was...determined that no one should get the idea he was subject to military control," said Cunningham. As soon as he got word of the attack, though, he "was [no longer] standing on his dignity."

The major concern of both was what to do with the 1,200 civilian workers. Teters agreed that the 180-or-so men who had previously volunteered for military training, would be given the opportunity to report to the Marines. Some of those were veterans of World War I.

It was also agreed that, for the moment, it was best to leave the rest of the work crews on the job during daylight hours. Since, for the most part, they were already scattered all over Wake and Peale, the normal dispersal provided by their jobs would do for the time being.

As Teters left, Ensign George Henshaw entered with a decoded message from Admiral Bloch at Pearl Harbor. "It ordered me to put into effect the provisions of a document known as WPL-46," said Cunningham. After an unsuccessful search for the elusive war plan, he realized that no copy of WPL-46 had ever been sent to Wake Island.

Following the unsuccessful search, Cunningham jumped onto his pickup truck and headed for the airfield. Minutes before he got there, four Grumman Wildcats, led by Paul Putnam, had taken off on their first wartime patrol of the island.

Over at Camp One, Major Devereaux had just concluded the first wartime briefing of his officers. One of those present, Major Walter Bayler, who had arrived twelve days earlier to help set up a ground to air communications network for Putnam's squadron, remembered what he said at the meeting. It was brief and to the point.

"He told us tersely that Japan had opened hostilities at Pearl Harbor," said Bayler. "Warned us we must expect to be attacked ourselves at any minute, and ordered us to battle stations."

When Devereaux broke the news, remembered Bayler, "for some reason there flashed into [my mind] the picture of the Japanese ambassador in Washington, plump, slant-eyed Nomura, who had been preaching Japan's desire for peace. I thought angrily, 'the big yellow bastard was there just to put over this fast one.' "

Since Major Devereaux had called them to arms at seven o'clock, with the realization that they were at war, Marines around Camp One had been hard at work digging fox holes, filling sandbags, and improving communications. Anticipating the worst, Devereaux decided to move his command post into the brush just east of the runway.

The NCO in charge of the Marines moving the switchboard from his office to the new site, looked at his watch. It was eight o'clock.

"At ease. At Ease, men," he said. "It's oh-eight-hundred." The men stopped in their tracks, and, without further word, turned toward the flagpole. All knew it was "Morning Colors," a tradition carried out every day at eight at every Marine post in the world.

Alvin Waronker, the bugler (known in the Marines as Field Music or Music), was well-known on the island for his sour notes, particularly while blowing "Colors." As Major Devereaux said, "His vain struggles with that call were something of a battalion joke."

"[But] this morning we heard something none of us will ever be able to explain," remembered the Marine commander. "I doubt even Waronker could. He just stood there and sounded off as the flag went up...every note was proud and clear. It made a man's throat tighten to hear it....It was the only time it ever happened."

Every Marine within hearing distance at Camp One "stopped whatever they were doing to straighten up and face in [that] direction," witnessed Major Walter Bayler. "I'm sure there were a lot of moist eyes and tightened throats as Old Glory was broken out at the top of the flagpole." The flag was not lowered again until the Japanese captured the island 16 days later.

A few minutes later, as Commander Cunningham was nearing Camp One, he glanced up at the 52-foot water tower. Two men were silhouetted against the low cumulus clouds that were covering the sky that morning. "[One] had a pair of field glasses to his eyes," he remembered. "Hardly the most modern system for guarding...against [air] attack."

He was right. Gunner Harold Borth, a pair of binoculars, and a Marine with a field telephone, solely represented Wake's early warning system against air and surface attack. There was no radar and no sound detector. There wasn't even an air raid alarm, which couldn't be heard anyway over the continual roar of the surf.

Walter Bayler remembered looking up at the tower too, hoping the two men would "never relax their vigilant pose for a split second."

After a short meeting with Devereaux, Cunningham started back for Camp Two. As he drove the six miles back to his headquarters, he began thinking about the *Clipper*.

"Someone...had mentioned it might be a good idea for [it] to make a long-range reconnaissance flight for us," he said, "going farther than our little fighters [could go]."

Cunningham had no reason to oppose the idea. The pilot was a Naval Air Reserve officer who had served under him back at Oakland. "He knew his job...as a civilian pilot and as a reserve flying officer."

Clipper skipper John Hamilton was, as Cunningham remembered, "enthusiastically in favor of the idea, and Mr. Cook gave us the go-ahead on behalf of the airline."

As the cargo was being unloaded to lighten the big Martin seaplane, Cunningham and Hamilton drove over to the airfield for a conference with Devereaux and Paul Putnam, whose four-plane patrol had just returned to Wake. After a quick refueling, they were in the air again, Putnam turning the patrol over to Captain Hank Elrod.

"We gave Hamilton the approach [to] make, and [the] approximate time he should return so my gunners would be expecting him," said Devereaux. "Commander Cunningham decided that the *Clipper*, escorted by two fighters, would take off after lunch and make a search for a hundred miles around the island."

They also decided to fuel the plane with enough gas for the patrol and for the flight to Midway, which Cunningham had okayed upon its return.

11:58 a.m. (PH plus 6 hrs. 28 min.): As it neared noon, anticipation of the attack that had not yet come, gave way to the normal lunchtime routine. Rations were delivered to Marines at their gun positions in the field. Construction crews close enough to Camp Two poured into their mess hall. Over on Peale, *Clipper* passengers were coming in for lunch in the fancy Pan American Hotel dining room.

In the squadron tent on the edge of the parking apron at the airfield, nine men, including Major Putnam and Walter Bayler, had gathered for lunch. It was 11:58 a.m.

"We were lounging under the tent fly, waiting for food," remembered Bayler, "when we heard, even above the roar of the surf, the sound of many engines. We piled out from beneath the fly and looked southward to see 24 big planes coming straight toward us."

"Those must be our B-17s," someone said.

"B-17s hell! They're Japs."

In his office at Camp One, a mile east of the field, Major Devereaux was on the phone with Lieutenant Wally Lewis, commander of 3-inch anti-aircraft Battery E on the westernmost point of Wake.

"I was on the phone...to Lieutenant Lewis at Peacock Point," said Devereaux, "when he suddenly broke in: Major, there's a squadron of planes coming in from the south. Are they friendly?"

Before he could answer, Devereaux heard someone yell on the other end, "Look! Their wheels are falling off!" and Wilson respond with, "They're dropping bombs!"

"The next instant, I heard the bombs explode," said Devereaux.

Thirty-six enemy planes had come in completely undetected until they reached their bomb-release point. As luck would have it, Putnam's Wildcats, at that moment, were 50 miles out on the northern leg of their patrol.

Again, as luck would have it, the Japanese, making their approach from the opposite side of the island, had dropped down to 2,000 feet to take advantage of a squall line off Wake's southern shoreline. With engines feathered to avoid sound detection until a mile from the island, they had appeared so suddenly that few ever saw them or were aware of the attack until the first bomb fell.

Commander Cunningham, two miles away in his office at Camp Two, had just finished reading the latest message from Pacific Fleet Headquarters, ordering him to "Execute submarine and air warfare on Japan," when he heard the sound of several explosions.

Thinking it was a local accident, as he ran to the door, he was shocked to find out that it was bombs falling. "There had been no warning of the approach of the enemy," he said.

The focal point of the attack was the airfield. With the same surprise they had achieved in Hawaii and the Philippines, in 12 minutes the Japanese would all but insure complete success of their mission.

Walter Bayler, who survived the attack on the airfield, remembered most vividly what happened there.

After it sunk in that the approaching planes were Japanese, most of those who were with him in the tent ran for a patch of woods some 200 feet away, despite the fact that it was "toward the oncoming planes."

"I saw the first V directly over me as I got to the woods," he remembered. "I threw myself flat on the ground at the base of a small tree...

"Then the Japs were upon us. An appalling crash made the ground tremble, as a salvo of bombs hurtled down on the edges of the runway and area adjacent to it. My body was shaken by the explosions as if I were astride a bucking earthquake.

"For me during those first few minutes, the whole world was nothing but one great aerial maelstrom of sound and fury and stunning confusion."

As the enemy attack ended, and relative peace descended on the island, Bayler looked at his watch. It was ten minutes after twelve. The attack had lasted only 12 minutes, "a 12-minute foretaste of hell," he said.

The attack on Camp Two had also been hell. Commander Cunningham, who realized the explosions he had heard from across the lagoon were bombs falling on the airfield, dove under a wooden desk when "machine gun bullets began splattering through the roof of the building."

When the raid passed, his first thought was to get to the airfield. "I ran out of the office," he said, "past the twisted silence of dead men and the screams of wounded on the ground at Camp 2..."

Over 50 construction workers, who had gathered for lunch at the camp mess hall, had been killed or wounded. The exact number was never determined, however, because immediately after the bombing, several gathered up what food and supplies they could carry, and scattered into the fields of dense brush and trees that dominated most of the undeveloped part of the island. They would not be seen again until after the surrender.

Over on adjacent Peale Island, John Hamilton driving from his office.to the Pan Am hotel for lunch, found his way blocked by several five-foot drainage pipes left in the road by construction workers.

"I left the car to walk," he said. "At that moment they came over, nine planes in closed pyramid formation, flying at about 1,500 feet. I ducked into one of the drainage pipes.

"They were over the island for about 5 minutes. The bombs fired the hotel, destroyed the Pan American buildings and the dock, but did not hit the *Clipper*. There were 16 bullet holes in the plane, however, but [none] struck a vital spot."

Although none of the passengers were hit, ten Pan Am employees, all Chamorros from Guam, had been killed, and several were wounded. Later, after inspecting the damage on Peale, Devereaux said that the island "looked like a junkyard."

The scene at the airfield that greeted Major Bayler as he limped out of the woods, and Commander Cunningham as he pulled up in his pickup truck, was staggering. If crippling Wake's air defense was the Japanese's objective, then it had been accomplished.

"I was not prepared for the desolation and destruction that awaited me," said Cunningham. "The whole area was a shambles. Dead airplanes lay about the parking area....Drums of gasoline burning everywhere."

Bayler was more descriptive. "Everywhere things were burning. [I could feel] the searing heat from the 25,000-gallon gasoline tank and some 600 [50-gallon] drums [that] still blazed fiercely. Seven of the eight precious planes...were burning. Tents were burning; a few that escaped the incendiaries had been riddled by shrapnel and bullets."

And then there was the human toll. "In every direction that I looked," remembered Bayler, "I saw our dead. There were twenty-three of them. I saw our wounded; eleven of them, their bodies torn, burned, and shot through with shrapnel and riddled by machine gun bullets.

"I recognized the bodies of two officers who had been with me in the tent, waiting for lunch. Like me, they had headed for [the woods, but] had been just far enough behind to catch the full fury of the exploding bombs."

When the attack came, the field was buzzing with activity. Mechanics were working on the four planes that were due to relieve the patrol in the air. The two that were to escort the *Clipper* were being warmed up. Lieutenants George Graves and Bob Conderman, who were to pilot the escorting Wildcats, were being briefed in the ready tent. Most of the relief pilots were there too.

In the brief moment between the bombs from the first and second waves of enemy bombers, Graves and Conderman and two other pilots made a dash for their planes. They didn't make it, but Graves came the closest.

Despite 16 bullet holes in its hull, the *Hawaii Clipper*, seen here in dock at Wake Island, was able to make it safely from Wake to Hawaii on December 8.

Pan American Airways

According to eyewitnesses, he was in the cockpit when his plane took a direct hit from a 100-pound fragmentation bomb. The explosion, which killed him instantly, catapulted his lifeless body onto the ground under the burning right wing of the plane.

"A minute-or-so later," remembered one man, "the [100-pound] bomb hanging on the wing directly over him, was exploded by the heat of the burning fabric, further mutilating his already dead body."

Bob Conderman nearly reached his plane when he got hit. His legs had been blasted out from under him. Two Marines who saw him fall, ran to help.

"Let me go," he insisted, as they started to move him. "Take care of them," he said, gesturing back toward the other two pilots that had rushed out of the tent with him.

One of them didn't need any help. It was Lieutenant Frank Holden. Walter Bayler, who later identified his body, said, "We found Frank stretched on his back on the runway...legs crossed, one arm thrown carelessly across his chest...looking like a man who had just lain down and gone to sleep."

The fourth pilot, Lieutenant Harry Webb, like Conderman, had his legs blown out from under him. Bayler and another Marine moved both him and Conderman off the field.

Ripping a burlap curtain from a nearby latrine to make a crude litter, "we went for the two wounded officers and carried them, one after the other [off the runway]," said Bayler. "Both had been struck, head to foot, with shrapnel."

Webb was conscious. "As we put him on the ground," remembered Bayler, "he raised his left leg slightly and said, 'Look at that damned foot!' " Part of the boot had been ripped away, "and ripped away with it were the smaller toes of the foot."

When they got Conderman, they noticed that he had suffered compound fractures of both legs above the knee.

"He was conscious, too," said Bayler, "and spoke to me quite naturally....'Walt,' he said, 'be careful of the legs.' "

"That same night, calm, collected, and courageous to the end, he died..."

Another wounded man Bayler helped carry off the field was Sergeant Andrew Paszkiewicz. Shrapnel from one of the first bombs had shattered the tough sergeant's leg, and wounded him in both arms. Paszkiewicz, leaving a trail of blood behind him, painfully crawled off the field, where, during the brief lull between the first and second waves of enemy bombers, he found a piece of wood. Fashioning a makeshift crutch, he struggled to his feet, but instead of seeking cover as bombs from the second wave were falling, he headed back toward the field.

Lieutenant David Kliewer, a Marine pilot, witnessed him hobbling and stumbling about on his crude crutch, from wounded man to wounded man, giving first aid and encouraging them to hang on.

As men began searching through the rubble of what had been the headquarters area of Marine fighter squadron VMF 211, they found everything had been destroyed.

The squadron tent, where Bayler and his fellow officers were waiting for lunch, had taken a direct hit. Two clerks in the rear of the tent when the bombs began to fall, were killed. "...nobody had more than about 5 seconds in which to seek shelter," calculated Bayler.

Three more men had been killed in a direct hit on the ordnance tent, just a few yards from the squadron tent. "They could never have known what hit them," said Bayler, who found their remains.

Commander Cunningham, who reached the field about ten minutes after the raid, saw Paul Putnam walking amongst what, moments before, had been eight brand new Grumman F4F fighters. Looking down the row of destroyed and burning planes, it appeared that there was nothing left of any of them. Sixty percent of VMF 211's personnel and two-thirds of its planes had been knocked out in 12 minutes.

"[As he] strode toward me through broken bodies and bits of what had once been men," said Cunningham, "his face was white with incredulity and rage. He was bleeding, and he waved an old Springfield rifle in his hand."

A man, protecting himself from bombers with a rifle, reflected the island commander later, truly represented "the futility of the situation."

A few minutes later, as pilots of the four planes who had been on patrol caught sight of the island, they were at first puzzled by the smoke and fires they saw rising from the airfield. There was also smoke above Camp Two and the Pan American area on Peale. As they got closer, they were shocked at what they saw. Bomb craters, burning and destroyed planes, and squadron tents and buildings either gone or smashed beyond recognition.

By some miracle, the runway itself had not been touched. Three of the planes landed safely. The fourth fighter, piloted by patrol leader Hank Elrod, unavoidably ran into a pile of bomb debris on the runway, resulting in a bent propeller and badly jarred engine. VMF 211 was momentarily down to only three flyables.

Meanwhile, Major Devereaux, who was responsible for both antiaircraft as well as beach defense, had checked on the results and well-being of his batteries after the attack. All was well with the latter, but return fire results from the 3-inch anti-aircraft batteries on Peacock, Toki and Kuku Points, were negative. "They came in too low and too fast," said one battery commander. Although the .50 calibers had put up plenty of fire at the low-flying enemy planes, no significant results were observed.

1:15 p.m. (PH plus 7 hrs. 45 min.): Commander Cunningham had just returned to his damaged office at Camp Two, when *Clipper* captain John Hamilton came to see him.

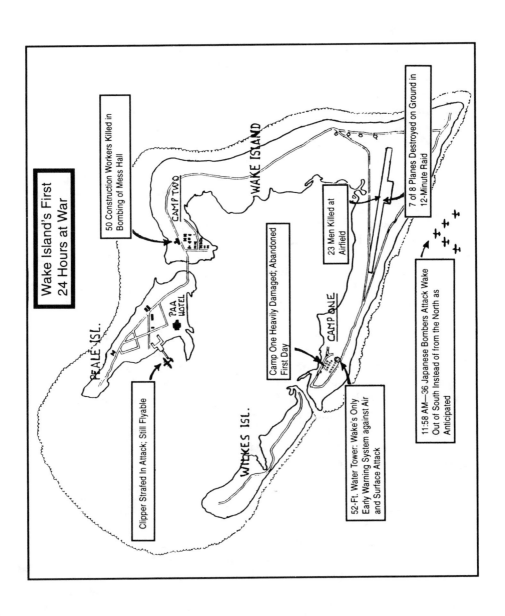

Wake Island's First
24 Hours at War

PEALE ISL.

PAA HOTEL

WILKES ISL.

CAMP TWO

WAKE ISLAND

CAMP ONE

50 Construction Workers Killed in Bombing of Mess Hall

Clipper Strafed In Attack; Still Flyable

Camp One Heavily Damaged; Abandoned First Day

23 Men Killed at Airfield

7 of 8 Planes Destroyed on Ground in 12-Minute Raid

11:58 AM—36 Japanese Bombers Attack Wake Out of South Instead of from the North as Anticipated

52-Ft. Water Tower: Wake's Only Early Warning System against Air and Surface Attack

Hamilton told him that Mr. Cook had directed him to load his passengers and all the Pan American personnel, and take off for Midway and Hawaii.

"I approved," said Cunningham. "Wake was no place for any civilians who could be evacuated." Takeoff time was scheduled for one o'clock.

The mail and cargo, which had already been removed in anticipation of the now-cancelled *Clipper* patrol, made it possible to take everyone, except the surviving Chamorros. Although Pan Am employees, they were refused passage. "...it seemed to me an [inappropriate] time to draw the color line," said Cunningham, when he learned of the decision. No doubt the two Chamorros who were caught trying to stow away on the big plane, also agreed with the island commander.

It was exactly one o'clock when the big *Clipper* pulled away from the damaged loading dock at Peale, and began taxiing toward its takeoff point in the lagoon.

The passenger list, including eleven crewmen, had thirty-nine names on it, but only thirty-seven had been checked off. Two were missing. One was Herman Havenor, of the Budget Bureau, sent there to keep an eye on construction costs. Apparently he had failed to see the 1:00 p.m. departure notice. "...a rather drastic lesson in the wisdom of punctuality," reflected Devereaux later.

The other man, a Pan Am employee named August Ramquist, who had volunteered to drive wounded men from the airfield to the hospital at Camp Two, was somewhere on the road when the plane pulled away.

As Captain Hamilton taxied the big Martin flying boat toward the western end of Peale, where he could take advantage of the longest run across the lagoon, he could tell by its sluggishness in the water that the plane was near its maximum weight for takeoff. He knew it would be close.

He was right. It was close. Two times Hamilton tried, but ran out of room both times. On the third try, he taxied the plane between the marker buoys at the western end of the island, extending the 2,000-yard takeoff distance by another 200 yards.

The combination of the additional distance and Wake's flat, near sea-level terrain near Camp One, over which the giant *Clipper* skimmed at near tree-top level, proved to be just enough.

Many of the Marines who had cheered as the plane passed over the camp, continued to watch until it was out of sight, each probably wondering if the only chance of escape was disappearing over the horizon.

At Wake's only hospital at Camp Two, trucks and the island's only ambulance had been bringing in wounded steadily since the attack ended. Known as the Contractor's Hospital, it was a T-shaped building, with two wards, an operating room, and a clinic. It was staffed by a civilian, Doctor Lawton Shank, who had been joined by navy doctor Gus Kahn and nine medics, who had operated the dispensary at Camp One before the bombing.

Before the attack, the hospital had less than a dozen patients, including an enlisted sailor off the submarine *Triton*, who had been put ashore with appendicitis a week earlier. By mid-afternoon, the tiny facility was filled to capacity.

No one knew what to do with the dead. There wasn't enough time or manpower to bury them. Someone suggested using the camp's giant cold storage boxes, located in one of the contractor's storehouses. By ten o'clock that night, more than 35 bodies had been placed in the temporary morgue. The last three to be brought in arrived in the ambulance. They were two sailors and a civilian, whose bodies were found late that afternoon a half a mile west of Camp One, near the Wilkes Channel end of the island.

Earlier when Captain Hank Elrod inadvertently taxied his plane into a pile of debris on the runway at the airfield, it was mentioned that that incident "momentarily" left Wake with only three flyables.

It was true. Major Bayler said that "our mechanics got busy in a hurry, [taking] a propeller from a strafed plane and fixing it in place..."

Fortunately, two of the wrecked planes could be cannibalized for parts. Unfortunately, however, the squadron had lost every bit of its maintenance equipment, and had been left without a single qualified mechanic.

Of the twelve Wildcat pilots who had ferried their planes in off the carrier *Enterprise* on December 4, only seven were left. Because of the circumstances, it was decided that if air patrols were to continue, the responsibility of keeping planes in the air had to be accepted by the men who were flying them. It was a unique situation, pilots taking over ground crew responsibilities.

The important job of making sure the planes were mechanically sound and combat ready, went to Lieutenant John Kinney and Technical Sergeant William Hamilton, the only enlisted pilot in the squadron, and Navy Machinist Mate J.J. Hesson.

Of the efforts of the three men, Major Putnam would later write, "Ever since the first raid, they traded parts...back and forth until not one plane could be identified. They swapped engines, junked, stripped and rebuilt them....It's solely due to their efforts that the squadron [remained in operation]."

Lieutenant David Kliewer took over squadron communications, while Captain Herbert Frueler remained as ordnance officer. It was a Frueler-designed rack that had made it possible to attack 100-pound bombs under the wings of the F4Fs.

Captain's Elrod and Frank Tharin took over supervision of the pick-and-shovel work. They dug fox holes, shelters, and defensive positions around the squadron area. By dawn of the next morning, the six bomb-proof revetments promised by the construction company were also finished—18 hours too late.

Walking over the field later that afternoon, Major Putnam and Bayler were dismayed by the accuracy displayed by the Japanese. They thought it "unreasonable" that they had destroyed seven of the eight planes, "in view of the care with which [they] had been dispersed."

They paced off the distance between bomb craters, finding them "identical—roughly 50 feet." They observed that, although areas adjacent to the runway "had been pounded, the runway itself had not received a single hit."

"[Their] marksmanship [was] so close to being one-hundred percent perfect," said Bayler, "it was all of keeping with human fallibility."

The undamaged runway worried them the most. If it had been omitted on purpose, it was possible the Japanese were planning to use it to fly in invasion troops. To eliminate this possibility, the entire strip on both sides was mined with dynamite charges placed at 150-foot intervals, and connected to generators located near machine gun positions at each end of the runway.

7:00 p.m. (PH plus 14 hrs. 30 min.): The return of the evening air patrol at sunset announced the end of Wake's first day at war.

At Commander Cunningham's office at Camp Two, Ensign John Lauff reported that submarines *Triton* and *Trambor,* which had been on a simulated war patrol off the atoll for several days, had radioed that they were surfacing to recharge their batteries.

Staying submerged during the day, they were puzzled at the scattered fires they saw when they surfaced. "...they didn't even know the war had begun," remembered Cunningham. "They had submerged for their day's patrolling and thus lost radio contact."

Cunningham sent them a message telling them that Pearl Harbor had been attacked, and about what happened at Wake. He also forwarded the 14th Naval District communique that had come in 8 hours earlier, ordering them to "Execute unrestricted submarine warfare...against Japan."

Over at the airfield, at the sound of bulldozers working on the six blast-proof revetments that it would take all night to complete, Marines had fallen in for muster.

After it was over, Bayler said, "It was dark by the time the mournful business was ended. The roll call told us definitely, for the first time, the full extent of our casualties."

By then, any idea he had of going over to Camp One for the night was forgotten. "Scores of tents were unusable," he said, "including mine." Although no one had been killed there, both mess halls had been wiped out, as well as the Officers Club and the shower, "which had been such a comfort [to me, but] was now a memory." The refrigerator at the Officers Club that was usually filled with ice cold beer, would also be missed.

An almost deserted Camp One, in fact, indicated that Bayler and most of those Marines not on duty, had decided, as he had, to "spend the night in the scrub."

So had Major Devereaux. After his switchboard was hooked up, "I moved my CP into the brush," he said. "It was dark and unpleasant, but we were concealed there. Nobody got any sleep. Marines and civilian volunteers worked on the defenses all night."

Not everyone had left the camp, however. On the water-observation tower, which, by some miracle, had remained unscathed in the bombing, the silhouette of two men scanning the fading horizon could still be seen long after the sun had gone down. Although the Japanese raiders had avoided their detection that morning, as one man remembered, it was comforting knowing they were there anyway, "like sentinels against the setting sun."

Around ten o'clock, a cold drizzle began to fall over the island. It was a depressing and almost fitting epilogue to Wake's disastrous first day at war.

CHAPTER 6

"THIS MORNING THE JAPANESE
ATTACKED MIDWAY ISLAND..."

TIME DIFFERENCE: 1 HOUR 30 MINUTES.

6:00 a.m. (PH minus 30 min.): As dawn was breaking over Sand Island, the westernmost of the two islands that make up the Midway atoll, the sounds of PBY patrol planes taking off across the quiet lagoon was heard over the incessant roar of the surf crashing into the surrounding barrier reef.

Seven PBYs had taxied into takeoff position. The first two planes, carrying the markings of the Dutch Navy, headed west for Wake Island, the next leg of their island-hopping flight to the Netherlands East Indies.

The remaining five planes of Midway's patrol squadron, VP-21, then took off on what had become routine "dawn patrol" search missions of the waters around the two islands.

Since alerted by the Navy Department's November 27 "war warning," Sundays on the island had become just like any other day.

On Sand's seaplane ramp, two more PBYs were being given their final check-up before leaving for a noon rendezvous with planes of the aircraft carrier *Lexington*.

At that moment, 420 miles southeast of Midway, the pilots and crews of 18 Navy SB2U Vindicators on the *Lexington* were themselves preparing for a noon launch and meeting with the two PBYs, who were assigned to guide them back to the air strip on Midway's Eastern island. Their assignment, once there, was to act as escorts for the anticipated large number of B-17s on their way to the Philippines.

6:35 a.m. (PH plus 5 min.): At 6:35, the teletype machine at the Navy Communication Center on Sand Island clattered out an uncoded message:

From: CINCPAC   7 DEC 41
                              -URGENT
AIR RAID ON PEARL HARBOR   THIS IS NO DRILL

A few minutes later, a second message came in from the 14th Naval District Commander, Admiral Claude Bloch, confirming the report, and ordering the implementation of WPL-46—the basic war plan to be put into effect in the event of war with Japan.

Commander Cyril Simard, island commander on Midway, quickly recalled the Dutch PBYs, then notified Marine Lieutenant Colonel Harold Shannon, who immediately ordered his 6th Defense Battalion to general quarters.

Not untypical of reactions all over the Pacific that day, at first no one believed the Japanese foolish enough to attack Pearl Harbor. Even after Colonel Shannon informed those in the officers mess to "have their men ready to man battle stations within the hour."

"My feelings at the time," remembered Captain Jean Buckner, commander of 3-inch anti-aircraft Battery D on Sand Island, "was that this was a realistic war game...[and] that Colonel Shannon also doubted that the warning was a report of a real attack."

Nevertheless, "we notified our men to be ready to march to the batteries...and hurriedly finished our breakfast," said the skeptical gun commander.

The 6th Defense Battalion had been there since September, and consisted of 34 officers and 750 men. Along with beach defense responsibility, they manned three 5-inch coastal defense batteries, and the island's two 3-inch anti-aircraft batteries. Although there was an excellent runway on Eastern, there were no combat planes on the islands.

When the two PBYs returned a half an hour later, Simard officially commandeered them, then reassigned search areas for all seven planes.

Figuring that an attack, if it came, would likely come out of the southwest, each plane was assigned to patrol an ark of roughly ten degrees by 400 miles in that direction.

Still anticipating having to escort planes in from the *Lexington*, the two PBYs assigned to that task were held on the ground, but not for long.

An hour or so after the announcement of the attack on Pearl Harbor reached the *Lexington*, a dispatch was received from Admiral Kimmel, "INTERCEPT AND DESTROY ENEMY BELIEVED RETREATING ON A COURSE BETWEEN PEARL AND JALUIT. INTERCEPT AND DESTROY." With that message, *Lexington* notified Midway of the change in plans, then turned south in pursuit of the elusive enemy, which, at that moment, was located 200 miles in the opposite direction from where they were heading.

Meanwhile, preparations for a defense against air or surface attack on the two islands were in full swing. Fox holes and shelters were dug or improved; gun positions were hurriedly camouflaged; beach and anti-aircraft defenses were manned; ammunition was issued; and vital communication networks were established and checked.

By five o'clock, all seven PBYs had returned to their base on Sand Island, each crew reporting that they had seen no sign of enemy ships or planes.

Darkness brought no relief, however. At 6:42 p.m., an hour before the sun went down, a Marine lookout from high atop the communications tower on Sand, reported seeing a flashing light southwest of the island.

Pre-war aerial photo of Midway's Sand and Eastern, *foreground*, Islands.

US Navy

Unknown to the sailors and Marines on Midway, the light the young Marine had seen came from one of three enemy ships, of what the Japanese called the Midway Neutralization Force. This small naval unit, composed of destroyers *Ushio* and *Sazamani*, and the tanker *Shiriya*, had left Japan on November 28. Its objective was to bombard and neutralize the air and seaplane bases on Sand and Eastern Islands, thus insuring the safe withdrawal of the Pearl Harbor attack force to Japanese home waters.

9:30 p.m. (PH plus 15 hrs.): With both islands now fully alerted, just before 9:30 p.m., radar on Sand Island picked up what appeared to be a surface target from the same direction as the flashing light. At the same time, two observers, scanning the horizon with powerful night glasses, verified the radar report, prompting Lieutenant Alfred Booth, searchlight battery commander, to request permission to illuminate the target. His request was turned down, however, for fear of prematurely giving away Marine positions.

Booth's request was also denied because, as Marine commander, Colonel Harold Shannon said, the islands were already "visible for miles..."

"There was a bright moon," remembered Shannon, "[and] all the new construction glistened in the moonlight. The reflection of the moon on the white buildings...and on the black-and-white squares of the water tower must have been visible for miles at sea. The sand looked like snow, and the beaches on the reef clearly outlined the island. It was an ideal night for such an attack."

Five minutes later, at exactly 9:35, his fears were realized, as lookouts on the communication tower spotted orange flashes in the distance. "They've opened fire!" a Marine excitedly yelled down.

He was right, but the first salvo landed in the lagoon, 100 yards short of the beach. The next one exploded on the beach in front of Marine positions.

The third salvo from the closing enemy ships, however, struck home. One landed near Battery A's 5-inch gun position, and severed the all-important communication lines running to its fire control station. Unable to get necessary target information, one of the most prominent coastal batteries on Sand Island was forced to remain silent during the entire attack.

Another shell from the salvo, which bracketed the island's concrete power plant and Battery C command post, whistled through the air-vent and exploded inside the bunker. Although no one was directly killed in the blast, battery commander, Lieutenant George Cannon, was fatally wounded. The concussion from the explosion knocked him across the room, bredking both legs and crushing his pelvis in the process. Shrapnel wounds from the blast left him bleeding severely. Another man in the room, battery switchboard operator Harold Hazelwood, was also blasted from his chair, suffering a compound fracture of the left leg.

As severely wounded as both men were, neither would leave their posts until other wounded men were evacuated, and Hazelwood had the switchboard back in operation. With communication re-established with battery guns, both allowed themselves to be carried out. Although Hazelwood would live to receive the Navy Cross for his action in the face of the enemy, Lieutenant Cannon would never know that he was the first World War II

Marine Lieutenant George Cannon, posthumously awarded the Medal of Honor for his heroic refusal to abandon his post despite fatal wounds received during the Japanese shelling of Midway on December 7.

US Navy

Marine to receive the Congressional Medal of Honor, for, as it says on his citation, "refus[ing] to be evacuated...until after his men, who had been wounded by the same shell, were evacuated, and [continuing to] direct the reorganization of his command post until forcibly removed." Lieutenant George Cannon died from loss of blood on the way to the aid station.

Although Battery A's guns were unable to fire, Captain Jean Buckner, from his Battery D parapet, at first mistook the enemy's shell bursts as Battery A's 5-inch guns firing at the reported enemy ships.

"I assumed that the flashes...were caused by Battery A's guns," said Buckner, "and those we observed at a distance were caused by [its] projectiles striking the water and exploding. In view of the fact that no real target was visible, I was quite amused by the antics of Battery A."

A minute or so later, while still trying to discover what Battery A was firing at, several guns flashed relatively close to the island "at great enough range not to be mistaken for Battery A," said the suddenly sobered Buckner. "My illusions...were further shattered when something that sounded like a freight train passed immediately over our heads, followed by explosions in the vicinity of the powerhouse. Needless to say, the tops of parapets were deserted without order."

With no searchlights or counterbattery fire from the Marines, the Japanese opened fire again, this time hitting the Pan American radio installation on Sand, the island laundry, and navy repair shops.

Shells from the same attack also hit the seaplane base hangar. Corporal Dale Peters, in the base tower on top of the hangar itself, was blown through the open tower window and on to the roof by the concussion.

Staggered and shocked but unhurt, as Peters crawled to his feet, he realized that the hangar was burning. Remembering that there were 100-pound bombs stored in the hangar, the young Marine climbed back in the tower so he could get down off the roof and help.

In the smoke and confusion, however, he slipped, falling through the hatch, 14 feet onto the hangar floor, and barely missing a group of sailors working below. Again shaken and in shock, but still unhurt, Peters was able to help remove the bombs from the hangar before it burned. For his doggedness, he too received the Navy Cross.

Finally, at 9:53, 12 minutes after the order to open fire was given, the only searchlight left functioning on the southern tip of the island came on. Able to illuminate a target up to eight miles at sea, the lead Japanese destroyer, caught broadside to the island at about a mile and a half, was suddenly transfixed by the bright light.

"[The] searchlight...illuminated the ship steering at high speed at a range of about 3,000 yards," said Buckner. "Through binoculars a large Japanese flag was plainly visible flying from the foremast." At that point, Buckner ordered all four of his 3-inch anti-aircraft guns, as ill-prepared to fire at surface targets as they were, to commence firing.

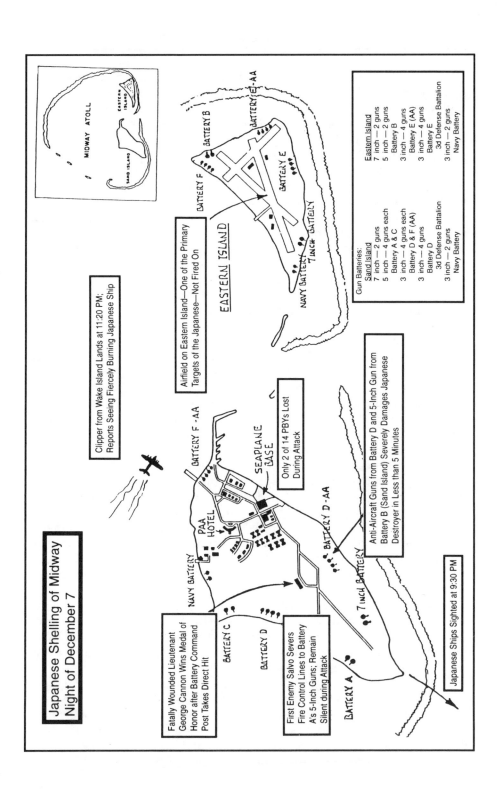

Japanese Shelling of Midway
Night of December 7

Clipper from Wake Island Lands at 11:20 PM; Reports Seeing Fiercely Burning Japanese Ship

Airfield on Eastern Island—One of the Primary Targets of the Japanese—Not Fired On

Only 2 of 14 PBYs Lost During Attack

Anti-Aircraft Guns from Battery D and 5-Inch Gun from Battery B (Sand Island) Severely Damages Japanese Destroyer in Less than 5 Minutes

Fatally Wounded Lieutenant George Cannon Wins Medal of Honor after Battery Command Post Takes Direct Hit

First Enemy Salvo Severs Fire Control Lines to Battery A's 5-Inch Guns; Remain Silent during Attack

Japanese Ships Sighted at 9:30 PM

EASTERN ISLAND

BATTERY E-AA

BATTERY B

BATTERY F

BATTERY E

NAVY BATTERY   7 INCH BATTERY

MIDWAY ATOLL

EASTERN ISLAND

SAND ISLAND

BATTERY F-AA

SEAPLANE BASE

PAA HOTEL

NAVY BATTERY

BATTERY C

BATTERY D

BATTERY D-AA

7 INCH BATTERY

BATTERY A

Gun Batteries:
Sand Island
  7 inch — 2 guns
  5 inch — 4 guns each
    Battery A & C
  3 inch — 4 guns each
    Battery D & F (AA)
  3 inch — 4 guns
    Battery D
      3d Defense Battalion
  3 inch — 2 guns
    Navy Battery

Eastern Island
  7 inch — 2 guns
  5 inch — 2 guns
    Battery B
  3 inch — 4 guns
    Battery E (AA)
  3 inch — 4 guns
    Battery E
      3d Defense Battalion
  3 inch — 2 guns
    Navy Battery

"With the range being only about 3,000 yards," said the battery commander, "the angle of elevation was very small. Gunnery Sergeant M.C. Pulliman...realizing the gun angle would be low, passed the word to commence firing, 'but' he said, 'check your line of fire and be sure you don't hit the battery in front of you.' "

For Gun 2, the angle was so low that the gun captain found that it was pointing directly at Colonel Buckner's bunker.

"He informed my gunnery sergeant of this fact over the phone," said a relieved Buckner, "and wisely held fire during the entire action." The gun captain of Gun 1 also held fire for fear of "delivering fire dangerously close to the heads of the men at Gun 3."

The captains of both Guns 3 and 4, because of the dangerously low angle of elevation, actually held the breeches of their guns open in order to sight through their bores, to make sure their projectiles would clear the dunes between them and the target.

Gun 3 fired six rounds and Gun 4, seven, before a near miss knocked out the searchlight.

In his action report, Colonel Buckner wrote:

"Immediately after the battery commenced fire, the ship began to make a black, heavy smoke from its stack. The results of Battery D fire appeared to me to be approximately three hits in the superstructure....I particularly watched for short splashes, [but since] I observed [none], it can be assumed that the shells passed either over the ship, hit the superstructure or passed directly into the hull before exploding, in which case the flash would not have been visible from the battery."

A few seconds after the searchlight on Sand Island was knocked out, a searchlight on Eastern Island began probing for the target. For Buckner's battery on Sand, however, it provided a few moments of apprehension.

"Immediately after the searchlight on Sand had gone out," wrote Buckner, "a searchlight on Eastern Island struck arc and proceeded to direct its beam directly onto my Battery D. This made us feel as if we were in a goldfish bowl before the eyes of those aboard the Japanese ship. We were all very thankful when the beam was trained out to sea in search of the enemy."

Moments after the searchlight picked up the withdrawing enemy ships, Marines on Sand Island heard guns firing from behind them toward the Japanese. The volleys were coming from Lieutenant Rod Handley's 5-inch battery on Eastern Island. None of the nine rounds fired by his battery were seen to hit the target, however.

As suddenly as it started, it was over. Although it only lasted a little over five minutes, it's possible, although never confirmed, that the Marines made a good account of themselves. Spotters supported Buckner's claim that three of Battery D's 3-inchers had hit one of the ships. The fact that the Japanese broke off the attack immediately after the second searchlight came on, indicated to some that "the Japs had had enough."

Possibly unknown to the island commander on Sand, two U.S. submarines, *Trout* and *Argonaut,* were on patrol several miles off Midway when the Japanese attacked that night. Although both were aware of what was going on, *Trout* was too far east to get in on the action. That left it up to *Argonaut,* who was in position to take on the two withdrawing enemy destroyers.

The sub's captain, Stephen Barchet, however, believed the bombardment was part of and preliminary to an invasion of the islands. If that was so, he thought, chances were the troop ships would be escorted by half a dozen cruisers and destroyers. Exercising caution as a better part of valor, Barchet took *Argonaut* down to 125 feet, where, sadly, the enemy "invasion force" was allowed to withdraw without challenge.

11:20 p.m. (PH plus 16 hrs. 50 min.): By eleven o'clock that night, damage to the islands had pretty well been assessed. One of the primary targets of the Japanese—the airfield on Eastern Island—had not been touched. On Sand, aside from the still-burning seaplane hangar, all other fires were out. Two PBYs had been lost, one in the hangar, and the other from shellfire. Twelve others were untouched. Four men had been killed in the attack, two Marines and two sailors. Nineteen had been wounded.

Also by eleven o'clock, technicians had the radio in Pan American's communication center back in working order, in time to receive a message from the *Philippine Clipper,* inward bound from Wake Island, requesting landing instructions.

About the same time, radar reported aircraft approaching from roughly the same southwesterly direction as the Japanese ships. Marines were called to battle stations, but were quickly told that the plane was friendly.

Because of the bright moonlit night, *Clipper* captain John Hamilton, 34-year-old veteran of 16 round trips to Hong Kong and Singapore, agreed to the navy's request for a lights out landing, that he made without a hitch at 11:20.

Marine and naval officers, anxious to hear about what happened at Wake Island, were also told about the two warships the *Clipper* had flown over some 40 miles out from Midway. They were sailing in a southwesterly direction. Smiles came across the faces of those listening, when Hamilton told them one of the ships was burning fiercely.

It is interesting to note that just five minutes of intense fire from Marine guns almost led to a second attack on the islands. As some correctly surmised, the Japanese ships retired after the brief fire fight, reporting that they had failed to achieve their objective of neutralizing the Midway air bases. Unknown to the sailors and Marines on Midway, the original Japanese plan called for a second attack on the islands by planes from retreating Pearl Harbor attack force carriers if this occurred. Fortunately, that was thought too risky, and was cancelled.

CHAPTER 7

"AMERICAN SHIPS HAVE BEEN REPORTED TORPEDOED ON THE HIGH SEAS..." SINKING OF THE *CYNTHIA OLSEN*

TIME DIFFERENCE: ZERO HOURS ZERO MINUTES.

12:00 a.m. (PH minus 5 hrs.): Saturday night, December 6, was the third night out for the tiny, 2,100-ton lumber schooner *Cynthia Olsen*. She had left the mainland on the fourth for Honolulu with a load of lumber for the army.

With a thousand miles to go, the clock on the ship, which had been advanced to correspond with the current time zone, read midnight.

Unknown to the *Olsen*, the clock on another ship a few hundred yards away, showed the time to be eight o'clock in the evening. The ship was Japanese submarine *I-26*. The clock was set to Tokyo time, where, one day ahead, it was already Sunday, December 7, 1941.

I-26 was the newest sub in the Imperial Navy, launched on November 6, one month to the day, from Kure Naval Yard in Japan. It was one of nine subs from what was called the Special Submarine Attack Unit. Their specific job was to attack U.S. merchant shipping lanes once the war started.

While running on the surface, *I-26* spotted the *Olsen*'s navigational lights around 11:30, and by twelve o'clock, had pulled up even with the ship, where it was tentatively identified as an American merchantman.

The sub's commander, Minoru Yokata, had been given strict orders not to launch an attack until after 3:00 a.m., Tokyo time, on December 8, the scheduled time for the attack on Pearl Harbor. Outside of Malaya, Pearl Harbor was the triggering event for Japanese attacks throughout the rest of the Pacific that day. It was feared that an act of aggression occurring before that time, might put the Americans on the alert, and cost the Japanese the element of surprise at Pearl.

5:00 a.m. (PH plus 0 hrs. 0 min.): It was barely daylight when Yokata surfaced *I-26* two and a half miles off *Cynthia Olsen*'s starboard bow. On board the freighter, the few crewmen that were up at that time were enjoying their first cup of coffee, when someone yelled "Submarine!" As they dashed to the rail to get a look at the sub, a 5.5 inch shell from *I-26's* deck gun whistled across *Olsen's* bow.

Several things must have crossed the captain's mind at that moment as to what the shot meant. It was obviously a warning shot, but the U.S. was not at war with anybody. For whatever the reason, his first thought must have been that it was a mistake, prompting him to quickly raise the flag in hopes that by identifying the ship as American, the error would be realized before it went any further.

A few minutes later, however, as *I-26* continued to move in, the enemy sub picked up an SSS, the international signal for "being attacked by submarine,"from the *Cynthia Olsen*.

With still nothing to show that the attack had been in error, the order to abandon ship was given. Captain Yokata, seeing two lifeboats being lowered, held fire until the crew had pulled safely away from the ship before beginning the attack. It was exactly 3:30 a.m., Tokyo time.

With only ten out of a capacity of seventeen torpedoes on board, and restricted to an Imperial Navy regulation allowing only one torpedo per merchant ship, Yokata decided to sink the little wooden ship with his 5-inch deck gun.

Holding the attack until the lifeboats were at a safe distance, twenty shots were fired at near point blank range before *I-26*, fearing the SSS signal would bring American planes, submerged without recording the results.

Chief Gunner Saburo Hayashi remembered that when no planes showed up, *I-26* surfaced again. Although they found the *Olsen* on fire, it was still afloat, prompting them to launch a torpedo at the floundering freighter.

"One torpedo was fired...from 400 meters," said Hayashi. "...our first torpedo of the Pacific War. We were dismayed because [it] went wild, turned in mid-course, [and] missed the target by as hair's breadth."

Again *I-26* submerged, resurfacing again later only to find the stubborn little ship, although listing heavily to starboard, still somehow afloat.

"The gunners went back to the deck for more shooting," said Hayashi, firing twenty more shells into the doomed merchant ship, before breaking off the attack for the last time.

11:30 a.m. (PH plus 3 hrs. 30 min.): Unable to officially record the *Cynthia Olsen* as sunk after an attack that lasted over three hours in duration, at 7:00 a.m., Tokyo time, Captain Yokata ordered the crew to stand down from battle stations.

How long it took for the little ship to go down will never be known. The only eyewitnesses, the 25 *Olsen* crewmen in the two lifeboats, were lost at sea.

Cynthia Olsen's SSS signal had been picked up by the SS *Lurline,* at that moment not quite a day and a half out from Honolulu en route to the

U.S. mainland. The message was received and forwarded by radio opera-
tor Leslie Grogan, who, after failing to get through to Honolulu and San
Francisco, did reach a remote U.S. Coast Guard station at Point Bonita,
California. The fate of the message from that point on is not known.

According to Captain Yokata, after breaking off the attack, *I-26* headed
south on the surface. That was perhaps fortunate for the 784 passengers
and crew of the *Lurline,* for had he decided to head west instead, there was
a chance that the liner would have become the second victim of *I-26.*

Captain Yokata, who changed his name to Hasagawa after the war,
claims the *I-19,* one of nine Japanese submarines assigned to attack West
Coast shipping lanes, spotted the *Olsen*'s two lifeboats around the middle
of December. *I-19* supposedly dropped off food before continuing to a position off San Pedro, California.

Both *I-19* and *I-26* were to leave their marks on World War II naval
history before being sunk in 1943 and '44, respectively. *I-19,* after torpedo-
ing the lumber ship *Absoroka,* a mile and a half off Los Angeles Harbor on
December 24, 1941, was credited with perhaps the most miraculous shot in
World War II. Off Guadalcanal on September 15, 1942, *I-19* fired a spread
of four torpedoes at the carrier *Hornet.* One hit the *Hornet,* which eventually sunk. Although the other three missed their assigned target, one went
on to hit and eventually sink the destroyer *O'Brien.* The third hit the battleship *North Carolina,* doing severe damage.

On June 20, 1942, *I-26* surfaced off Estevan Point on the west coast
of Vancouver Island, where it fired seventeen rounds at the Estevan Point
lighthouse and wireless station. On November 13, 1942, off Guadalcanal,
I-26 fired a torpedo at the cruiser *San Francisco.* It missed, but hit the
cruiser *Juneau* instead, which blew up, killing 700 crewmen. Among those
killed were the five Sullivan brothers.

CHAPTER 8

SHANGHAI

TIME DIFFERENCE: 5 HOURS 30 MINUTES.

3:10 a.m. (PH plus 40 min.): By the morning of December 8, only two ships of the American and British Yangtze River Patrol were left in China—the tiny, 370-ton, 160-foot-long gunboat USS *Wake*, and the 310-ton HMS *Peterel*. Both were anchored near midstream on the Whangpoo River, opposite the famous Bund in the International Settlement of Shanghai.

As far as the Americans were concerned, war with Japan had been anticipated for quite some time. On November 3, Washington had ordered the 4th Marine Regiment to evacuate Shanghai for Subic Bay in the Philippines. Outside of four Marines left to take care of unfinished business affairs, China had seen the last of the famous Shanghai Marines by November 28.

On November 24, Rear Admiral William Glassford, commander of the Yangtze Patrol, ordered the *Wake*, at that moment 600 miles up river near Hankow, to Shanghai. When the little gunboat arrived four days later on November 28, its captain, Lieutenant Commander Andrew Harris, was surprised to hear that the Yangtze River Patrol was being disbanded. He and most of his crew were being transferred to the two waiting gunboats, *Oahu* and *Luzon*, which were leaving immediately for the Philippines.

The *Wake* and Commander Harris' replacement, Lieutenant Commander Columbus Smith, were left with a skeleton crew of fourteen, six naval reserve crewmen and eight radiomen. It was felt that the older and smaller *Wake* was not seaworthy enough to chance the 1,100-mile, open sea voyage to Manila. Also, with its powerful radio, the *Wake* could be used as a communications link for the U.S. Consulate in Shanghai.

Along the notorious Shanghai riverfront opposite the Bund, things had been happening since midnight. Most notable was the arrival of a Japanese gunboat, which dropped anchor on the opposite side of the river from the *Wake*. Since its arrival, signal lights had been flickering back and forth between it and the cruiser *Idzumo*, moored a half mile down river near the bend in the Whangpoo.

YANGTZE RIVER GUNBOATS

U. S. S. Oahu Patrolling the Yangtze River

Powerful light draft naval vessels protect American lives, alleviating distress and assisting commerce on the upper Yangtze River. These gunboats penetrate regions over 1300 miles from the sea in a land where transportation and communication is primitive.

1931 U.S. Navy recruiting poster depicting gunboat USS *Oahu* on patrol on Yangtze River.

The presence of the *Idzumo*, flagship of Japan's China Fleet, ensured that if a fight broke out, there would be no contest. Not counting the newly arrived Japanese gunboat, compared to *Peterel*'s two 3-inch guns, the 10,000-ton enemy cruiser's four 8-inch and eight 6-inch guns would make sure it was over in a hurry. *Wake*, without its crew and stripped of most of its armament, was not prepared to resist. Captain Smith, who had kept most of this men on shore at night, had been ordered to blow the bottom out of the old ship in the event war broke out. Explosive charges had already been in place for over a week in anticipation of the attack.

At 3:00 a.m., secure in the fact that the attack on Pearl Harbor had been carried out 30 minutes earlier, a launch carrying two officers and a dozen Japanese marines set out from the enemy gunboat toward the *Wake*. Without opposition, they quickly secured the little ship. By 3:10 a.m., the only American warship to strike its flag during the entire war, did so within 40 minutes of the beginning of the conflict. Once secured, the launch, joined this time by a picketboat of 50 more marines from the *Idzumo*, headed for the *Peterel*.

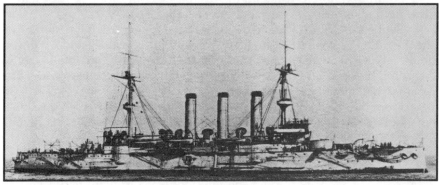

Fire from the Japanese cruiser *Idzumo* sunk the British gunboat *Peterel* on the morning of December 8, in Shanghai.

Although Commander Stephen Polkinghorn of the *Peterel* had been ordered to scuttle the ship in the event of war, unlike the *Wake*, the crew of the tiny British gunboat had remained on board.

When the Japanese launch drew alongside, and he was presented with an order to surrender the ship, Commander Polkinghorn was not surprised. Less than ten minutes earlier he had received a message from the British consulate in Shanghai, saying that Pearl Harbor had been bombed. In fact, he had already ordered the crew to make preparations to scuttle the *Peterel.*

Stalling for time while the crew readied the ship to be scuttled, the 63-year-old veteran gunboat captain drew the wrath of the Japanese officer who had presented him with the surrender demand. At his final demand for an immediate reply, Polkinghorn angrily told him the answer was "no," and ordered him off the ship.

When the launch was a safe distance from the *Peterel*, two red flares were sent up. Searchlights on the Japanese gunboat came on, followed by a blast from the 3-inch deck gun. At just 600 yards, they couldn't miss, nor could the 6-inch guns from the *Idzumo*, anchored a half a mile down river. Fire from several army field pieces that had been wheeled in along the opposite shore were also contributing. If there was any opposition from the *Peterel*, it was probably from Lewis machine guns, and it was over in a hurry. Within moments, the little gunboat was engulfed in smoke and fire, punctuated by explosions.

On shore, Commander Columbus Smith, deposed captain of the *Wake*, agonized as he watched the *Peterel* being helplessly pounded by the Japanese guns. Like Commander Polkinghorn, he too had been informed of the attack on Pearl Harbor a little before 4:00 a.m., with a phone call from his quartermaster. "The message said it was no drill," exclaimed the excited sailor.

Smith told him to wake up the rest of the crew, because they had to blow up the *Wake* before the Japanese could take her.

By the time Smith walked out of his hotel and reached the pier opposite the little gunboat, it was too late. He was held up at least half a dozen times, talking his way past armed Japanese patrols. By the time he got to the *Wake*, it was over. The ship was there, but the *Wake* was gone. The Japanese had already re-named it the *Tatara*.

From the top floor of the Shanghai Club on the Bund, American businessman John Potter was awakened by the series of explosions. At first he thought the Japanese were celebrating another German victory. "I thought Moscow had fallen," he said. "But the firing was too heavy."

"I ran to the window. There on the river...just before the club was a vivid scene of war. Just under the window were brilliant explosions as field pieces fired and shells struck the target up river. Reddish streaks made by tracer bullets chased one another in low arcs.

"From further downstream, at the bend of the river...the Japanese flagship *Idzumo* [was also firing].

"I knew they were firing at the ...*Peterel*. Quickly she burst into flames [and] was battered to pieces."

From another window overlooking the unfolding scene on the Whangpoo, young James Ballard was also watching the one-sided battle.

"...there was a huge explosion from the center of the river," remembered Ballard, looking down from his parents' tenth floor suite at the Palace Hotel. "Like rockets in a fireworks display, burning pieces of the *Peterel* soared into the air and then splashed into the water." Yet, "every few seconds there was...a flickering of light from its center, [indicating] the British sailors on the *Peterel* were fighting back. They manned one of the guns and were returning fire at the [Japanese]."

On board the *Peterel*, commander Polkinghorn quickly destroyed his code books, and ordered the ship's launch around to the starboard side, away from the enemy fire. Then he gave the order to abandon ship.

As the little cutter pulled away from the sinking *Peterel*, Japanese marines on the captured *Wake* opened fire with machine guns on the boat and the British sailors swimming for shore.

The fire did not let up even after the launch reached the shallow mud flats at the edge of the river. As bullets whizzed around them, the crewmen, most of them wounded, began wading through the waist-deep mud toward shore.

Meanwhile, on shore, several Britishers had run over from the Shanghai Club to help their English comrades. One was young Jim Ballard's father, who, business suit and all, jumped in and helped rescue a wounded petty officer off the ship.

"True to the British tradition," said American businessman John Potter, who watched the one-sided battle to the end, "the *Peterel* went down fighting. Her hopeless resistance...the only defense Shanghai was to know."

Even the Japanese officer who had delivered the surrender ultimatum to commander Polkinghorn on the *Peterel*, saluted the *bushido* displayed by the English sailors. Raising a glass of sake to an unofficial representative of the British government later that day, he said, "I ask you to accept the admiration of the Imperial Japanese Navy for the noble action of the *Peterel*."

10:00 a.m. (PH plus 7 hrs. 30 min.): Five hours after they had struggled ashore from the *Peterel*, the crew of the old gunboat, along with their British civilian rescuers, were still sitting on the mud flats along the edge of the river. They had been kept there by Japanese soldiers to witness a ceremony on board the new Imperial Navy ship, *Tatara*.

At exactly ten o'clock, the Japanese flag was hoisted to the mast of the old *Wake*, amidst a parade of Japanese marines strutting along the Bund waterfront, and the claim that the Imperial Japanese Navy had "capture[d] a mighty American warcraft without the enemy being able to fire a shot."

A somewhat fitting but unintentional epitaph to the sad events of that morning on the Whangpoo River in Shanghai was noted by American John Potter, "The day was bleak and cold," he wrote, "and the sun did not shine."

CHAPTER 9

NORTH CHINA MARINES

TIME DIFFERENCE: 6 HOURS 30 MINUTES.

7:45 a.m. (PH plus 6 hrs. 15 min.): It was 1:25 a.m., Tientsin time, when the first Japanese bomb fell on Pearl Harbor. Six hours later, at the U.S. Marine legation there, a puzzling four-word message came through from the Secretary of the Navy in Washington. Marked "URGENT," it read, "Execute WPL-46 against Japan." This was followed a few seconds later by a second short message from the Secretary of State Cordell Hull, that somewhat explained the first. It read, "Japanese have bombed Honolulu."

A couple of minutes later, an out of breath Marine handed the two messages to Captain John White, executive officer of the 49-man Marine contingent in Tientsin.

Ironically, White, who had just had his breakfast interrupted by a call from an English-speaking Japanese officer, knew something was up. He was told that the Imperial Army was taking over the British Concession in Tientsin that morning, and that they didn't want any trouble from the U.S. Marines. He was also told that a Major Omura would be calling on them at 9:00 a.m.

White assured him that it was not the Marines' mission to defend the British Concession, and that he would meet Major Omura when he arrived.

The United States, in the agreement that ended the Boxer Rebellion in 1901, was allowed to keep a military presence in Shanghai, and in the northern China cities of Peking, Tientsin, and Chinwangtao. Despite the Japanese capture and occupation of North China in 1937, the U.S. still remained. In the spring of 1938, the army's 15th Infantry Regiment was replaced by American Marines.

Actually, the few Marines and naval personnel still remaining in China, which included 141 U.S. Embassy Guards in Peking, 49 in Tientsin, and 22 at Chinwangtao, a small seaport 140 miles northeast of Tientsin, were all well aware that relations between the United States and Japan were at the tenuous stage. Of course, if war broke out between the two countries, the Marines in North China would be doomed.

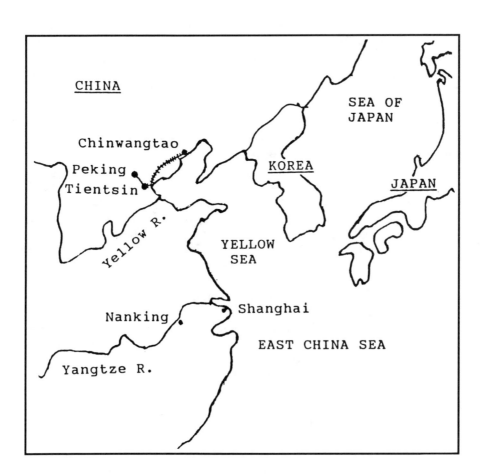

Because of this, on November 11, Asiatic Fleet Commander, Admiral Thomas Hart, in Manila, ordered the Marines to prepare to leave China. First to go was the 750-man strong Fourth Marine Regiment in Shanghai, which left for the Philippines on November 27 and 28 on the SS *President Harrison* and *President Madison*. Immediately after unloading, the *Harrison* started back to pick up the remaining 212 Marines and navy personnel in China.

On December 4, as relations with Japan reached the critical stage, Admiral Hart ordered all secret codes and confidential papers burned.

Anticipating the return of the *Harrison* on December 9, all gear, including machine guns and automatic weapons, was sent to Chinwangtao. Each man was allowed to keep his own rifle and sixty rounds of ammunition. The *Harrison* was scheduled to leave Chinwangtao for Manila on December 10.

As scheduled, at 9:00 a.m., Major Omura, with five men, including an interpreter, and a truckload of Japanese soldiers, appeared at the main gate. Captain White escorted the six men to the office of the commanding officer, Major Luther Brown.

Major Omura handed a note to Brown demanding the surrender of the U.S. Marines in Tientsin and Chinwangtao by 1:00 p.m. that day.

Ironically, the same three officers had met the day before in the same office, and hoisted a glass of American beer to Major Omura's toast, "No war between Japan and the United States." He had called in response to Major Brown's farewell visit a few days before to General Koyjoi Tominaga, commanding officer of Japanese occupation forces in Tientsin. Because of the effort put forth by Brown, relations between the Marines and the Japanese had remained friendly. It would pay off.

"...I must demand that you and your men lay down your arms and give me your unconditional surrender," continued Omura through his interpreter. "Please give me your answer immediately."

"The United States Marines," said Brown, "are stationed here...under the terms of the Boxer Protocol of 1901." Reminding Omura that it was agreed to as a settlement to the Boxer Rebellion, in which both the U.S. and Japan were signatories, and that, under the existing circumstances, it allowed "reparation" of military forces to their home countries, he said, "Will you please tell General Tominaga that I shall...surrender in response to your proposal only if [you] observe the terms of the Boxer Protocol."

Major Omura, taken aback by the response, telephoned General Tominaga for advice. It was quick in coming.

"The general will investigate your status under the Boxer Protocol," said Omura. "He personally guarantees the safety of each member of your command."

With the Japanese already in control of the telephone system, Omura told Brown that he had arranged for him to telephone his superiors in Peking for any further instructions.

A minute or so later Brown was talking to Colonel William Ashurst, commander of all Marine forces in North China.

Ashurst told him that since the embassy was not required to maintain 24-hour communication with the Asiatic Fleet's command radio circuit, this was the first official word of the outbreak of hostilities with Japan he had received.

Unofficially, however, the presence of a large number of Japanese troops that had surrounded the embassy compound at dawn, and the complete absence of the hundreds of Chinese coolies with their vegetable carts that usually gathered on the street outside the wall, indicated that something was up.

Until he could communicate with Admiral Hart in Manila to get the official word, Ashurst advised Brown to comply with the Japanese demand.

Brown hung up, then dictated the following reply to his clerk, who typed, "I accept the terms of your proposal and shall be ready to meet your party at 1:00 p.m."

A few minutes later, when Captain White returned from escorting Major Omura and his party to the front gate, Major Brown showed him the radio message that had come in from Colonel Ashurst while he was gone.

At that moment both men wondered if the 7:45 a.m. message from Secretary Knox, ordering them to execute WPL-46, directed them to do something else.

"We never did have [a copy of War Plan 46]," said White. "I don't think...it intended that I draw my pistol, throw a couple of hand grenades in that truck and shoot the first seven who try to get out."

"...do you know this is the first time a United States Marine command has surrendered without a fight?" lamented Brown, his voice choked with emotion.

The way things were stacking up with the Marines—at Chinwangtao, however, there was still a chance the command would not give up without putting up a fight after all.

Second Lieutenant Richard Huizenga, officer in charge of the 21 Marines at Chinwangtao, was supervising the stockpiling of crates for loading on to the *President Harrison* when it came in the next day, when a truck driver, who had just arrived from Camp Holcomb, told him that they heard over the radio that the Japanese had just bombed Pearl Harbor.

When Huizenga and the truckload of men he brought with him from the docks entered the camp gate near the railhead, he found his men surrounded at a distance by Japanese troops. Chief Marine Gunner William Lee, in charge of unloading the boxcars, had already broken out several machine guns and BARs, and was in the process of preparing a defensive position behind the packing boxes.

Realizing the untenable position he was in, but not unwilling to make a fight of it, Huizenga met with a Japanese officer, who demanded his immediate surrender. The young lieutenant said he would have to check with his superiors at Tientsin before he could give him an answer. A few minutes later, the following radio message came through for Major Brown:

"Have set up machine guns and think we have a chance to stand them off. Request instructions. Huizenga."

Brown had Captain White send the following message in reply:

"Do not repeat not resort to fire except if self defense. Comply with demand of Japanese Army Forces."

Disappointed, the small 22-man detachment of U.S. Marines turned over their weapons and, as prisoners of war, were put on a train for Tientsin later that afternoon.

1:00 p.m. (PH plus 11 hrs. 30 min.): As agreed, Captain White was at the main gate in Tientsin when the Japanese arrived at one o'clock to officially take over the post. After turning over their small cache of weapons, White took the four officers on an inspection of the compound.

"It took about three hours for me to take [them] through every building, office, mess hall, and living quarters," said White. "[They] seemed satisfied that we gave up all our arms and ammunition."

On his way back to his quarters, White ran into Sergeant Robert Smith. There were tears in his eyes.

"He pointed up and for the first time I missed the flag," said White. "The American flag that for 40 years had graced the top of the pole, had been replaced by the Japanese flag."

Smith, who was the only Marine there to see the "Stars and Stripes" lowered, said, "I snapped to attention and saluted as they lowered our colors, then bawled like a baby."

Seventy miles to the north in Peking, bugler Carrol Boucher, accompanied by a Marine color guard, sounded "Retreat" as the flag was lowered for the last time from the U.S. Embassy flag pole. It was presented to Colonel Ashurst, remembered Captain James Hester, a witness to the event. "[Ashurst] in turn gave them to the Japs. Boucher then broke his bugle over his knee and with tears in his eyes threw it aside."

The Boxer Protocol that the Marines counted on was never honored by the Japanese. The 212 Marines and U.S. Navy medical personnel remained prisoners of war until the end. The SS *President Harrison* never made it to Chinwangtao. Instead, the skipper of the ship, Captain Orel Pierson, purposely ran it aground outside the entrance to the harbor at Shanghai. It was later salvaged by the Japanese and renamed the *Kachidoki Maru*. It was sunk by a U.S. submarine on September 12, 1944. Four-hundred-thirty Australian and British POWs perished on the unmarked prison ship.

CHAPTER 10

NETHERLANDS EAST INDIES

TIME DIFFERENCE: 7 HOURS 30 MINUTES.

6:30 a.m. (PH plus 5 hrs. 55 min.): It was 12:25 a.m., December 8, Netherlands East Indies time, when the first Japanese bomb fell on Pearl Harbor. In London, England, it was 6:25 in the evening. The first the British, including Winston Churchill, heard of the attack was from a 9:00 p.m. news broadcast, that had placed the event third on its list of important war news of the day.

The prime minister, who at first "...did not personally sustain any direct impression [from the broadcast]," was made aware of its impact when his butler came into the room. "It's quite true," the butler said. "We heard it ourselves. The Japanese have attacked the Americans."

After absorbing the significance of what he had just heard, Mr. Churchill later wrote of that moment, "I knew the United States was in the war, up to the neck and to the death. So we had won after all!"

An hour later, the phone rang at the London residence of Queen Wilhelmina, exiled monarch of the Netherlands, who had fled Holland before it fell to the Germans in May of 1940. Although she was told of the Japanese attacks, and that they had not yet struck the East Indies, there was no hesitation on her part in deciding not to wait for the inevitable to happen.

All Netherlanders knew that when war came, the riches of Java, Sumatra, and the oil of Borneo would make the Dutch East Indies a key, if not primary, objective of the Japanese.

After notifying the governor general of the Indies in Batavia of the attack, she told him to announce that the Netherlands East Indies had declared war on the Japanese Empire.

Said Queen Wilhelmina in her declaration of war speech early the next morning: "You know how Germany...attacked many countries in Europe, one after another. Japan, motivated by the same spirit of aggression and...disregard for law, follows the same footsteps of her Axis partners."

After mentioning the Japanese attack on the Americans at Pearl Harbor and the British at Hong Kong, she said, "The Kingdom of the Netherlands considers itself in a state of war with Japan because the aggression...can only be halted through a strong coalition....Our course is righteous and our conscience clear, we accept the challenge, together with our powerful Allies."

Ironically, not only was the Netherlands the first country in World War II to officially declare war on Japan, it was the only country to do it prior to being attacked.

At 4:30 a.m., on the other side of the world in Batavia, Java, the phone rang at the home of United Press correspondent Jack Raleigh. His wife, Betty, answered it.

"I stood several feet away, watching her face grow pale in the single desk lamp she had lit," said Raleigh.

After hanging up the phone, she turned and said, "Jack, the Japs have bombed Pearl Harbor, and the Netherlands East Indies are formally declaring war on Japan at six-thirty. The governor general is delivering an address over the Royal Dutch Indian radio informing the peoples of the Indies that they're at war."

"I suppose I stood for fully three minutes trying to absorb what Betty had said," remembered Raleigh.

Ironically, earlier that night, "feeling like hell," he had called the doctor. After diagnosing his condition as an attack of malaria, he had been ordered to bed for five days.

"Whatever happened to that attack of malaria or whatever it was, I will never know," said Jack, who yelled at Betty to get his clothes.

Realizing that the first thing to do was to write a "news flash" for the United Press on the governor general's speech, he sat down at the typewriter. "The message simply said that the governor general would declare to the rest of the world, that the Netherlands East Indies were at war."

After "bribing" their chauffeur over the phone to come pick them up, Jack, in pajama bottoms, coat and sun helmet, and Betty, piled into the car and headed for the post office to file the cable.

"Well, Bets, this is it!" said Jack, as they pulled away.

"Yes, Jack, this is it! Thank the Lord it's come at last."

"Several things occurred to me," remembered Raleigh. "First, I felt a physical surge of heartfelt hatred. All the...nasty practices and cruelty of the Japanese in Shanghai and Nanking were to be avenged. Then and there the new order in East Asia was finished....They're going to get what's coming to 'em at last."

As scheduled, at 6:30 on the morning of December 8, the governor general addressed the people of the Netherlands East Indies. He said, in part: "Fellow citizens, by sudden attacks on the United States and British territories...the Japanese Empire has consciously chosen the way of force.

"These attacks...have involved the United States of America and the British Empire in an active war with Japan....This greed of conquest is also...directed at the Netherlands Indies.

"The Netherlands Government hereby accepts this challenge and takes up arms against the Japanese Empire..."

Imediately after the governor general's speech, an order went out for the internment of all Japanese subjects in the islands. Two-thousand people were rounded up by noon. Almost twice that number would have been picked up if 1,500 had not left Batavia and Surabaya for Japan the week before on the *Fuzi Maru*. All Japanese-operated barber shops, stores, and restaurants also closed their doors that same day.

Japanese males who were rounded up on the eighth were forbidden to bring anything with them. Dutch officials, reflecting on the fate of Holland prior to the Nazi invasion in 1940, confidently said that there would be "no such attack from within" in the Indies.

That night, when Jack Raleigh, who doubled as a correspondent for the Columbia Broadcasting System in the United States, got to the radio station to file a report, it was, as he said, "graphically brought home to me that the Indies were at war. As I ran into the radio station I was abruptly stopped at the point of a bayonet. Frantically I held up my papers and passport, and, after matching my face with my passport photo, was allowed to pass."

Early in the afternoon on December 6, two British PBY patrol planes spotted a large number of Japanese troop transports in the Gulf of Siam, heading northwest toward the coast of Thailand and Malaya.

British intelligence had previously reported that two convoys of ships had left Camranh Bay and Saigon on December 4 and 5 respectively, heading south towards the Gulf. Now that they had been spotted well inside Gulf waters, it seemed obvious that their objective was the invasion of Malaya or Thailand or both, within the next two or three days.

When word of their presence reached Vice Admiral Conrad Helfrich, commander of the Royal Dutch Navy in the Indies, on the sixth, he pleaded for permission to attack the Japanese transports with his submarines, one of which was on patrol in gulf waters at the time. Response from the exiled Dutch Government in London was, of course, negative.

The lone Dutch submarine operating in the Gulf was under the command of Lieutenant Commander A.J. Bussemaker. On the night of December 6, while cruising on the surface, he was forced to make an emergency crash dive because of two fast-approaching Japanese destroyers that bore down on him without warning out of the darkness.

The next night it was different. Notified early on the eighth that his country was at war with Japan, Bussemaker spent most of the day searching for the enemy. Late in the afternoon, about 75 miles north of the Thai-

Malayan border, he spotted a large Japanese transport crammed to the rails with enemy troops, heading in the direction of the small Siamese coastal town of Patani.

With the possibility that the transport might lead him to other enemy ships, Bussemaker, staying submerged, decided to follow the Japanese ship rather than attack. It would pay off.

As they rounded Laem Pho Point, the headland forming the eastern edge of the bay known as Patani Roads, Bussemaker was forced to surface because of shallow water. Fortunately, it was too dark for them to be seen. It wasn't too dark for them to see that the enemy ship had led them into a nest of three other transports, however, all in the process of unloading troops and supplies for their push against Malaya and Singapore.

Quickly lining up on his unsuspecting targets, Bussemaker fired all four forward tubes, then, as he turned to head out of the bay, let go with his stern torpedoes. All six were observed to explode. As the Dutch submarine rounded Laem Pho Point for open water, it appeared as if all four enemy transports were burning or sinking.

By successfully attacking the four Japanese ships, Bussemaker's Royal Dutch Navy submarine became the first Allied ship to draw blood in the 18-hour-old Pacific war.

Sadly, 24 hours later, only one man would be alive as an eyewitness to the attack at Patani Roads. All but the ship's quartermaster, Cornelius de Wolf, were lost when Lieutenant Commander Bussemaker's sub went down after hitting a mine off the east coast of Malaya. De Wolf was on the bridge when the mine was struck. He was picked up by an Australian rifleman as he staggered up the beach after being in the water for thirty-five hours.

Interestingly, the Japanese did not declare war on the Netherlands East Indies until January 10, 1942.

CHAPTER 11

USS *ENTERPRISE*

TIME DIFFERENCE: ZERO HOURS ZERO MINUTES.

6:15 a.m. (PH minus 1 hr. 45 min.): At 6:15 on the morning of December 7, the carrier *Enterprise*, that had delivered twelve Marine fighters to Wake Island on December 4, was eight hours sailing time from Pearl Harbor. If it hadn't been for bad weather holding up the entire thirteen-ship task force most of a day, it would have arrived at Pearl Harbor at dawn on December 7. The ships had lost a day's sailing time because stormy seas had prevented *Enterprise* from refueling its escorting destroyers.

Although the task force itself was 210 miles from Pearl, at 6:15, twenty SBD Dive Bombers from the big carrier were preparing to take off for Ford Island. It was a flight that would put them over Pearl Harbor around 8:00 a.m.

First plane off was Air Group Commander Brigham Young's SBD, whose rear seat was occupied by Lieutenant Commander Bromfield Nichol, carrying classified material regarding the Wake operation to Admiral Kimmel in Pearl Harbor. Next off, following Young's wingman, was Lieutenant Commander Halsted Hopping, skipper of Scouting Six, followed by the squadron's remaining seventeen Dauntlesses.

7:58 a.m. (PH plus 3 min.): Task Force Commander, Admiral William Halsey, who had observed the launching, had gone below after it was over, where he "shaved, bathed, put on a clean uniform, and joined [his] flag secretary, Lieutenant Douglas Moulton, at breakfast."

At 7:58, while the two men were at breakfast, down in the ship's code room a radioman began reading the plain-language message coming in on the teletype machine. It was from Lieutenant Commander Logan Ramsey, who had run into the command center at Ford Island and sent the message after realizing they were under attack by the Japanese. It read: "Air raid Pearl Harbor. This is not drill."

The young sailor quickly passed it on to Commander Charles Fox, duty officer in the code room.

"We were on our second cups of coffee when the phone rang," remembered Halsey. "Doug answered it. I heard him say, 'Moulton....What?....Roger!' 'Admiral,' he said, with a puzzled look on his face, 'the staff duty officer says he has a message that there's an air attack on Pearl.' "

"My God," yelled Halsey, jumping to his feet, "They're shooting at my own boys! Tell Kimmel!"

Halsey hadn't notified Pearl of the arrival of his planes, so his first reaction was "that some trigger-happy AA gunners had failed to recognize them."

"Just then my communications officer...came in and handed me a dispatch," he said. It was from Kimmel. It read:

From CINCPAC (Commander-in-Chief Pacific Fleet)
TO: All ships present
AIR RAID PEARL HARBOR X THIS IS NO DRILL

Ten minutes later, a second message came in from the same source that announced: "Hostilities with Japan commenced with air raid on Pearl Harbor."

"We notified all hands over the loud-speaker and sent the ship to general quarters," said Halsey.

Eleven minutes later at 8:23, CINCPAC sent out a third message: "Alert X Japanese planes attacking Pearl and air fields on Oahu."

8:30 a.m. (PH plus 30 min.): Ironically, the assertion Halsey made some 30 minutes earlier that "they're shooting at my own boys," was now true, only most, but not all fire was coming from the Japanese.

Commander Brigham Young and his wingman were the first to arrive over Oahu. Discounting the planes he saw circling over the Marine Air Station at Ewa as army aircraft, he noticed black puffs of what looked like anti-aircraft bursts over the harbor. He thought it was strange, that they would be holding target practice on Sunday, and couldn't figure out how he was supposed to get through it to land. Brom Nichols, his passenger, remembered thinking that the army had gone crazy, "having an anti-aircraft drill on Sunday morning."

Seconds later, Young noted that one of the "army" planes that had been circling over Ewa, had broken away and was heading towards him. Swinging in behind the SBD, the plane opened fire as it bore down on the still unsuspecting American. It was not until the wing was hit and the plane roared past the slower Dauntless, that the two men identified their attacker as Japanese.

Young, with his wingman close behind, dove for Ford Island, where, after losing the Japanese on the way down, they were shot at by trigger-happy gunners from their own ships as they came in to land.

"[We] went through the damndest amount of anti-aircraft fire and bullets...that [I] had ever seen..." recalled Nichols, as he and Young jumped from the Dauntless while the propeller was still spinning.

About ten minutes later, the first of Scouting Six's eighteen Dauntlesses arrived over Oahu. Down in *Enterprise*'s code room, men were listening on the radio to conversations between pilots of the squadron, when they heard the Spanish-accented voice of Ensign Manuel Gonzales.

"Please don't shoot! Don't shoot," he yelled. "This is an American plane." To his rear gunner, he said, "We're on fire! Bail out!" Then there was nothing but silence.

Ironically, had things remained as scheduled, Lieutenant Edward Anderson should have been flying in Gonzales' place. However, at the last minute, the two men traded places because Gonzales' wife resided in Honolulu. Anderson's didn't. Unknown to the young pilot, his wife was not there. She had left for the mainland on the *Lurline* two days before.

A few minutes after communication with Gonzales faded out, they heard another voice they recognized. It was Lieutenant Earl Gallaher, executive officer of Scouting Six, and senior pilot of the squadron.

"Pearl Harbor is under attack by enemy planes! May be Jap planes," said Gallaher, in a voice so calm that the men listening were sure the whole thing was a sham. Like everyone else, no one believed a Japanese attack on Pearl Harbor could ever happen.

Commander Charles Fox routinely relayed Gallaher's message to the bridge, where Halsey, who ten minutes earlier had received CINCPAC's "Japanese planes attacking Pearl and air fields on Oahu" message, immediately ordered the ship to battle stations.

Although nothing more distinguishable was heard over the radio, the remaining SBDs were in for plenty of trouble as they attempted to make it into Ford Island. When it was over, fourteen of the twenty Dauntlesses that took off from the *Enterprise* that morning, made it safely into either Ford or the Marine airfield at Ewa.

Of the six that didn't make it, one crash-landed on Burns Field, Kauai. Marines at Ewa Marine Air Station saw Ensign John Vogt's plane go down in a mid-air collision with a damaged Zero he had hit and over-run in a dog fight.

The planes, piloted by Lieutenant (jg) Clarence Dickenson and Ensign J.R. McCarthy, were somewhat behind the rest of the squadron when they reached the island.

Lieutenant Clarence Dickenson. This *Enterprise* pilot flew his SBD smack into the Japanese attack on Pearl Harbor. Although shot down, he survived and later led a search for enemy carriers.
US Navy

The first thing they saw were two distinct columns of smoke rising from the island. Discounting them as burning cane fields, commonly seen during harvest season, "I paid no heed to [it]," said Dickenson.

After identifying three destroyers and a cruiser off the entrance to Pearl as U.S. ships, he saw something unusual off to his right. "...a rain of big shell splashes in the water off the entrance to Pearl Harbor, recklessly close to shore....I supposed some Coast Artillery batteries had gone stark mad and were shooting wildly," he thought. "I remarked to Miller [his gunner], just wait! Tomorrow the army will certainly catch hell for that."

A few seconds later, as he banked his plane toward Ford Island, he saw that the biggest smoke cloud was rising from the harbor itself. Glancing up, he saw "thousands of black balls of smoke," which explained the splashes in the water. Suddenly realizing that they were anti-aircraft bursts, he yelled to Miller, "Pearl is under attack!"

After unsuccessfully chasing a B-17, identified as a Japanese bomber, into a cloud, "...Mac and I [turned] back towards Barbers Point for another look," recalled Dickenson. "[Suddenly], two fighters popped out of the cloud in a dive and made a run at us."

In the lopsided dog fight that ensued, Dickenson saw McCarthy's plane "burst into yellow flame," but saw him bail out just before hitting the ground.

"In that same second, four or five...Zeroes dove out of the smoke and sat on my tail," said Dickenson. "Miller was firing away and giving me constant reports on what was happening. Then in a calm voice, he said, 'Mr. Dickenson, I've been hit, but I think I got one of the sons of bitches.' "

"In one glance I saw our Jap go down in flames, saw Ensign McCarthy's parachute open, and then again my eyes were wide open for those Jap fighters behind us....You get a queer feeling looking at those guns when they are shooting," recalled the young pilot. "They seem to be winking at you, but you know each wink is an effort [to] kill you...

"[The Japs] were having a field day, all of them in a scramble to get me; each wildly eager for the credit.

"Then one of them got on target....Bullets clattered on my metal wing like hail on a tin roof....I could hear [them] explode and saw the first tongue of [fire] as [a] bullet went into the gas tank in my left wing."

"Are you all right?" Dickenson yelled back to Miller.

"...I've [used] all six cans of ammunition," he replied, then suddenly screamed. "I have never heard any comparable human sound," remembered the startled pilot. "It was a yell of agony. I believe Miller died right then.

"[I was now] in one hell of a fix. The plane did not respond to the stick, [and] eight or nine hundred feet from the ground, I went into a spin."

"Then I started to get out," said Dickenson. "I shoved out on the right side because that was the inside of the spin."

As he pushed himself clear of the plane, the rush of wind blew his goggles off. Reflecting back, he remembered that his first thought, as he leaped free of his ship, was that he hoped he didn't have to pay for the goggles.

"They were experimental," he said, "and weren't any good in the first place."

He also remembered that "there was a savage jerk. [From] where I dangled," he said, "my eyes followed the shroud lines up to the most beautiful sight I had ever seen—the stiff-bellied shape of my parachute. Fortunately I had jumped so low that neither the Japs overhead nor the Marines defending Ewa Field had time to get a shot at me."

Both Dickenson and McCarthy, whose leg was fractured by the tail as he attempted to push clear of his plane, survived.

Not far behind Ensign Gonzales were two SBDs flown by Ensigns Edward Deacon and Bill Roberts. Flying at 500 feet, as they neared the island they spotted a large formation of planes heading toward them and away from Oahu.

Unknown to the two Americans, they were part of the first wave of Japanese attack planes that had just gotten through working over the island, and were on their way back to their carriers.

Ironically, as they approached each other, both mistakenly believed they were passing their own planes. Roberts and one of the Japanese actually waggled their wings at each other as they passed.

As the loose formation of planes slid beneath them, both men thought the red "meatball" insignias they saw painted on their wings, meant that the army must have had them specially painted for war games. Not very smart, thought Roberts, "someone might mistake them for Japanese."

When the island came into view a few minutes later, both were baffled by the huge clouds of smoke rising from Pearl Harbor. Moments after failing to contact the tower at Ford Island, a familiar voice over the radio told them what was going on. "Please don't shoot! Don't shoot! This is an American plane!" Then, "We're on fire! Bail out!" It was Ensign Gonzales, and he was under attack. Both men now knew that the red "meatball" insignias really were Japanese.

With Ford Island and the Marine air base at Ewa obscured by smoke from the now fiercely burning *Arizona*, the two decided to try for Hickam Field. Unfortunately, in order to land at the army base, they were forced to pass by Fort Weaver, site of the Fleet Machine Gun School.

On the ground at Weaver, Machine Gun School guns and anti-aircraft batteries of the 97th Coast Artillery had already been blasting away at Japanese planes when the two SBDs started in for Hickam.

Assuming, by now, that everything in the air had to be Japanese, Deacon and Roberts came under fire as they passed the trigger-happy gunners at Fort Weaver.

Deacon, who was first in, was shot down before he reached the Hickam runway. Coming down in the water some 200 yards from shore, the young ensign, who had suffered a minor bullet wound in the left leg, quickly broke out the rubber life raft, then pulled his badly wounded gunner, Audrey Coslett, out of the rear seat, and began paddling for shore.

Not satisfied that they had shot down an "enemy plane," as soon as the men on shore spotted the raft, they opened up on the two survivors. Fortunately, they were saved when an army crash boat from Hickam, whose job it was to rescue downed flyers, rushed out and picked up the two navy men.

Bill Roberts, whose plane was also hit, was able to land safely at Hickam. Neither he nor his gunner, Donald Jones, were wounded.

Undaunted by the fact that they were sitting on the ground, when Hickam came under strafing attack by the Japanese planes a few minutes later, Jones jumped into the rear seat and blasted away at them with his .30 caliber machine gun until his ammunition ran out.

9:21 a.m. (PH plus 1 hr. 21 min.): Back on the *Enterprise,* at 9:21, CINCPAC sent the following message to Admiral Halsey, that directed his actions throughout the rest of the day. It read:

FROM: CINCPAC
TO: Task Forces 3-8-12
RENDEZVOUS AS CTF-8 DIRECTS X FURTHER INSTRUCTIONS WHEN ENEMY LOCATED.

The *Enterprise* and its twelve-ship escort had been designated as Task Force 8. The message directed Task Force 3, under Vice Admiral Wilson Brown, whose six-ship force had just finished a simulated bombardment and landing exercise on Johnston Island, 700 miles southwest of Oahu, and Rear Admiral John Newton's Task Force 12, the carrier *Lexington,* and eight escorts, at that moment 420 miles southeast of Midway, to rendezvous with Task Force 8. Their job, once the enemy was located, was to go after them. "CTF-8" indicated that commander of Task Force 8, Admiral Halsey, had been placed in command of the combined 26 ships. Halsey signaled to the two task forces that he had chosen Kaula Rock, 150 miles west of Pearl Harbor, as the rendezvous point.

While heading for the selected location, Halsey received the following message from Admiral Kimmel at 10:18 a.m., indicating where the enemy fleet might be. Addressed to "All Ships," it read:

SEARCH FROM PEARL VERY LIMITED ACCOUNT MAXI-
MUM ONLY TWELVE VP [patrol planes] SEARCHING FROM PEARL
X SOME INDICATION ENEMY FORCE NORTHWEST OAHU X
ADDRESSEES OPERATE AS DIRECTED CTF-8 TO INTERCEPT EN-
EMY X COMPOSITION ENEMY FORCE UNKNOWN.

Ironically, Kimmel's assumption was correct, but a misinterpretation of an intercepted Japanese message by Naval Intelligence at Pearl Harbor resulted in directing U.S. search efforts in the opposite direction.

Admiral Kimmel's 10:18 message had apparently been picked up by a Japanese submarine, and subsequently passed on to Admiral Nagumo's task force north of Oahu. At that point, the navy-operated radio-direction finder at Heeia, on the east side of Oahu, was able to track the response from the Japanese to a line 358 degrees north, 178 degrees south. Whether the enemy fleet was on the northern or southern end of the line could not be determined, however, and it was left up to Kimmel's War Plans Division to make a guess.

Since Naval Intelligence had believed the Japanese could have come out of the Marshall Islands, and that most U.S. ships at sea were already in or close to southern waters, it was decided to redirect their search south.

Therefore, at 10:46, Kimmel sent the following message to "All Ships": "D/F [direction finder] bearings indicate enemy carriers bearing 178 from Barbers Point."

After receiving Kimmel's message, Admiral Wilson Brown was led to the conclusion that "the enemy might be withdrawing...toward Jaluit [in the Marshall's]." He therefore decided to turn back toward Johnston Island, from which they had been steaming since the 9:21 a.m. order to rendezvous with Halsey at Kaula Rock.

The heavy cruiser *Minneapolis*, at that moment a few miles off Barbers Point on her way home from the Fleet operating area, having seen no carriers in the described vicinity, quickly responded to Kimmel's message. However, the radioman who was told to signal "No carriers in sight," somehow sent "Two carriers in sight"—a mistake that almost led to the *Minneapolis* itself being attacked.

Hawaiian Air Force Commander, Major General Frederick Martin, got word of the enemy ships off Barbers Point, and was able to launch four A-20 Havocs at 11:30, with the mission of "trying to find the carrier that was south of Barbers Point." Fortunately, the pilots recognized the only ship they saw as a U.S. cruiser and returned to Hickam.

A second attack was narrowly avoided when the cruiser *St. Louis* literally fought its way out of Pearl Harbor during the attack, and reacted to the same message. Only a last-minute identification of the "enemy carrier" as the *Minneapolis* averted an attack on the big cruiser.

12:00 p.m. (PH plus 4 hrs.): If there was one group of men who knew there were no enemy ships off Barbers Point, it was the pilots of Scouting Squadron Six from the *Enterprise*, who, as Lieutenant Clarence Dickenson said, "...had flown in from the west, scouting over an area so wide that no ship could have moved across it since we had seen it."

Dickenson, after parachuting from his plane and hitchhiking his way over to Ford Island, had just joined the remnants of his squadron, when word of Japanese ships off Barbers Point came in. Of the 18 Scouting Six planes that had taken off from the *Enterprise* that morning, only seven had made it to Ford.

Despite knowing that there were no Japanese ships off Barbers Point, Lieutenant Commander Halsted Hopping, skipper of the squadron, decided to take a look anyway.

"Unwilling to tell us to go on what he considered a useless flight, he went himself," said Dickenson, "and nearly got shot down by our own people.

"Almost before his plane was off the runway the shooting began; to us watching...it seemed as if all the guns in Pearl Harbor were trying to bring the skipper down.

"There was kind of a contagion about it. Somebody manning a machine gun on a destroyer was the first; after that others simply took it for granted that the plane was a Jap."

Despite the friendly fire, Hopping was able to complete his mission, landing back at Ford Island around eleven o'clock.

"He searched an area 30 or 35 miles off the island," said Dickenson, "and sighted nothing."

At twelve noon, with the attacking Japanese planes well on their way back to their carriers, the pilots from the *Enterprise* were ordered to search for the enemy ships. The remaining seven Scouting Six planes were joined by two from Bombing Squadron Six.

"We headed north-northwest and although went out to sea about 200 miles and searched for four hours; we saw no trace of the Jap fleet," said the young lieutenant. "We searched as long as our gasoline supply allowed and then started back.

"As we were flying over Wheeler Field on our way back, a couple of their machine guns opened up on us. They did no damage except to our nerves and tempers. We got back to Pearl Harbor, and, miracle of miracles, landed on Ford Island runway without being shot at."

At 1:20, the *Enterprise* received a message from one of its escorting destroyers, the *Benham*, that it had detected the presence of a submarine. Halsey immediately changed course away from the identified location and increased speed. *Benham* proceeded to drop eight depth charges on the target, later reporting that an oil slick and debris was seen on the surface following the attack.

Not long after that, what turned out to be a second case of mistaken identity, occurred, only this time bombs were dropped.

U.S. Navy PBY patrol planes had been patrolling the waters both north and south of the island since dawn. One of the planes that was scouting the area southwest of Oahu reported sighting a Japanese carrier and cruiser "well south of Pearl Harbor." "Dropped two bombs on carrier which was zigzagging at high speed," the pilot radioed back to Pearl.

A quick check of the nearest American ships to the enemy carrier by Kimmel indicated that Task Force 3, under Wilson Brown, was within 90 miles of the reported coordinates.

Brown's response to CINCPAC's order to "get the carrier," however, was puzzling. A few minutes earlier he had received a message from the heavy cruiser *Portland,* who, along with the destroyer *Porter,* had separated from Admiral John Newton's *Lexington* task force, in order to help out on the search for the retiring Japanese fleet south of Oahu.

Admiral Brown signaled to CINCPAC that he believed the *Portland* had been bombed by mistake, bringing Pearl to signal *Portland,* "Were you bombed this afternoon?" The captain of the cruiser replied, "Yes, a plane dropped two bombs narrowly missing me astern."

During the Japanese attack on Hickam Field earlier that morning, Captain Brooke Allen, acting C.O. of Hickam's bombers, had rushed out to his B-17 and successfully taxied it out of harm's way.

When General Martin got word of the enemy carriers off Barbers Point, Allen decided he'd get in on it. After loading his B-17 with bombs, he was off.

On board the USS *Enterprise,* four bells had just sounded, when "All hands man your battle stations!" was suddenly announced throughout the ship. An unidentified bomber was reported approaching out of the south.

The "unidentified" plane was Captain Allen's B-17. Unknown to both the anxious bomber pilot and the *Enterprise* gunners who had been tracking the big plane, the fourth case of mistaken identity that day was about to occur.

After sighting what Allen described as "this beautiful carrier," which had begun firing at him, he started his bomb run. Suddenly, as he drew closer, he recognized the ship. It was the *Enterprise.* "God had a hand on me," he said afterward, reflecting back on what would have happened had he sunk the big carrier by mistake.

Allen quickly moved out of range of the carrier's guns, deciding to continue north, where he originally believed the Japanese attack force to be. About an hour and a half later, after finding no sign of the enemy ships, he headed back, spotting the *Enterprise* on the way in. Only this time he was greeted by two F4F Wildcats, whose pilots looked him over before returning to the ship.

By the time Allen set his B-17 down on Hickam, it was close to four o'clock in the afternoon. The mistaken identity problem that had plagued the U.S. since the attack began, was far from over, however.

The U.S. submarine *Thresher* was about 50 miles outside the entrance to Pearl Harbor when she received word of the attack at eight that morning. Captain William Anderson's sub, returning from a long patrol off Midway, had just rendezvoused with the old four-stack destroyer that had been assigned to escort it in.

About 30 miles off the entrance, the two ships were passed by a task force of cruisers and destroyers, under command of Rear Admiral

Milo Dreamel, who was racing to join Admiral Halsey at the Kaula Rock rendezvous.

At that point, the escorting destroyer announced that it was joining up with the task force, and left. Because of the possibility of being attacked by Japanese planes, Anderson, who signaled Pearl of what had happened, decided to submerge until dark, then make his way into the harbor alone.

As *Thresher* was going under, a message came through from Rear Admiral Thomas Withers, commander of submarine operations at Pearl, instructing Anderson to recall the escort, and not, under any circumstances, attempt to come in alone.

A little after 4:00 p.m., a four-stacker destroyer was spotted heading toward what Captain Anderson had designated as the rendezvous point of the two ships. *Thresher* surfaced, only to find the rapidly approaching American was not the escort after all.

On board the ship, which turned out to be the destroyer-minelayer *Gamble*, battle stations had been sounded as the sub surfaced. Believing it to be Japanese, *Gamble* turned toward *Thresher*, opening fire with her 5-inch gun as she bore in to ram.

Anderson quickly dove to 250 feet and rigged for a depth charge attack, which, fortunately, never came.

Gamble's log showed that it had attacked a "surfacing submarine" at 4:32 p.m., but that it had escaped. It was fortunate for both ships that the old four-stacker, whose duties had been converted to minelaying, was not carrying depth charges.

Reports of enemy ship sightings showed no relief as the afternoon wore on. One involved Admiral Dreamel's task force. Task Force One, as it had been quickly designated that morning, had received a report that a PBY patrol plane had spotted several Japanese ships northwest of Barbers Point. Dreamel decided to go after them. After fruitlessly searching for over an hour, he gave up. Unknown to the frustrated commander, he had actually been searching for his own task force.

Unfortunately for Admiral Halsey, he too was unable to distinguish between real and illusionary reports of Japanese ship sightings.

Later that afternoon, responding to possibly the same report as Admiral Dreamel had, Halsey later wrote, "The only weapons I had left were 21 planes of Torpedo Six. I launched them all, accompanied by six smoke planes and six fighters. Again they found nothing. The fighters continued on to Pearl..."

The fighters did "continue on to Pearl," and to the biggest mistaken identity tragedy of the day.

8:50 p.m. (PH plus 12 hrs. 50 min.): It was dark when squadron commander, Lieutenant Fritz Hebel, radioed Ford Island for landing instructions. Admiral Halsey had notified 14th Naval District Headquarters to expect the fighters around 8:30. "...all ships present and army anti-aircraft units" had been notified of their anticipated arrival. To make sure, the warning was repeated twice.

It was 8:50 when Hebel, who was told to turn on his landing lights, led the six F4Fs in. All was well until he passed over the drydocked USS *Pennsylvania.* With everyone still tense and trigger-happy after the attack that morning, there was chance that one shot from one gun could force all hell to break loose. Tragically, that one shot came from the *Pennsylvania,* and all hell did break loose.

The typical reaction was noted in the log of the seaplane tender *Curtiss.* Like everyone, the crew of the *Curtiss* had been expecting the *Enterprise* planes. When the fighters were heard approaching from the south, they correctly assumed they were from the big carrier. The excuse the *Curtiss* made for "joining in," however, was that "...the planes zoomed up from the landing field and AA batteries from the whole fleet commenced firing on them."

As soon as the shooting started, it was every man for himself. Lieutenant Hebel, who was able to escape the sudden inferno, headed for Wheeler Field, some 20 miles away. As luck would have it, however, his plane was hit by ground fire from army gunners near the field, who had been alerted by the sight of ack-ack fire and tracers arcking over Pearl Harbor. Unable to make Wheeler, he crashed in a cane field near Aiea. He died later that night from injuries sustained in the crash.

Of the remaining five planes, one was forced down, two were shot down, one landed, and one ran out of gas, forcing the pilot to bail out.

Ensign Gayle Hermann's engine was hit, forcing him to make a deadstick landing on Ford Island. The next morning he counted 18 "friendly fire" bullet holes in his plane. Unbelievably, some of the holes were made after he had landed.

Herbert Menges, second behind Hebel, was probably the first to go down. His plane crashed and burned near Pearl City. His charred body was not identified until December 11.

Last in line, but second to go down, was the F4F of Eric Allen. After successfully bailing out over the harbor and avoiding being killed by trigger-happy marines as he drifted down in his parachute, he landed in the water near the battleship *California.* A few minutes later he was rescued by a boatload of armed sailors, who were disappointed when they learned he was an American.

Ensign David Flynn, who was able to successfully escape the "friendly fire" holocaust, was deciding what to do next when his engine quit somewhere over Barbers Point, forcing him to bail out. He was picked up in a field by army troops, who, like the sailors when they reached Eric Allen, were disappointed to find he was not a Japanese pilot.

Last in, and the only one to the six *Enterprise* planes to land safely and unscathed at Ford Island, was Ensign James Daniels. Fifth in the approaching line of six F4Fs, Daniels was able to avoid the heaviest ground fire. Low on gas and having no other alternative, he waited as long as he could for things to quiet down before heading again for Ford Island.

With orders from the tower to come in with lights out and as fast as he could, Daniels hit the field at 30 or 40 knots faster than normal, forcing him to ground-loop his "Wildcat" at the end of the runway. Undamaged, and thinking it was at last over, as he taxied his plane toward the squadron hangar, a marine in a sandbagged anti-aircraft emplacement opened fire with his .50 caliber. Fortunately, he was unable to depress his gun enough to hit Daniels. Gayle Hermann, who had walked over to greet his fellow pilot, actually had to smash the trigger-happy marine over the head with a rifle butt to make him stop firing.

As Daniels climbed shaken but safely from his cockpit, what had happened to the six *Enterprise* planes that night pretty well capsulized the response of those on the ground who had lived through the attack. There were no friends in the sky over Pearl Harbor that day or night.

Wrote Admiral Halsey in his diary about the events of that day, "So many false reports...from unknown sources concerning presence of enemy ships...that it was very difficult to glean the truth from the false." Needless to say, he should have added that it was just as difficult to identify friend from foe.

In tribute to three *Enterprise* airmen who were killed that day, Lieutenant Clarence Dickenson's gunner, William C. Miller, Ensign Walter M. Willis, and Ensign Herbert H. Menges, the navy named a destroyer-escort in honor of each of them.

On December 10, Lieutenant Dickenson successfully bombed and sunk Japanese submarine *I-70* a few miles off Oahu.

CHAPTER 12

WASHINGTON, D.C.

9:00 a.m. (PH minus 4 hrs. 30 min.): At 8:30 on the morning of December 7, Colonel Rufus Bratton, intelligence chief of the War Department's Far Eastern Section, was handed the final pages of a long, 14-part message from Tokyo to the Japanese ambassadors in Washington. The first 13 parts had been intercepted and deciphered by U.S. intelligence the night before. Part 14, which had come in earlier that morning, had just been deciphered when Bratton read it. The message, for presentation to the U.S. Government in response to a November 26 State Department proposal, was without instruction as to when it was to be delivered.

Bratton, after reading it, defined it as "merely the formal announcement...of a break [in diplomatic relations] which [now] seemed inevitable." President Roosevelt, after reading a copy dropped off at the White House, simply said, "It looks like the Japanese are going to break off negotiations."

By the time Bratton finished reading the final page, however, he was handed two more intercepts that galvanized the meaning of the 14 parts. The first ordered the two ambassadors, Nomura and Kurusu, to "submit to the United States Government our [14-part] reply to the United States at 1:00 p.m. on the seventh, your time." The second instructed the Embassy to "destroy at once the remaining cipher machine and all machine codes," plus "all secret documents."

Putting all three together, Bratton was convinced that the 1:00 p.m. deadline meant that the Japanese could launch an attack against the United States in the Pacific anytime after that. There was only one man in the War Department with the authority to issue a warning to the Pacific commands—Chief of Staff, General George C. Marshall, who Bratton hurried over to see.

When he arrived at Marshall's office in the Munitions Building at nine o'clock, he put a call through to the general's home across the Potomac at Fort Myer. The call was answered by Marshall's orderly, who said the general was out horseback riding.

"You know where you can find him?" asked Bratton.

"Yes, I think I can find him," replied the orderly.

"Please go out at once...and find General Marshall. Tell him who I am and to go to the nearest telephone, that it is vitally important that I communicate with him at the earliest practicable moment."

10:00 a.m. (PH minus 3 hrs. 30 min.): "On Sunday morning, December 7, I went to my office, as I had done almost every Sunday since I entered the State Department," wrote Secretary of State Cordell Hull of that fateful day. Around ten o'clock, Secretary of War Henry Stimson arrived, followed by Navy Secretary Frank Knox. "The faces of my visitors were grim," remembered Hull.

Knox had just been handed the packet containing the "14-part" and "1:00 p.m. deadline" messages on the way into Hull's office. The three men spent the next two hours discussing the possible ramifications of the two intercepts.

"The [14-part] note was little more than an insult," said Hull. "It said that our proposal [of November 26] ignored Japan's sacrifices in...China...[and] menaced the Empire's existence itself..." Accusing the U.S. and Great Britain of conspiring "to obstruct Japan's efforts toward the establishment of peace in the Far East," it concluded by saying that "in view of the attitude of the American Government, [Japan] considers it impossible to reach an agreement through further negotiations."

"The note did not declare war. Neither did it break off diplomatic relations," said the Secretary. After examining the "1:00 o'clock" message, which he said was "zero hour," his comment was "that the Japs [are] planning some deviltry, and we are wondering where the blow will strike."

Despite the ominous content of the two intercepts, the major concern had not been that the Japanese might attack the United States. The worry was how to persuade Congress to declare war on Japan if, as it appeared, they attacked the British in Malaya. It was a response Roosevelt had secretly promised Churchill at the Atlantic Conference four months earlier. In anticipation of needing to convince Congress to go to war on behalf of the British, the President was armed with a 27-page speech that he was set to deliver the next day.

10:30 a.m. (PH minus 3 hrs.): It was nearly 10:30 when General Marshall returned Colonel Bratton's call. The "1:00 p.m. deadline" was now two and a half hours away. With panic in his voice, Bratton told Marshall about the "important message he must see at once," even offering to drive it over to Fort Myer himself. "No, don't bother to do that," said Marshall. "I'm coming down to my office. You can give it to me then."

Marshall, who personally disdained any exhibition of emotion, regardless of the circumstances, reacted to Bratton by deliberately taking his time showering and getting dressed, before making the 20-minute drive to the Munitions Building.

11:25 a.m. (PH minus 2 hrs. 5 min.): General Marshall finally arrived at his War Department office at 11:25, and had begun reading the 14-part message when Bratton and the assistant chief of staff, General Sherman Miles, entered the room. While waiting for Marshall, Bratton had phoned Miles, who rushed right over.

Whenever Marshall, who was reading the document aloud, paused between paragraphs, the two men tried unsuccessfully to get the general to skip to the "1:00 p.m. deadline" message.

When, after ten or twelve agonizing minutes, Marshall got around to reading it, he too realized "that one o'clock had some very definite significance. When they specified a day, that of course had significance," he said, "but not comparable to an hour. Something [was] going to happen at one o'clock."

General Miles at that point urged the "the Philippines, Hawaii, Panama and the West Coast be informed immediately that the Japanese reply would be delivered a one o'clock that afternoon, and to be on the alert."

Marshall agreed, and quickly wrote out the following message:

> Japanese are presenting at one pm eastern standard time today what amounts to an ultimatum also they are under orders to destroy their code machine immediately. Just what significance the hour set may have we do not know but be on the alert accordingly.

Before giving it to the message center, Marshall decided to call Admiral Harold Stark, Chief of Naval Operations, to see what he intended to do.

Ironically, Stark, who had also received a copy of the intercepts, had just decided not to bother Admiral Kimmel in Pearl Harbor about the two messages. After all, it was 5:00 a.m. in Hawaii—an ungodly time to disturb someone.

Telling Marshall that since they "had sent them so much [information] already," he didn't think it necessary to alert them further.

No sooner had Marshall hung up, than the phone rang. It was Admiral Stark again. Deciding that there might be "some...significance to the Japanese Ambassador calling on Mr. Hull at 1:00 p.m. [after all]," he asked the Chief of Staff to "include in his message...instructions to his people to inform their naval opposites."

Marshall agreed, adding, "Inform naval authorities of this communication" to the message, then handed it to Bratton with instructions to take it to the message center for dispatch "at once by the safest means."

By 12:11, the message had been sent out to three of the four defense areas, Panama, the Philippines, and the Presidio in San Francisco. Unable to get through to Hawaii because of severe atmospheric interference, at 12:17 it was sent as a regular, non-priority Western Union telegram, for delivery to the Hawaiian Defense command at Fort Shafter in Honolulu.

11:55 a.m. (PH minus 1 hr. 35 min.): As the meeting between Secretaries Hull, Stimson, and Knox was about to break up, the anticipated phone call from Ambassador Nomura requesting a one o'clock appointment came through. "I granted his request," said Hull.

At that point, Knox and Stimson left, with the Secretary of the Navy returning to his office for a meeting with Stark and War Plans Chief, Admiral Richmond Kelly Turner.

Henry Stimson, the Secretary of War and one of the three most important men relative to the anticipated "deviltry" planned by the Japanese that day, returned to his 20-acre estate at Woodley, for his usual mid-afternoon Sunday dinner..

1:30 p.m. (PH plus 0 hrs. 0 min.): In anticipation of the meeting with Nomura and Kurusu, Cordell Hull had just finished outlining his response to the 14-part message, that he knew the two ambassadors would be delivering, when the phone rang. It was from the Japanese Embassy.

"A few minutes after one," said Hull, "Nomura telephoned again to ask that the appointment be postponed until 1:45. I agreed."

Knowing in advance of how the Japanese government would respond to American diplomatic demands, was nothing new to the Secretary of State. Unknown to the Japanese, U.S. intelligence had broken their diplomatic code in September 1940, allowing Hull to anticipate every move and counter proposal since negotiations began.

Over at the Navy Department, Knox's meeting with Stark and Turner had just ended, when an officer from the communication center burst through the door with a message for the secretary. It was exactly 1:30 p.m.

Knox looked at it. "AIR RAID PEARL HARBOR X THIS IS NO DRILL," it said. "My God, this can't be true; this must mean the Philippines," said Knox, handing it to Stark. Recognizing the point of origin as CINCPAC, Stark said, "No sir, it's Pearl!"

Knox immediately called the White House. Harry Hopkins, who was lunching with the president, answered the phone. Like Knox, Hopkins' first reaction was that "there must be some mistake...surely Japan would not attack Honolulu," he said. Knox assured him it was the real thing.

Hopkins repeated the news to Roosevelt, who said that if it were true, and he thought it probably was, it had "taken the matter entirely out of my hands." It was a comment no doubt made in regards to his anticipated meeting with Congress on Monday, where he hoped to influence them to declare war on behalf of the British in far-off Malaya.

Over at the Munitions Building, an out-of-breath navy enlisted man rushed into the office of Colonel John Deane, one of the secretaries of the General Staff, with a penciled note that read,"Pearl Harbor attacked. This is no drill." Deane immediately phoned General Marshall, who was having lunch in the building. Marshall said he'd be right there, and to "contact Hawaii if possible and verify the message." It wasn't necessary. By the time the Chief of Staff came through the door ten minutes later, Deane handed him a copy of the official CINCPAC message, "AIR RAID PEARL HARBOR X THIS IS NO DRILL."

2:20 p.m. (PH plus 50 min.): Roosevelt immediately phoned Cordell Hull, whose secretary had just ushered Nomura and Kurusu into the diplomatic waiting room.

"There's a report that the Japanese have attacked Pearl Harbor," said the President.

"Has the report been confirmed?" asked Hull.

"No. I have it only from Knox," replied Roosevelt, suggesting he receive the envoys anyway but not mention Pearl Harbor.

Hull's legal adviser Green Hackworth, and Joseph Ballentine, a key adviser on Japanese affairs, were with him in his office.

"The president has an unconfirmed report that the Japanese have attacked Pearl Harbor," he told the two men. Reflecting on the content of the 14-part message, he said, "The ambassadors are waiting to see me. I know what they want. They're going to turn us down on our note of November 26. Perhaps they want to tell us war has been declared. I'm rather inclined not to see them."

With the attack yet to be confirmed, and, as he said, "one chance out of a hundred that it was not true," Hull decided to receive the two Japanese.

"Nomura and Kurusu came into my office at 2:20," wrote Hull later of their meeting. "I received them coldly and did not ask them to sit down."

Apologizing for having postponed the original meeting because of a decoding delay, Nomura handed him the 14-part message, which Hull "made a pretense of glancing through..."

Unknown, of course, to the secretary of state, the two envoys were completely unaware of the attack on Pearl Harbor, as Nomura unknowingly admitted when Hull asked him why he specified one o'clock in his first request for a meeting. "He did not know," said Hull. It was what he was instructed to do.

When he finished "skimming the pages," Hull turned to Nomura and said, "In all my 50 years of public service I have never seen a document that was more crowded with infamous falsehoods and distortions...on a scale so huge that I never imagined until today that any Government on this planet was capable of uttering them."

Taken completely aback by the usually phlegmatic secretary of state, Nomura struggled to say something, but was gestured by Hull to leave the room. "The Ambassadors turned without a word and walked out, heads down," he said.

Hull called the president shortly after the two men left. "By then he had received further reports on the attack on Pearl Harbor. I repeated to him what I had told them. He said he was pleased that I had spoken so strongly."

While the secretary of state was meeting with the two ambassadors, Roosevelt had been busy on the phone. After talking to Hull at 2:05, he called Henry Stimson, who took the call at the dinner table. "Henry," said the president, "come down here at once. The Japs have struck."

Thinking it would be news about the British, Stimson said he had heard that telegrams "...have been coming in about Japanese advances in the Gulf of Siam."

In "a rather excited voice," remembered the secretary of war, Roosevelt replied, "Southeast Asia, hell. Pearl Harbor." Like Roosevelt, a relieved Stimson later wrote of the news, "...now the Japs have solved the whole thing by attacking us directly in Hawaii."

Deciding that he better get the news out to the American people, Roosevelt called his press secretary, Stephen Early, who scribbled on a note pad, "The Japanese have attacked Pearl Harbor from the air and all naval and military activities on the Island of Oahu, the principal American base in the Hawaiian Islands."

"Better tell the press right away," he said.

Early was able to get the White House switchboard to connect him with all three major news services at the same time. With representatives from the Associated Press, United Press, and International News Services listening on the other end, at precisely 2:22 p.m. he read a brief statement from the president. It was a news flash that would literally reach every newspaper and radio station in the world. "The Japs have attacked Pearl Harbor and all military activities on Oahu Island. A second air attack is reported on Manila air and naval bases."

5:00 p.m. (PH plus 3 hrs. 30 min.): After a brief meeting with Hull and General Marshall earlier that afternoon, the president got a call from his son, Marine Corps Captain James Roosevelt, from his nearby home. He told his father that he had had a call from someone in the White House informing him of Pearl Harbor, and requesting him to come over as soon as he could.

When James walked in around four o'clock, the president said, "Hello, Jimmy. It's happened," then asked him to stand by in case he was needed.

Ironically, a few minutes before James arrived, Army Air Corps Lieutenant Elliot Roosevelt, in navigation school at Kelly Field, Texas, had called.

After listening to news of the attack, "I put through a call to Father," he said, "which took two hours to get through."

"What's the dope, Pop?"

"Well, it looks like we're really in for it," said Roosevelt. "What's new with you?"

Rumors were flying already. "...we heard that there was a Jap landing force in Mexico," said Elliot, "and that there'd be an attack on the Texas air bases any time now....Also that the Japs were getting ready a task force of ground troops to come up from Mexico across the border and attack Texas or California."

"Well, if you hear anything else, you'll be sure to let me know, won't you? Good luck to you, Son," said the president, hanging up the phone.

A few minutes after his conversation with Elliot, a call came through from London. It was Winston Churchill. Word of the attack had just come over the 9:00 p.m. nightly news broadcast in London.

Remembering his promise of November 11, to declare war "within the hour" if Japan attacked the United States, the prime minister asked that a call be placed to the president.

"In two or three minutes Mr. Roosevelt came through. Mr. President, what's this I hear about Japan?" he asked.

"It's quite true," said Roosevelt, "they have attacked us at Pearl Harbor. We're all in the same boat now."

"This certainly simplifies things," said the prime minister. "God be with you."

Aware that he had to prepare a speech before going before Congress the next day, around five o'clock, Roosevelt called his secretary, Grace Tully, to his study. "I'm going before Congress tomorrow," he said. "I'd like to dictate my message. It will be short." Reading from a handwritten rough draft, he started: "Yesterday, December 7, 1941—a date that will live in infamy—the United States was suddenly and deliberately attacked by the naval and air forces of the Empire of Japan..."

8:30 p.m. (PH plus 7 hrs.): 12:17 p.m. in Washington was 6:13 a.m. in Hawaii—one hour and forty-two minutes before "AIR RAID PEARL HARBOR..." and the exact time General Marshall's "be on the alert" warning was sent out by regular telegram to the Commanding Officer of the Hawaiian Department at Fort Shafter.

Through no fault of the RCA office in Honolulu, the telegram was not delivered until close to three o'clock in the afternoon, seven unbelievable hours after the attack, and an inexcusable eight hours and 42 minutes after the Message Center in the War Department sent it out with no mark to indicate that it was special or urgent.

At 8:20, a black sedan was checked through the outer gate and pulled into the portico in front of the White House. Out stepped Commerce Secretary Jesse Jones, the first cabinet member to arrive for a scheduled 8:30 meeting with the president.

Although news of the attack on Pearl Harbor had been released to the press at 2:30 that afternoon, it seemed that few of the cabinet members, outside of Hull, Stimson, and Knox, actually knew what the meeting was for. When Attorney General Francis Biddle entered the Oval Room for the meeting, the first thing he said was, "I'm just off the plane from Cleveland. For God's sake, what's happened?"

Another cabinet member who "just got off the plane" was Labor Secretary Frances Perkins. As she came into the Oval Room, she was shocked to find it "a clutter of communications equipment, maps pinned to the walls, chairs that had been brought in from other rooms, and Steve Early 'tearing around.' "

"The president was at his desk, very pale, very calm," she remembered, "completely concentrating on the papers that were being brought to him....Normally outgoing, he only looked up when, at nine o'clock, we all sat down."

Roosevelt opened with the sobering statement that this was "the most serious meeting of the Cabinet that had taken place since 1861."

Following an explanation of what had transpired throughout the Pacific that day, many questions were asked. Most involved the incredulous disbelief of how Pearl Harbor could have happened. And not all questions were from Cabinet members. Frances Perkins remembered that twice the president said to Navy Secretary Knox, "Find out, for God's sake, why those ships were tied up in rows."

Before the ten select members of Congress, who were scheduled to join the meeting at 9:45, arrived, the president read the message he was scheduled to deliver before the joint session the next day.

Although the majority liked the president's draft, Hull, who had also drafted a message, and Stimson suggested the U.S. declare war on Germany and Italy at the same time. After discussing it, however, they agreed that it was pretty much inevitable "the Germans would declare war on us," said Hull, and decided "to wait and let Hitler and Mussolini issue their declarations first."

As scheduled, at 9:45 the 10 congressmen were ushered in. Roosevelt briefed them on what had transpired in Hawaii that morning. "They sat in dead silence," remembered Stimson, "and even after it was over they had very few words."

One man who didn't remain silent for long was Senator Tom Connally of Texas, who stood up, slapped his hand on the president's desk and said, "They were supposed to be on the alert....I am amazed by the attack by Japan, but I am still more astounded at what happened to our navy. Were they all asleep? Where were our patrols? They knew negotiations were going on."

Turning to Knox, he said, "Didn't you say last month that we could lick the Japs in two weeks? Didn't you say that our navy was so well prepared and located that the Japanese couldn't hope to hurt us at all?"

The chairman of the Senate Foreign Relations Committee then blasted the secretary with, "When you made those public statements, weren't you just trying to tell the country what an efficient Secretary of the Navy you were?"

Knox didn't reply, nor did Roosevelt attempt to temper Connally. "Why did you have all those ships at Pearl Harbor crowded in the way you did," continued the senator, "and why [was there] a long chain across the mouth of the entrance to [the harbor], so that our ships couldn't get out?"

"To protect against Japanese submarines," Knox responded weakly.

"Then you weren't thinking of an air attack?"

"No," said Knox.

The meeting officially broke up around 11:30 p.m., but many of the Cabinet members had slipped out earlier.

Although it is not known if others sensed it, Secretary Frances Perkins came away from the meeting feeling as though something was wrong. It was enough to make her jot down her impression on a White House memo pad that same night.

Of course, the president was in anguish over the tremendous losses of men and ships at Pearl Harbor, but what bothered Perkins was "that [the] situation was not all what it appeared to be....His surprise was not as great as the surprise of the rest of us." He seemed to be relieved.

"...all [the] conflicts [over the possibility of the British being attacked and not the U.S.] which have harassed him for so many weeks or months, were ended. [He] didn't have to think about that anymore."

Frances Perkins knew her man.

Although the day was over for the most part, sometime after midnight Mr. Roosevelt met with news correspondent Edward R. Murrow, who had been a dinner guest at the White House that night. Forced to miss the occasion, the president asked Murrow to wait until the meeting was over.

In their meeting, Roosevelt filled Murrow in on the happenings of the disastrous day, leaving few details out. At one point, when the subject of American aircraft losses came up, the president pounded his fist on the table, exclaiming that almost all had been destroyed "on the ground, by God, on the ground!"

Interestingly, Murrow, who expected to see the chief executive emotionally down, found him almost unperturbed by the momentous events of the day. "Never have I see one so calm and steady," he wrote later. "He was completely relaxed." Had Murrow known the truth, he would know that what he really saw was a man more relieved than relaxed.

After Murrow left, remembered Roosevelt's son James, who would help him into bed at 1:00 a.m., "Father worked on the message to be delivered to...Congress the next day. He did not like [Undersecretary of State] Sumner Welles', draft, and Hull's was too long-winded."

"Father," said James, "...chose his own words to describe this 'date which will live in infamy.'"

5:00 a.m. (PH plus 15 hrs. 30 min.): It was a short night for the president, who was up "before the sun" at 5:00 a.m., drinking black coffee and scanning the latest dispatches for any news that could be used in his speech. During the night, one item had come in that the president added to his list of places attacked by the Japanese. Writing it in under "Last night Japanese forces attacked Wake Island," he wrote, "This morning the Japanese attacked Midway Island."

Finally satisfied that it was complete, Roosevelt handed it to his confidant, Harry Hopkins, to read. Hopkins studied the draft for a few minutes, then walked over to the president and handed him a piece of paper, suggesting he add the following words after the next to last sentence, "With confidence in our armed forces—with the unbounded determination of our people—we will gain the inevitable triumph—so help us God."

Roosevelt liked it, and the second of the two most emotional sentences of the speech was added to a speech that would be heard by more Americans than any other in history.

10:00 a.m. (PH plus 20 hrs. 30 min.): At exactly 3:00 p.m., London time, 10:00 a.m. in Washington, British Prime Minister Winston Churchill stood up before a jammed Parliament to deliver a speech announcing Britain's declaration of war on Japan.

The formal declaration itself had already been made by the King, who, under the British Constitution, merely had to be advised of the fact by the War Cabinet for it to take effect.

Churchill's speech held none of the dramatics heard by those who listened to President Roosevelt three and a half hours later. Despite the personal joy and relief he felt with the "United States [now] at our side," it was not his place to convey those feelings in the face of Japanese attacks on Hong Kong, Singapore, and Malaya.

Nothing was mentioned about the United States or the attack on Pearl Harbor, and only once did he subtly indicate that he knew things were going to get better. "In the past we have had a light which flickered," he said. "In the present we have a light which flames, and in the future there will be a light which shines over all the land and sea."

On the way out, one reporter was overheard saying, "Don't know why I came...wasn't hardly worth it."

12:00 noon (PH plus 22 hrs. 30 min.): A little after noon, the president was wheeled out of the White House into a waiting limousine. Unknown to Roosevelt, as his son James helped him into the back seat, under the existing circumstances, the Secret Service felt a bullet-proof car should be used for the short drive to the Capitol Building.

The only car in the government's inventory was the one seized from Al Capone as restitution for his tax evasion conviction in 1932. It presented quite a contrast. The president of the United States was on his way to deliver a speech that would plunge the whole world into the greatest conflict in civilized history, and was riding in the back seat of an automobile once owned by the most notorious gangster in the world.

As the president's motorcade made its way toward the Capitol Building, things inside had started to happen. At 12:09, Speaker Sam Rayburn banged his gavel and called the House to order.

Outside, things had been hectic, much of it over tickets to get into the gallery. Congressmen who had asked for two or three tickets, got one. Others stood in line for an hour to try to get in.

Although Representative Dewey Short of Missouri was a Republican, he was well known around Washington as a rabble-rousing isolationist, and bitter opponent of the president. When asked by a correspondent if he thought the U.S. ought to declare war on Japan, his reaction epitomized how the sneak attack on Pearl Harbor had galvanized even those most opposed to war. "Hell, it's the only thing to do," he said. "Shoot the God damned living hell out of them."

Not long after House members were seated, the Senate filed into the chamber, followed by the Supreme Court and the Cabinet. The representatives of the four branches of service, General Marshall, Hap Arnold of the Air Force, Marine Commandant General Thomas Holcomb, and Admiral Harold Stark, all in uniforms smelling, like Marshall noted later, "like mothballs," moved in and took seats at the left of the speaker's platform.

At last, the president arrived. He was received by a one-and-a-half-minute ovation as he walked slowly up the ramp to the speaker's platform on the arm of his son James, in his Marine officers' uniform. For the first time in over eight years, Republicans, as one, applauded Franklin Roosevelt.

Close to a thousand people had crowded in behind the rails in back of the Chamber, with another thousand in the galleries. The Press Gallery was jammed, forcing hundreds of reporters who couldn't squeeze in to peer through the doors.

The Executive Gallery was, of course, also jammed. Eleanor Roosevelt, in black hat and black dress, and wearing a silver fox fur, was sitting behind one of the steel girders that had been installed a year earlier to help support the House roof. "She had one of the poorest seats in the house," wrote one of the correspondents who spotted her "peering out from behind the girder."

Next to her was the widow of President Woodrow Wilson, who was present when her husband went before Congress in 1917 to make the same appeal as Mr. Roosevelt was about to make. In a little less than two hours, with Congress's approval, even the name of the war that Wilson sent American boys to help win would be changed forever. It would no longer be called the Great War. It would become the First World War. That day, Congress would lead us into the Second.

Little need be mentioned about the president's dramatic speech or the country's response. Outside of leaping to their feet with cheers and applause for one whole minute after, "No matter how long it may take us to overcome this premeditated invasion, the American people in their righteous might will win through to absolute victory," the next question was what Congress's response would be. Could the president of the United States have convinced an up to then reluctant Congress to send the country to war in a speech that took less than ten minutes to deliver?

1:00 p.m. (PH plus 23 hrs. 30 min.): As soon as the president left and the galleries emptied, the senators adjourned to the Senate Chambers, leaving the house members alone to see how its 389 representatives would respond to Mr. Roosevelt's plea.

In the Senate, Foreign Relations Chairman Tom Connally led off, followed by Arthur Vandenberg, then the roll call. It was never a question of whether Senate Joint Resolution 116 would pass. The drama was whether Senators Gerald Nye and Robert LaFollette, outspoken "America First," anti-war isolationists, would have the guts to vote their convictions. They didn't.

At precisely 1:00 p.m. it was over. The vote was 82 to nothing. As noted by *Time* magazine correspondent, Frank McNaughton, it was "a complete shut-out of America First [and] isolationism beyond even the expectations of the President's advisers."

1:26 p.m. (PH plus 23 hrs. 56 min.): On the floor of the House, meanwhile, although its Joint Resolution 254 to declare war on Japan, was never in danger of not passing, there were some fireworks.

Like the Senate, majority leader John McCormack immediately moved to suspend the House rules and vote. While debating if a second was necessary, Jeanette Rankin of Montana, who had voted "no" in 1917, stood up at the rear of the Chamber to protest. Sam Rayburn bluntly ruled that an objection could not be entertained.

From that point on, it's interesting to follow correspondent Frank McNaughton's version of what happened.

"McCormack...defended his motion, said Japan had attacked, moved its adoption. Joe Martin followed...reading [a] prepared speech....A plea for all-out unity, no more strikes, [etc.].

"There were yells of 'Vote, vote, vote,' from the Democratic side. Rayburn...shouted, 'It won't be long. Let us maintain order at this particular time.'

"Then Ham Fish said his piece...

"Again Jeanette Rankin rose to her feet. "Sit down sister,' yelled John Dingell of Michigan.

"Five more people stood up with something to say. The House was getting restless.

"At 1:04 p.m., Rayburn ordered the roll call. Again Jeanette Rankin tried to interrupt proceedings and stop the roll call. She was again brutally thrust off by Rayburn.

The largest number of people ever crowded into the House Chambers to hear President Roosevelt's "Yesterday, December 7, 1941..." speech on December 8.

AP

"Down the line, without a break, the isolationists voted for war. The clerk reading the roll call, called 'Rankin of Montana.' 'No,' Jeanette Rankin smiled. 'SSSSSSSS.' The hisses echoed through the House Chamber.

"A dozen Republican Congressmen rushed back to the rear of the Chamber, ganged up and sought to change her vote.

"She smiled, argued, refused. What did she tell them? That it might be a mistake, it might be propaganda. It might be another presidential ruse.

"There was [a] burst of cheering when, at 1:26 p.m., Sam Rayburn whammed the gavel and announced the vote as 388 Aye, 1 no."

1:32 p.m. (PH plus 24 hrs. 2 min.): There was only one step left to make it official. The House had to vote on the Senate's Joint Resolution 116, identical to the comma to its own number 254.

At precisely 1:32 p.m., eight minutes short of an hour since the president's speech, and 24 hours and two minutes since "AIR RAID PEARL HARBOR," it was over.

During that fateful 24-hour-and-two-minute period, the U.S. Pacific Fleet had been crippled at Pearl Harbor, half the air force in the Philippines had been destroyed on the ground, and there had been attacks and major Japanese invasions of Hong Kong and Malaya. Wake Island had been heavily bombed and cut off from all hope, and at that very moment, Guam was being overrun by hordes of Japanese troops.

BIBLIOGRAPHY

CHAPTER I

Barber, Noel. *A Sinister Twilight—The Fall of Singapore 1942.* Boston: Houghton Mifflin Co., 1968.

Brown, Cecil. *Suez to Singapore.* New York: Random House, 1942.

Caidin, Martin. *The Rugged, Ragged Warriors.* New York: E.P. Dutton and Co., 1966.

———, and Hirokoshi Jiro. *Zero.* New York: E.P. Dutton and Co. Inc., 1956.

Falk, Stanley. *Seventy Days to Singapore: The Malayan Campaign 1941–42.* London: Hale, 1975.

Gallagher, O.D. *Action in the East.* New York: Doubleday Doran, 1943.

Greenfell, Captain Russell, RN. *Main Fleet to Singapore.* London: Faber and Faber, 1951.

Kirby, Major General S. Woodburn. *The War Against Japan, Vol I—The Loss of Singapore.* London: Her Majesty's Stationary Office, 1957.

———. *Singapore: The Chain of Disaster.* New York: McMillan and Co., 1971.

Leasor, James. *Singapore—The Battle That Changed the World.* New York: Doubleday and Co., Inc. 1968.

McCormac, Charles. *"You'll Die in Singapore."* London: Robert Hale Limited, 1954.

McMillan, Norman. *The RAF in the World War.* London: George G. Harrap, 1950.

Morison, Samuel Eliot. *History of the United States Naval Operations in World War II, Vol. III—The Rising Sun in the Pacific.* Boston: Little Brown and Co., 1961.

Owen, Frank. *The Fall of Singapore.* London: Michael Joseph Ltd., 1960.

Richards, Denis and Saunders, Hilary St. George. *RAF 1939–1945,* Vol. II. London: Her Majesty's Stationary Office, 1954.

Toland, John. *But Not in Shame.* New York: Random House, 1961.

Tsuji, Colonel Masanobu. *Singapore—The Japanese Version*. New York: St. Martin's Press, 1960.

Weintraub, Stanley. *Long Days Journey Into War—December 7, 1941*. New York: Truman Books, Dutton, 1990.

CHAPTER 2

Ferguson, Ted. *The Desperate Siege—The Battle of Hong Kong*. New York: Doubleday and Co. Inc., 1980.

Guest, Captain Freddie. *Escape From the Bloodied Sun*. London: Jarrolds, 1956.

Marsman, Jan. *I Escaped From Hong Kong*. New York: Reynal and Hitchcock, 1942.

Weintraub, Stanley. *Long Days Journey Into War—December 7, 1941*. New York: Truman Talley Books, Dutton, 1991.

Newspaper Articles:

The London Times, December 8, 1941: "Japanese Ambushed"; "Enemy Bridges Thrown Across Frontier."

The New York Times, December 10, 1941: "Clipper Attacked By Swarm Of Planes."

CHAPTER 3

Gailey, Harry. *The Liberation of Guam*. Navato California: Presidio Press, 1988.

Hough, Frank, Ludwig, Verle, Shaw, Henry I. *History of U.S. Marine Corps Operations in World War II—Pearl Harbor to Guadalcanal*. Washington: Government Printing Office, 1958.

Karig, Commander Walter, and Lieutenant Welbourn Kelly. *Battle Report: Pearl Harbor to the Coral Sea*. New York: Farrar and Rinehart Inc., 1944.

Lodge, Major O.R. USMC. *The Recapture of Guam*. Historical Branch, Headquarters USMC, 1954.

Palomo, Tony. *An Island in Agony*. Self-published, 1984.

Tweed, George, and Blake Clark. *Robinson Crusoe USN*. New York: McGraw-Hill Book Co. Inc., 1945.

Weintraub, Stanley. *Long Days Journey Into War—December 7, 1941*. New York: Truman Talley Books, Dutton, 1990.

Newspaper Article:

The New York Times, December 10, 1941: "Minesweeper Sunk In Raids On Guam."

CHAPTER 4

Bartsch, William H. *Doomed at the Start*. Texas: Texas A & M University Press, 1992.

Brereton, Lewis H. *The Brereton Diaries*. New York: Morrow, 1946.

Caidin, Martin. *The Rugged, Ragged Warriors*. New York: E.P. Dutton and Co. Inc., 1966.

Craven, Frank, and James Cate. *The Army Air Forces in World War II, Vol. I—Plans and Early Operations*. Chicago: University of Chicago, 1948.

Crouter, Natalie. *Forbidden Diary*. New York: Burt Franklin and Co., 1980.

Dyess, Colonel William E. *The Dyess Story*. New York: G.P. Putnam & Sons, 1944.

Edmonds, Walter D. *They Fought With What They Had*. Boston: Little Brown, 1951.

Grashio, Colonel Samuel C. *Return to Freedom*. Oklahoma: MCN Press, 1982.

Heinl, Colonel Robert, USMC. *Soldiers of the Sea*. Maryland: U.S. Naval Institute Press, 1965.

Hoyt, Edwin P. *The Lonely Ships*. New York: David McKay Co. Inc., 1976.

Ind, Allison. *Bataan—The Judgement Seat*. New York: McMillan Co., 1944.

James, D. Clayton. *The Years of MacArthur, Vol. II, 1941–1945*. Boston: Houghton Mifflin Co., 1975.

Karig, Commander Walter, and Lieutenant Welbourn Kelly. *Battle Report: Pearl Harbor to the Coral Sea*. New York: Farrar and Rinehart Inc., 1944.

Lee, Clark. *They Call It Pacific*. New York: The Viking Press, 1943.

MacArthur, General Douglas. *Reminiscences*. New York: McGraw-Hill Book Co., 1964.

Manchester, William. *American Caesar*. Boston: Little Brown and Co., 1979.

Messimer, Dwight. *In The Hands of Fate*. Maryland: Naval Institute Press, 1985.

Morison, Samuel Eliot. *History of the United States Naval Operations in World War II, Vol. III—The Rising Sun in the Pacific*. Boston: Little Brown and Co., 1961.

Morris, Eric. *Corregidor—The End of the Line*. New York: Stein and Day, 1981.

Morton, Louis. *The Fall of the Philippines.* Washington, D.C.: Office of the Chief of Military History, U.S. Army, 1953.

Sakai, Saburo. *Samurai.* New York: Nelson Doubleday Inc., 1957.

Toland, John. *But Not In Shame.* New York: Random House, 1961.

Wainwright, Jonathan M. *General Wainwright's Story.* New York: Doubleday and Co., 1946.

Weintraub, Stanley. *Long Days Journey Into War—December 7, 1941.* New York: Truman Talley Books, Dutton, 1990.

Whitcomb, Edgar D. *Escape from Corregidor.* Chicago: Henry Regnery Co., 1958.

White, W.L. *Queens Die Proudly.* New York: Harcourt-Brace and Co., 1943.

Unit Histories:

Army Air Action in the Philippines and Netherland East Indies 1941–1942. Study No. 111. Washington, D.C., 1945.

Headquarters Far East Air Force: "Summary of Activities, 8 December 1941–24 February 1942."

AAF Historical Narratives: Army Air Forces In the War Against Japan 1941–42.

CHAPTER 5

Bayler, Walter. *Last Man Off Wake Island.* New York: Bobbs-Merrill, 1943.

Blair, Clay, Jr. *Silent Victory: the U.S. Submarine War Against Japan,* Vol. I. New York: Lippincott Co., 1975.

Cunningham, W. Scott. *Wake Island Command.* New York: Popular Library, 1962.

Devereaux, James P. *The Story of Wake Island.* Philadelphia: Lippincott, 1947.

Heinl, Lieutenant Colonel R.D., USMC. *The Defense of Wake.* History Section U.S. Marine Corps, 1947.

Hough, Frank, Ludwig, Verle, Shaw, Henry I. *History of U.S. Marine Corps Operations in World War II—Pearl Harbor Guadalcanal.* Washington: Government Printing Office, 1958.

Karig, Commander Walter, and Lieutenant Welbourn Kelly. *Battle Report: Pearl Harbor to the Coral Sea.* New York: Farrar and Rinehart Inc., 1944.

Schultz, Duane. *Wake Island—The Heroic, Gallant Fight.* New York: St. Martin's Press, 1978.

Sherrod, Robert. *History of Marine Corps Aviation in World War II.* Washington: Combat Forces Press, 1952.

Smith, S.E. *The United States Marine Corps in World War II*. New York: Random House, 1969.

Toland, John. *But Not in Shame—The Six Months After Pearl Harbor*. New York: Random House, 1961.

Newspaper Article:

The New York Times. December 11, 1941: "Liner And Clipper Escape Invaders."

CHAPTER 6

Heinl, Robert. *Soldiers of the Sea*. Maryland: U.S. Naval Institute Press, 1962.

————. *Marines at Midway*. Historical Section, Headquarters, United States Marine Corps, 1948.

Hough, Frank, Ludwig, Verle, Shaw, Henry I. *History of U.S. Marine Corps Operations in World War II—Pearl Harbor to Guadalcanal*. Washington: Government Printing Office, 1958.

Karig, Commander Walter, and Lieutenant Welbourn Kelly. *Battle Report: Pearl Harbor to the Coral Sea*. New York: Farrar and Rinehart Inc., 1944.

Morison, Samuel Eliot. *History of United States Naval Operations in World War II, Vol. III—The Rising Sun in the Pacific*. Boston: Little Brown and Co., 1961.

Prang, Gordon. *At Dawn We Slept*. New York: McGraw-Hill Book Co., 1981.

Sherrod, Robert. *History of Marine Corps Aviation in World War II*. Washington: Combat Forces Press, 1952.

Newspaper Article:

The New York Times, January 28,1942: "Midway Guns Hit 2 Enemy Warships."

CHAPTER 7

Prang, Gordon. *December 7, 1941: The Day the Japanese Attacked Pearl Harbor*. New York: McGraw-Hill Book Co., 1988.

Toland, John. *Infamy—Pearl Harbor and Its Aftermath*. New York: Doubleday and Co., Inc., 1982.

Webber, Bert. *Silent Siege II: Japanese Attacks on North America in World War II*. Oregon: Webb Research Group, 1988.

Weintraub, Stanley. *Long Days Journey Into War—December 7,1941*. New York: Truman Talley Books, Dutton, 1991.

CHAPTER 8

Ballard, J.G. *Empire of the Sun*. New York: Simon and Schuster Inc., 1984.

Brooker, Edna Lee, and John S. Potter. *Flight From China*. New York: McMillan Co., 1945.

Hoyt, Edwin P. *The Lonely Ships*. New York: David McKay Co. Inc., 1976.

Karig, Commander Walter, and Lieutenant Welbourn Kelly. *Battle Report: Pearl Harbor to the Coral Sea*. New York: Farrar and Rinehart Inc., 1944.

Weintraub, Stanley. *Long Days Journey Into War—December 7, 1941*. New York: Truman Talley Books, Dutton, 1991.

Willmott, H.P. *Empires in the Balance*. Maryland: Naval Institute Press, 1982.

CHAPTER 9

Hough, Frank, Ludwig, Verle, Shaw, Henry I. *History of U.S. Marine Corps Operations in World War II—Pearl Harbor to Guadalcanal*. Washington: Government Printing Office, 1958.

Weintraub, Stanley. *Long Days Journey Into War—December 7, 1941*. New York: Truman Talley Books, Dutton, 1990.

White, John A. *The United States Marines in North China*. Self-published.

North China Marines POW Bulletin, January 1993.

Conversation with Ray Haberman.

CHAPTER 10

Karig, Commander Walter, and Lieutenant Welbourn Kelly. *Battle Report: Pearl Harbor to the Coral Sea*. New York: Farrar and Rinehart Inc., 1944.

Raleigh, John McCutcheon. *Pacific Blackout*. New York: Dodd-Mead and Co., 1943.

CHAPTER 11

Blair, Clay, Jr. *Silent Victory: The U.S. Submarine War Against Japan*, Vol. I. New York: J.B. Lippincott Co., 1975.

Cressman, Robert J., and J. Michael Wenger. *Steady Nerves and Stout Hearts—The Enterprise Air Group and Pearl Harbor, 7 December 1941*. Montana: Pictorial Histories Publishing Co., 1990.

Dickenson, Lieutenant Clarence E., USN. *The Flying Guns*. New York: Charles Scribners and Sons, 1942.

Halsey, William F. and Bryan, J. *Admiral Halsey's Story*. New York: McGraw-Hill Book Co., 1947.

Karig, Commander Walter, and Lieutenant Welbourn Kelly. *Battle Report: Pearl Harbor to the Coral Sea*. New York: Farrar and Rinehart Inc., 1944.

Layton, Rear Admiral Edwin T. *And I Was There*. New York: William Morrow and Co., 1985.

Morison, Samuel Eliot. *History of the United States Naval Operations in World War II, Vol. III—The Rising Sun in the Pacific*. Boston: Little Brown and Co., 1961.

Prang, Gordon. *At Dawn We Slept*. New York: McGraw-Hill Book Co., 1981.

————. *December 7, 1941: The Day the Japanese Attacked Pearl Harbor*. New York: McGraw-Hill Book Co., 1988.

Stafford, Edward. *Big E—The Story of the USS Enterprise*. New York: Random House, 1962.

CHAPTER 12

Burns, James McGregor. *The Memoirs of Cordell* Hull. New York: Harcourt, Brace Jovanovich Inc., 1970.

Churchill, Winston. *The Grand Alliance*. Boston: Houghton Mifflin Co., 1951.

Farago, Ladislas. *The Broken Seal*. New York: Random House, 1967.

Hodgson, Godfrey. *The Colonel: Life and Wars of Henry L. Stimson 1868–1950*. New York: Alfred Knoph, 1990.

Hull, Cordell. *The Memoirs of Cordell* Hull, Vol. II. New York: The McMillan Co., 1948.

Lash, Joseph P. *Roosevelt and Churchill: The Partnership That Changed the West*. New York: W.W. Norton and Co., 1976.

Morgan, Ted. *FDR—A Biography*. New York: Simon and Schuster, 1983.

Morison, Elting E. *Turmoil and Tradition: A Study of the Life and Times of Henry L. Stimson*. Boston: Houghton Mifflin Co., 1960.

Mosely, Leonard. *Marshall: Hero of Our Time*. New York: Hearst Books, 1982.

Prang, Gordon. *December 7, 1941: The Day the Japanese Attacked Pearl Harbor*. New York: McGraw-Hill Book Co., 1988.

By the Correspondents of *Time, Life* and *Fortune*. *December 7–the First Thirty Hours*. New York: Alfred A. Knoph, 1942.

INDEX